Suicide Terrorism

SUICIDE TERRORISM

Ami Pedahzur

polity

The right of Ami Pedahzur to be identified as Author of this Work
has been asserted in accordance with the UK Copyright, Designs
and Patents Act 1988.

First published in 2005 by Polity Press

Polity Press
65 Bridge Street
Cambridge CB2 1UR, UK

Polity Press
350 Main Street
Malden, MA 02148, USA

ISBN: 0-7456-3382-X
ISBN: 0-7456-3383-8 (pb)

A catalogue record for this book is available from the British
Library.

Typeset in 11 on 13pt Berling Roman
by Servis Filmsetting Ltd, Manchester
Printed and bound in Great Britain by MPG Books Ltd, Bodmin,
Cornwall

For further information on Polity, visit our website:
www.polity.co.uk

Contents

Acknowledgements

The research for this book was a long journey during which I required and received a lot of help. I would like to thank the National Security Center at the University of Haifa and its Head, Gabriel Ben-Dor, who encouraged me to undertake this project. A wonderful group of young scholars was of vital assistance in the different stages of research for this book. Especially, I would like to thank Shirley Kenny, a brilliant graduate student, who spent days and nights putting pieces of data together and corroborating facts. Alexander Bialsky, a promising scholar of social networks and terrorism, helped tremendously in gathering data about the suicide bombers. I am also grateful for the invaluable assistance of Einat Holander, Asaf Rovner, Adi Sela, Moran Yarchi and Sagie Meiri.

Arie Perliger, an outstanding scholar and a dear colleague, accompanied the research from its initial stages. This book would not have been completed without his priceless help and I would like to thank him from the bottom of my heart.

I had the privilege of completing the manuscript as a Donald D. Harrington Fellow at the University of Texas, Austin. I would like to extend my gratitude to the Donald D. Harrington Fellows Program and especially to John D. Dollard, Christine Marcin and Julie Ewald, who made my stay in Austin an unforgettable experience. Above all, I would like to thank John Higley, Chair of the Department of Government, and Ian Manners, Chair of the Department of Middle Eastern Studies and Head of the Center for Middle Eastern Studies, for their friendship and support.

I had the honor and privilege of receiving advice and encouragement from Bruce Hoffman, to whom I owe so much. Leonard Weinberg offered me his wisdom and friendship and I am indebted to him for that.

As always, Dan Schlossberg, a wonderful editor, stood by my side, took very good care of the manuscript and made sure that my ideas would be communicated in a clear and coherent way. I would also like to express my gratitude to Olga Sagi, who helped me in the last stages of the editing work.

Special thanks to Ellen McKinlay, Sarah Dancy and the wonderful people at Polity Press. Above all, I would like to thank Louise Knight, who was always there for me and offered her help at some very critical junctions of the work.

I would also like to thank a special group of colleagues and friends who listened to my ideas and offered their own ideas as well as friendship: Yael Yishai, Avraham Brichta, Daphna Canetti-Nisim, Zoltan Barany, Gary Freeman, Gary J. Jacobsohn, George Gavrilis, Jeffery K. Tulis, Patricia Maclachlan, Cas Mudde, Devin Stauffer, R. Harrison Wagner, Raul Madrid, Rogelio Alonso, Sergio Herzog, Shylashri Shankar, Andre Eschet, Annabel Herzog, As'ad Ghanem, Assaf Moghadam, Badi Hasisi, Clement Henry, Clive Jones, David Rapoport, Fernando Reinares, Kenneth D. Wald, Peter Trubowitz, Lorraine Pangle, Thomas Pangle, Mia Bloom, Mohammed Hafez and Terri Givens.

Finally, I would like to thank Galit, Rotem, Shahar and Doron, whom I love so much.

This book is dedicated to my student, Nir Regev, and all the other victims of suicide terrorism.

List of Figures

1
What is Suicide Terrorism?

I will never forget that sunny, peaceful Saturday in my home town on 4 October 2003. Weekends at the beginning of the Israeli autumn are an ideal opportunity for family get-togethers, nature trips or attempts to enjoy the last moments of the hot summer sun on the beach. The Saturday quiet was disrupted by the screaming sirens of police cars and other rescue vehicles as the weekend calm was irrevocably shattered. A few minutes later, cellphones started ringing and anxious relatives could be heard on the other end of the line, sighing with relief and then uttering remarks such as, 'Thank God, you're OK', and, 'Turn on the TV, quick'.

At that point, it was evident to me that another suicide terror attack had taken place somewhere in Haifa, my home city. The pictures flashing on the television screen were hard to look at and, at first, it was difficult to identify the site of the incident. All one could make out on the small screen were the skeletal remains of a building surrounded by dozens of ambulances and police. However, the calm sea in the background did not leave any room for doubt. These were the remains of *Maxim*, a Middle Eastern restaurant under the joint ownership of Jews and Arabs, located for more than forty years on one of the most beautiful sites overlooking the Haifa coastal area. Due to the restaurant's convenient location on the main road leading from Haifa to Tel Aviv and its relaxed atmosphere, it became a 'pilgrimage' site for many of the city's residents, as well as for passers-by who happened to come this way and stopped for a Middle Eastern meal en route to their destination.

The suicide action in *Maxim* was perpetrated by Hanadi Jaradat, a twenty-nine-year-old female lawyer from the city of Jenin, which is under the control of the Palestinian Authority. As far as I was concerned, it was not the same as the hundreds of suicide attacks that preceded it. Each act of terrorism in a small city such as Haifa brings you one step closer to the people who are the casualties of such an attack. The first question that strikes me each time the rumour spreads like wildfire regarding a new attack in the city is: do I know the whereabouts of all my nearest and dearest? Immediately after having ensured that my family members are safe and sound, the fear then dawns on me that one of my friends or colleagues may have been at or near the site. In a similar incident which took place a year and a half ago, also at a Middle Eastern restaurant in Haifa, which I myself frequented quite regularly, fifteen people were killed. Among them was Suheil Adawi, the restaurant cook whom I knew quite well because he would often leave the kitchen to assist his younger brother in serving food and in the meanwhile also engage in conversation with his customers. About one year later, a suicide terrorist exploded himself on bus line number 37 which drove along its fixed route from the downtown part of the city to the University of Haifa, which lies along the crest of the Carmel mountains. In this attack, fifteen people were killed, most of them schoolchildren, and among them was Yuval Mendelevitch, thirteen and a half years old, whose mother was participating in a seminar that I was teaching.

However, this time, the noose was drawn a little bit tighter. The attack at *Maxim* took the lives of twenty-one people, and among them were students from the University of Haifa. One of them, Nir Regev, was a political science undergraduate who was studying the subject of terrorism, which is how I had become acquainted with this bright student and his work.

On that same sunny Saturday, Nir was spending time on the beach. As it neared lunchtime, he asked his friend, Olga, if she would like to join him for lunch at the popular restaurant. When Jaradat activated the heavy explosive charge she carried on her body and which, besides the explosives, also contained a great number of screws and pieces of metal, Nir was sitting with his back to her and was hit by flying screws and metal scraps. Tragically, the screws that penetrated Nir's head killed him on the spot.

The truth is that during the course of his studies at the University, my encounters with Nir were few and inconsistent. My closer acquaintance with him, strangely enough, began after his death. On the visits I made to the Regev family house during the formal seven days of mourning, I learnt quite a lot about this young man whose life was cut short at the age of twenty-five. Like many of his age group, he had stood with one leg in the world of youth and the other in the adult world. Only a small number of papers remained in order for him to complete and receive his bachelor's degree in political science and statistics, and he was indulging himself just a little while longer in his student days. At the same time, he had already started a professional career in the banking business. His personal life also reflected the transition from youth to adulthood. Nir, who had always been surrounded by friends and girls, was known for his youthful playfulness. Yet, in the last few months of his life, he had left his parents' house in Nahariya, rented an apartment of his own in Haifa and started a fresh chapter of his adult life.

Hanadi Jaradat was only four years older than Nir. Not long before, she had also completed her academic studies and was certified as a lawyer. Unlike Nir who, just several days before his death, returned from a vacation with his friends in Sinai, Jaradat's last days were more sombre. After her brother, an operative in the Palestinian Islamic Jihad organization, was killed by IDF (Israeli Defence Force) soldiers, most of the burden of caring for her cancer-ridden father fell on her shoulders. The last few weeks of her life were dedicated to efforts to bring her father, a resident of the Palestinian Authority, for medical treatment at the Rambam hospital in Haifa.

Despite the fact that, after the incident, there were those who told of the despair that overtook her, in the last moments before she activated the explosives belt, Jaradat was completely at peace with herself. Quite unlike numerous suicide bombers before her, she was in no hurry to set off the explosive charge attached to her body. She sat for quite a while in the crowded restaurant, ate to her heart's content and had time to linger and observe the restaurant patrons, including one-year-old Noya Zer-Aviv, whose baby carriage stood fairly close to her. Only after rising to pay her bill, did she press the button that activated the explosives belt.

A short while after the suicide explosion at *Maxim*, there were comments directly associating the difficult experiences Jaradat underwent in the last few months of her life with the act she had just committed. On the face of things, these contentions sounded logical. The desire for revenge is indeed known as one of the most powerful forces that can drive a human to commit horrific acts. And yet, the deeper I probed into the study of suicide terrorism in the Palestinian arena, as well as in other locations, I realized that this argument sheds light on only part of a phenomenon whose explanations are immeasurably more numerous and complex.

The principal goal that I took upon myself in writing this book was to try to understand the phenomenon of suicide terrorism. Although much has been written on the theory of its development in different places all over the world, it is my estimation, regarding all aspects of this phenomenon, that we are still at the beginning of the road, and I therefore hope this book will help us take several steps forward.

The book is divided into three major parts. In the first section, it is my intention to define the phenomenon of suicide terrorism and to demonstrate its features and manifestations. The most significant section, however, is the second part, where I consider the causes for the emergence and dispersion of suicide terrorism. I will present a model and put it to the test by drawing a broader comparison among several suicide terrorism campaigns that have taken place in the last two decades in different areas in the world. In the third part, and summary, I will examine the effects of suicide terrorism on the countries where it is prevalent and I will offer a number of ideas on ways to deal with it.

The Symbiosis between Terror and Death

Terrorism and death are closely intertwined. From the first appearance of modern terrorism, the majority of acts were directed at taking people's lives. However, death was not only the fate of terrorism victims. It cast its long, dark shadow on the terrorists themselves. I still remember quite well the picture of Ulrike Meinhof, leader of the German Red Army Faction, who committed suicide by hanging herself in prison in 1976. In addition, her four colleagues, led by Andreas Baader, also took their own lives after it was evident that their chances of being liberated from prison were nil in the wake of the failure of the Lufthansa jet hijacking in 1977. No less gruesome were the descriptions of the slow deaths of ten IRA (Irish Republican Army) men who, in the famous hunger strike of 1981, starved themselves to death in their prison cells in Belfast after realizing that their petition to be recognized as political, instead of criminal, prisoners was rejected by the British authorities.

Scores of lives of other terrorists were cut short in the midst of terrorist actions in which they played a part. Towards the end of the nineteenth century, these included Russian anarchists, members of the Narodnaya Volya, and, a few years later, also members of the IRA, who died accidentally while assembling crude bombs that blew up in their hands before reaching their destination. Many members of the Irgun and Stern Gang organizations who fought to establish an independent Jewish state in the land of Israel were killed in their attempts to attack British targets or were executed shortly after their capture. The same can be said for FLN (Front de la Libération Nationale) activists in their struggle for independence in Algeria. Throughout the 1960s and 1970s, with the emergence of worldwide radical left-wing terrorism, members of terrorist groups such as the Italian Red Brigades, the Popular Front for the Liberation of Palestine and the Japanese Red Army deliberately fought against countries that declared they would not succumb to terrorists' demands and would engage with full resolve in counter-actions against these groups. A great deal of counter-terrorist action led to the deaths of terrorists. It can therefore be argued, with a not inconsiderable degree of accuracy, that terrorism is a dangerous business and those who elect to take part in acts of terrorism by and large are conscious of the risks involved. However, there is a genuine difference between taking risks and wilfully setting out on what is going to be one's certain death.

The number of terrorists setting out on suicide missions has assuredly been increasing in the last few decades, and this tendency has provided a genuine challenge for social scientists. The lion's share of research dealing in the broader subject of suicide addresses the phenomenon in which an individual takes his/her own life, most often without physically involving others and usually as the consequence of personal circumstances. Suicide terrorism significantly strays from this description. It generally exemplifies a phenomenon whose principal goal is the physical injury of others, while the death of the person committing the suicide is merely a means of achieving this goal.[1]

In the first comprehensive study of suicide at the conclusion of the nineteenth century by Emile Durkheim, it is already possible to detect, albeit partially, reference to this kind of incident. On the basis of Durkheim's typology of suicide types, the most familiar type is the egoistic suicide (also contemporarily known as individualistic); however, the French social scientist also addressed altruistic and fatalistic suicide types which over the years were driven to the margins of sociological research.[2] According to Durkheim, and quite contrary to egoistic suicide, whose motives are individual, committing the act of altruistic suicide intends to serve the will of the collective. This kind of suicide is the product of situations in which a person undergoes a highly compelling process of integration into a social group which champions the act of suicide. As a result, the interests and desires of the individual become secondary to the group and he/she will take any step needed to help it advance its goals.[3]

The signs of fatalistic suicide have already made their mark early on in the twenty-first century. This pattern of suicide is associated with an environment in which the individual or social category to which he/she belongs has been subject to a persistent oppression, thus leading to feelings of despair and a belief that the future does not portend any guarantee of improvement in these conditions. Although this brand of despair may rise from hopelessness stemming from economic conditions, this nevertheless does not preclude the possibility that similar feelings can arise under the circumstances of the restriction of political liberties.[4]

Years before the upsurge of suicide terrorism, it was argued that the difference between altruistic and fatalistic suicide types was not so significant. In contrast to the individualistic types of suicide which appear mostly in post-industrial societies, the altruistic and fatalistic types are more common in traditional societies that have undergone political, social and economic transformation.[5] The principal difference between altruistic and fatalistic types can be found in the social interpretation given to the suicide act. When a person with a sense of a profound calling takes his/her own life as part of a social role required of him or her, the action is designated altruistic suicide, whereas if he or she performs this act from within a sense of deep despair, in most cases, this will be referred to as fatalistic suicide.[6] However, this does not exclude the probability that this despair might coalesce into a sense of social vocation and will thus create an additional combinative type of fatalistic-altruistic suicide.[7]

Whereas the greater part of Durkheim's interest was focused on incidents where persons took their lives due to circumstances noted above, while not necessarily intending to do harm to others, in more recent times it appears that similar circumstances may lead to situations where suicide is just a means in the fulfilment of a considerably broader purpose, specifically, the intentional and more extensive harm to other people.

What is Suicide Terrorism?

Before plunging into the discussion of the question of the definition of modern-day suicide terrorism, the boundaries of the phenomenon should be defined. The most problematic question in this regard is what actions can be designated as suicide terrorism? For example, was Ibrahim Hasuna, the man who, in March 2002, sprayed automatic gunfire at customers who sat in the Tel Aviv *Seafood Market* restaurant and did not cease firing until he was overpowered, a suicide terrorist? Or should Baruch Goldstein, the man who performed a similar act of unrestrained killing of Muslims praying in the Cave of the Patriarchs in Hebron some nine years earlier, also be classified as a suicide terrorist? Or should the definition apply solely to acts such as the woman terrorist who detonated her explosives belt in a crowd of people waiting in line for a concert in the heart of Moscow? Or to the terrorist who drove a car loaded with dynamite straight into a recruitment office building of the new Iraqi army? Certain researchers tend to refer to all these terrorists as suicide terrorists.[8] I am inclined to accept this approach. I believe that the phenomenon of suicide bombings, which will be at the centre of this book, is a contemporary manifestation of suicide terrorism and should be referred to as a sub-category of this phenomenon.

Suicide terrorism includes a diversity of violent actions perpetrated by people who are aware that the odds they will return alive are close to zero.[9] Suicide terrorists do not take the trouble, in most cases, to prepare a getaway route and often leave behind some kind of testament in which they declare their conscious and willing intention to go to their deaths. The most common tactic employed by the contemporary suicide terrorist, apart from suicide bombing, is an attack by one or more terrorists wielding automatic guns and grenades and aimed at a populated target. The length of the operation is not predetermined; it comes to an end only after the terrorists have been overpowered by armed forces who were present or eventually reached the scene or by individuals who were able to evade the deadly assault of the terrorists.[10]

Despite the fact that terrorist organizations in different parts of the world still use other suicide tactics,[11] I accept the contention that these tactics have proven to be an anticipatory stage laying the foundations for suicide bombings,[12] which can be described as one of the most dramatic developments in the history of terrorism. Prior to defining this contemporary form of suicide terrorism, it would be interesting to take a look at the various acts of suicide which have been carried out by terrorists throughout history.

There is evidence of this type of terrorism as early as the beginning of the second millennium. The Shiite sect of the Assassins operated in the mountainous area between Syria and Persia (Iran) during the eleventh to thirteenth centuries and trained young men to commit murders against prominent political notables with the aim of toppling the Sunnite reign in the region. The Assassins were termed *fida'is* and their primary weapon was the stiletto. They did not prepare getaway routes in advance and considered death in action a source of pride. The fact that they did not fear death augmented significantly the effectiveness of their operations. Substantiation of the impact of their methods is evidenced by the annals of time which show how, in addition to the killing of two kalifs, wazirs, sultans and other figures of the ruling regime and administration, their campaign also had a far-reaching strategic impact on the whole area by successfully sowing seeds of fear and anarchy and undermining the stability of the Sunnite rule.[13]

During the rule of the Spaniards in the Philippines, there were also episodes of suicidal acts of terrorism. These were carried out by members of Muslim tribes who objected to

Christian expansion in the southern islands of the Sulu Archipelago. Methods of warfare of tribal members were not significantly different from those of the Assassins. Seeming to appear from nowhere, they used to raid places with concentrations of people and, brandishing sharp weapons in their hands, they would stab as many victims as possible until they were defeated and killed. Unlike the Assassins, however, the Filipino murderers did not act within a systematic organizational framework but rather carried out their aggression on their own initiative. Nevertheless, before setting out on a raid, every person who chose to sacrifice himself first appealed for the blessing of his parents, relatives and occasionally even the Sultan, who was the chief political and religious authority in the area.[14]

With the termination of Spanish rule in the Philippines in 1898, the Americans took control of the country, including the Muslim areas. American attempts to establish direct control over these areas led to the same methods of warfare. Once again, history showed the considerable strategic advantages of a warrior who is willing to sacrifice his life; after protracted decades of a war of attrition between the American forces and Muslim martyrs, the former conceded defeat and enabled the institution of a partial autonomy in areas where there was a Muslim majority.[15]

In recent years, following the reappearance of suicide terrorism, mostly in the form of suicide bombing, the term has been defined in numerous ways, and while there is similarity among the various explanations, it is also possible to arrange these definitions along a continuum leading from minimum to maximum. The minimum definition perceives suicide terrorism as a diversity of actions that necessitate the death of the terrorist in order to ensure the success of the action.[16] In a slightly expanded definition, Mia Bloom adds that the terrorist executes the action in order to achieve a political goal and with the complete awareness that he is going to his death.[17] Another definition proposed by the same scholar stresses the tactical aspect: that is, unlike other terrorists, a suicide terrorist blows himself up together with his victims.[18] The broadest or maximum definition focuses on the goals of suicide terrorism and states that the suicide attacker's intention is to cause harm to as many people as possible (in most cases these are civilians), and with the ultimate purpose of effecting some type of political change. According to this definition, the terrorist's action is in fact aimed at the destruction of a chosen target. However, the means for bringing about political change are anchored in the psychological pressure applied to a much greater populace than the group of people who are directly affected by the action.[19]

So, what conclusions can be drawn from the above definitions? Similar to other acts of terrorism, suicide terrorism also aims at destroying or damaging a specific target. However, its real intention is to create an atmosphere of terror amidst a population not necessarily exposed directly to the incident, but rather those who are informed about it from a secondary source. As the terrorists perceive it, public pressure in the wake of this collective anxiety should also be translated into political gains. The principal difference between contemporary suicide terrorism and other types of terrorism, including manifestations of suicide terrorism in history, is embedded, therefore, in a tactical perspective, noted in Bloom's definition. Or, in other words, the terrorist's death by means of the detonation of an explosive charge is an integral part of the execution of the operation and constitutes an essential condition of its success.

Deploying suicide bombers brings with it a wide range of advantages for the organization dispatching the terrorist. First of all, the organization predetermines the target which the terrorist will attack, but the terrorist himself decides on the precise location and timing of execution. In this way, by leaving room for some flexibility, the terrorist has a greater chance of succeeding in his mission.[20] Second, suicide bombing has the benefit of some unique features which promote the likelihood of causing greater harm in comparison to other types of terrorism. Research based on reports filed by the American State Department shows that since the recent emergence of suicide terrorism in the form of suicide bombing, attacks employing this method have constituted only 3 per cent of the sum total of terrorist incidents in the world; however, their toll has been disproportionately much higher: 48 per cent of the fatalities. Third, the use of suicide bombing has in effect amounted to a break with all the previous, conventional rules of the exercise of violence in relatively low-scale conflicts. By upgrading their violence, these organizations are signalling that there are practically no means of dissuading them with traditional approaches.[21] Fourth, in addition to the fact that methods have yet to be found that are able to deter organizations from sending suicide bombers off on their missions, it should frankly be noted that effective methods of protecting the assaulted populations are also wanting.[22]

After establishing the definition of modern-day suicide terrorism, the next stage will be to present its features in further detail, as well as the similarities and differences among its various manifestations. The following discussion is divided into two parts. In the first, I will demonstrate facts pertaining to suicide terrorism all over the world as shown by previous research; in the second part, I will focus on the tactical features of this type of terrorism based on the research I conducted.[23]

General Features of Suicide Terrorism in the World

To begin with, contrary to the assumption held by many Westerners who believe that suicide terrorism is a phenomenon perpetrated primarily by religious zealots acting on impulse or unable to restrain an uncontrollable drive, today it is quite evident that these attacks are, for the most part, organizational undertakings. Ninety-five per cent of the acts of suicide terrorism were devised by some type of organizational structure which was part of an ably planned and well organized network that continued to operate effectively over a period of time.[24]

In the second place, again departing from an opinion shared by many, the decisive majority of conflicts in which suicide attackers have been mobilized were territorial conflicts involving the struggles of ethnic or nationalist groups opposing the presence of foreign military forces on what they defined as their homeland or native soil. The goal of these organizations was to bring about the withdrawal of the conquerors or expropriators, as the case may be, from these same lands. This applied to the struggle of Hezbollah and other Lebanese organizations opposed to American, French and Israeli military presence in Lebanon, as well as to the Palestinian campaign against Israeli control over the West Bank and Gaza Strip. The same can be said for the Tamil minority's struggle in Sri Lanka to seize sovereignty from the Sinhalese majority in areas where there is a Tamil dominance, for the Kurdish minority's battle in Turkey for independence in Turkish Kurdistan, for the Chechens' fight for independence from Russia, and for the Kashmir region campaign for independence. A more recent addition are the suicide missions of recent years aimed at the American military in Saudi Arabia,[25] as well as against the Western military presence in Afghanistan and Iraq.

Third, only on rare occasions does a suicide terrorist act occur as an isolated event. In most cases, the suicide attack is part of a string of incidents extending over a certain period, which may be called a 'campaign' of terror. The majority of suicide terrorist campaigns were led by a single organization with a definite goal, and suicide operatives were dispatched in order to blow up targets related to that goal.[26] Each campaign of this type consists of a starting point, a climactic period and an ending. During the course of the campaign, there are stages in which suicide attacks are more frequent and some which are less intense.

Fourth, nearly 70 per cent of suicide terrorism occurrences in the world were aimed at democratic countries or at least at countries which uphold fundamental democratic properties such as Israel (33.5 per cent of the incidents), Sri Lanka (19.1 per cent), Russia (4.9 per cent), Turkey (4.1 per cent) and India (2.4 per cent). These countries are perceived by terrorist groups as more vulnerable because their public is not willing to endure protracted and relentless security threats and is liable to express its dissatisfaction at the voting booth. Furthermore, there is a view according to which terrorist groups assume that democratic countries, in contrast to more authoritarian countries, will tend to be more restrained in their reactions towards the organization which dispatches the suicide assailant and the population which condones or supports the attack. As well as this view, an open, democratic environment is more convenient for introducing suicide bombers and advertising their actions in comparison to countries that are more tightly controlled and where there are many restrictions on the freedom of movement and expression.[27]

Fifth, the dynamic of rapid diffusion that has marked other terrorist strategies, such as the use of bombs or hijacking planes, has also occurred with suicide terrorists. Along with the assessment that terrorist organizations around the world are closely watching one other and will replicate modes of operation that appear successful to them, there is also the question of whether the dispersion of this type of terrorist device is, to a great extent, a direct result of inter-organization collaboration. So that, for example, militants of the Iranian Revolutionary Guard carried the suicide tactic over to Hezbollah fighters in Lebanon.[28] These allegedly passed on information to members of the LTTE (Liberation Tigers of Tamil Eelam) in Sri Lanka and, further, cooperated with them in instructing Al-Qaeda operatives on aspects of activating suicide bombers.[29] Further evidence of cooperation and the conveying of information among organizations can be found in the case of Hezbollah and Hamas. The beginning of the collaboration of these two groups was near the end of the 1980s, and it intensified after the Government of Israel decided to expel 400 Hamas activists to Lebanon in 1992.[30] In recent years, the extent of cooperation between the organizations has reached a point where Hezbollah was regularly transmitting to Hamas and other Palestinian organizations precise directions and means for fabricating explosives belts.

Tactical Features of Suicide Terrorism

Methods of operation

Following the description of the general features of suicide terrorism, it seems appropriate now to focus on its operative aspects. Despite the tendency to view suicide operations as cast from a single mould, attention should be paid to the broad diversity of operational methods employed by the different organizations. According to the findings I have analysed, it is possible to see that the most common modus operandi, and the one most preferred by the majority of organizations, is the detonation of an explosives belt directly attached to the militant's body. So far, this method has been in use in 53.3 per cent of the cases of suicide terrorism in the world.

Other frequently used methods are driving a car or a truck rigged with explosives of some kind towards the operation target with the intention of smashing into it (25.1 per cent and 5.3 per cent from the sum of all incidents, respectively). Some less conventional methods are carrying the explosive charge in a handbag (4.5 per cent), activating explosive boats (4.1 per cent), detonating hand grenades (3.3 per cent), use of booby-trapped bicycles (1.7 per cent), and, as demonstrated by the events of 11 September 2001, even hijacking a means of transportation with the purpose of crashing it into a chosen target.[31]

Over the course of years, a trend developed in which most organizations chose one method and stayed with it, so that, for example, the first suicide aggression in Lebanon was executed by means of a car bomb which was detonated in front of the Iraqi embassy in Beirut in December 1981.[32] The use of vehicles loaded with explosives remained a common terrorist technique in the Lebanese arena in the following years. Out of the sum total of suicide attacks mounted by the Lebanese organization Hezbollah, 70.6 per cent were initiated by means of car bombs and truck bombs. A similar trend is noticeable in the Al-Qaeda organization, where 62.5 per cent of suicide operations employed booby-trapped cars. The Sunnite forces in Iraq also prefer the use of booby-trapped cars; 58.6 per cent of all the operations used this method.

The hypothesis regarding the way in which an organization decides on its preferred method of operation assumes that organizations are inspired by each other, either by imitation and learning from afar, or by way of simple cooperation. However, in many cases, after adopting the idea of staging suicide attacks, they are required to adapt this technique to the specific properties of the environment in which they operate.[33]

This hypothesis is further confirmed in the circumstances of Palestinian suicide terrorism. Hamas, which, under the inspiration of Hezbollah, embarked upon its campaign of suicide attacks with the detonation of a car bomb in the settlement of Mechola in the Jordan valley, quickly shifted its customary method to terrorists who carried bombs on their person. A review of attacks committed by the organization in the years 1993 to 2004 shows that the percentage of attacks employing explosives-clad terrorists gradually increased over the years and presently stands, on the basis of a general calculation, at 63.4 per cent of the sum total of suicide actions perpetrated by the organization. At the same time, the emphasis on suicide attacks using car and truck bombs decreased and now stands, on the basis of a general calculation, at only 20 per cent of all incidents.

A similar profile can be seen in operations of Palestinian Islamic Jihad. Like Hamas, this organization also prefers the use of explosives belts. The percentage of assaults with explosives belts is 64.3 per cent of all the attacks, whereas car bombs have been used in only 23.8 per cent of the incidents. In regard to Fatah (its military wing, called the Al-Aqsa Martyrs Brigades, is responsible for dispatching suicide attackers), the picture is even more striking. It appears that the heads of the military arm of the Fatah – who joined the cycle of suicide terrorism only in the beginning of the year 2002, nearly ten years after Hamas and Palestinian Islamic Jihad had already instigated this method – quite capably internalized the lessons of their precursors. Except for the Kurdish PKK

(Kudistan Workers' Party), Fatah became the organization making the greatest use of explosives-belt-wielding terrorists (85.7 per cent out of the sum total of actions) and the fewest attempts at car bombs (8.6 per cent). The fact that all Palestinian organizations employ similar modes of action may in fact attest to a trend of mutual imitation and learning, but, at the same time, it is worth noting that all these organizations are up against the same, single enemy – Israel – and operate in a specific part of the world, that is the West Bank and Gaza. Therefore, it seems that constraints created by Israeli defence strategy, as well as terrain conditions, have an effect on the modes of action followed by the organizations and their adherence to these particular methods.

Other than the tactical orientation of the organization, local topographical features and tight security arrangements distinguishing countries already accustomed to terrorism (who attempt to make it difficult to penetrate defences with cars or trucks laden with explosives and driven by suicide operators into crowded areas), it is possible to detect two additional reasons that have made explosives belts the most prevalent tactic among organizations orchestrating suicide missions.

First, this type of weapon is very effective. While the average fatality quotient in shooting attacks is 2.11 individuals and in attacks executed by means of delaying mechanisms it is 2.01, the average number of fatalities in a suicide attack committed by a terrorist carrying an explosives belt on his/her body is 8.11. When the weapon is a car laden with explosives driven by a suicide terrorist, the average number of fatalities in effect rises to 19.08 dead and the record is 39.33, which is a direct outcome of the use of truck bombs handled by suicide operatives; however, dispatching suicide attackers in vehicles is a more complicated undertaking and its success rate is smaller.

Second, in most instances where explosives belts are used, the organization does not lose more than one terrorist, unless one is speaking of an operation that is executed in several places at the same time. In the detonation of a truck bomb, the average number of suicide attackers is 1.3; when it is a car bomb, the number increases to 1.4, whereas, in the case of a boat bomb, the number is 3.3. This economy in manpower is liable to lead to a reduction in the operation's dramatic effect; however, it will also prevent a more rapid depletion of suicide potentials in the organization.

Targets of suicide terrorism

In more recent years, it has become apparent that the primary target for the activation of suicide attackers has become concentrations of civilian populations. In 2002, this tendency reached a high point when 48 per cent of worldwide suicide assaults were directed at civilian populations. However, it would be inaccurate to assume that only civilian targets are the objects of terrorist interest. In the early years of suicide terrorism, the bulk of attacks were in fact aimed at targets that were not civilian. This becomes evident when calculating the long-term, total number of attacks against military and police installations: that is, 44.1 per cent, in comparison to civilian targets, specifically, 42.6 per cent.

An analysis of these events indicates a further and significant correspondence between the selected targets and the tactics employed against these targets. For example, while 54.5 per cent of the attacks employing truck bombs set their sights on military facilities or troops, only 18.2 per cent of the incidents using this same tactic were aimed at civilian targets. A similar tendency, although somewhat less prominent, can be perceived regarding the use of car bombs activated by suicide operatives. While 41.3 per cent of the operations using cars were directed at military targets, only 25 per cent were executed against civilians. On the other hand, a statistical analysis of the use of explosives belts worn by individual perpetrators gives an altogether different picture. In this case, 53.6 per cent of the actions were aimed at civilians, whereas only 28.6 per cent set their sights on military objectives.

Six organizations can be noted for their preference for civilian targets. The most prominent among them is Hamas which has launched some 74.3 per cent of its assaults against civilians. A close second is Fatah (68.6 per cent) and then Palestinian Islamic Jihad (61.9 per cent). In addition to these organizations, there are the Sunnite groups operating in Iraq (46.7 per cent), the PKK (43.8 per cent) and the Al-Qaeda network (31.3 per cent). In contrast, there are three organizations that are noteworthy in their preference for dispatching suicide attackers against police or military objectives. Hezbollah is the most prominent among them, with 88.2 per cent of its suicide actions perpetrated against soldiers and police. The LTTE is not far behind with 71.9 per cent, as well as Chechen rebel groups (60.9 per cent).

One of the assumptions regarding the preference of some organizations for civilian instead of military targets stems from the great difficulties involved in an attack on a military installation and the prolonged planning required for this purpose. Terrorist groups that nonetheless prefer military targets are generally those operating in an environment where this type of target is fairly prevalent and where penetrability is not too complicated. Another supposition is that the nature of the target will be determined according to the degree of legitimacy the organization has from the group or population in whose name it operates. As the conflict becomes more drawn out and violent, and the more the population represented by the organization perceives the stronger side in the conflict as ruthless, the prospect of broad public support in dispatching suicide attackers against civilian targets increases.[34]

Another type of target, which is entirely excluded from the activities of all Palestinian organizations but is significant in the schemes of other organizations, is the use of suicide terrorists in political assassinations. The organization responsible for the development and enhancement of this method is the LTTE. The target of nearly one quarter of suicide actions mounted by the organization was politicians, and the most prominent among these actions were the assassination of the Prime Minister of India, Rajiv Gandhi, in May 1991 and the fatal attempt on the life of the President of Sri Lanka, Premadasa, in May 1993. Iraqi organizations, the PKK and Al-Qaeda also dispatched suicide bombers in the attempt to carry out political eliminations on enough occasions to reach substantial percentages (20 per cent, 18.8 per cent and 12.5 per cent, respectively). One example is the assassination of the leader of the Northern Alliance in Afghanistan, Ahmad Shah Masoud, by two members of Al-Qaeda who masqueraded as journalists. This slaying became especially impressed upon many people's memories all over the world because it took place only two days before the attacks of 11 September 2001. Other organizations that employed this method of aiming to harm political figures, but with less frequency, were Chechen organizations (8.7 per cent) and Hezbollah (2.9 per cent).

Plan of the Book

In this opening chapter, I have presented some of the dilemmas involved in the definition of suicide terrorism. I then conceptualized the phenomenon of suicide bombing as a sub-category of suicide terrorism and evaluated its sources and features. After indicating the features of suicide terrorism, the ground is now prepared for chapter 2, in which I introduce the common explanations for the appearance of modern-day suicide terrorism and its rapid expansion in the last few decades, and offer my model for describing and explaining suicide terrorism. This model challenges the idea that suicide terrorism is related to a specific culture or religion, as well as the notion that it can be perceived as a grass-roots phenomenon. Rather, it looks into the different factors which bring elites of terrorist organizations to turn to suicide terrorism or, conversely, to cease from using it. Specific emphasis is given to the relations between the terrorist organization and its constituency. I then present an overview of the circumstances leading young people to join terrorist groups and to sacrifice themselves. Finally, I investigate the training process of the suicide potential in the terrorist organization, beginning from the moment he/she has been selected and recruited and concluding with the dispatch to the suicide mission.

The rest of the book's chapters follow this model. In chapters 3 to 5, I focus on the factors which led terrorist organizations in different corners of the world to start and end campaigns of suicide terrorism. Chapter 3 is devoted to a comparative analysis of the Lebanese Hezbollah and the Palestinian organizations. Chapter 4 focuses on the Tamil LTTE and the Kurdish PKK. In the first part of chapter 5 I look at Al-Qaeda, as well as other Islamic fundamentalist organizations, while in its second part I discuss the Chechen and Iraqi cases.

In chapter 6 I turn to an in-depth discussion of the individual motivations for suicide terrorism, with a special focus on the concepts of commitment and crisis. Following an account of life stories of suicide terrorists from different countries, I test my hypotheses by employing a quantitative analysis of a dataset, which includes rich data on the whole population of the Palestinian suicide bombers. Next, in chapter 7, I focus on the analysis of the recruitment, training and dispatching of suicide attackers. In this chapter I emphasize the important role of the surrounding community in facilitating the process. The first part of the concluding chapter is devoted to a discussion of the effects of suicide terrorism; in the second part I offer a new model for coping with this threat.

2
How can Suicide Terrorism be Explained?

The advent of suicide terrorism in the early 1980s caught security services and citizens off guard in many countries all over the world. For more than two decades scholars from the fields of humanities and social sciences have devoted much time, effort and considerable resources to finding an answer to the riddle of what makes human beings kill so many people and simultaneously sacrifice their own lives, sometimes, apparently, for political ends. Why has suicide terrorism spread around the globe, and so rapidly? And doesn't this act in effect go against one of the most fundamental instincts of most human beings, that is, the preservation of one's own life at almost any price? It therefore does not come as too much of a surprise that the scholars who first began to study this phenomenon placed the individual committing the suicide at the focal centre, and subsequently pursued the psychological, economic and social factors that allegedly compelled the person to commit this act.[1]

This orientation was also espoused by intelligence services seeking to compile the psychological and social 'profile' of the suicide terrorist, thereby facilitating efforts to apprehend potential suicide attackers. However, in-depth studies investigating the backgrounds of suicide terrorists did not lead to unambiguous conclusions regarding this enigmatic 'profile'.

In effect, many cases show that suicide terrorists do not differ in their psychological characteristics (and often also in their sociological features) from their peers; heated discussion continues among scholars on this matter.[2]

The only partial success in explaining the persistent expansion of suicide terrorism by focusing on the isolated suicide bomber led social scientists to redirect the spotlight onto the society and culture that produced these terrorists. This approach gained further appeal immediately in the wake of the events of 11 September 2001, and was considerably fuelled by the fact that the origin of all organizations dispatching suicide terrorists so far was in Asia and the Middle East. Before long, Samuel Huntington's idea of the clash of civilizations was adapted to account for suicide terrorism and an emphasis was particularly put on the struggle of Muslim culture with Western culture.[3] However, academic scepticism calls for redoubled caution. To be sure, the majority of groups activating suicide terrorists are organizations with Islamic origins, yet, having said that, one should not jump to the conclusion that all believers in the Muslim faith necessarily support this phenomenon, or that it can be exclusively associated with one culture.[4]

There are many cases underscoring the problematic aspects of trying to form an exclusive affinity between radical Islam and suicide terrorism. For example, a short time after the appearance of Shiite suicide terrorism in Lebanon in the first half of the 1980s, organizations consisting of members who were Muslim yet secular – occasionally, even communist – in their ideology, began to cast their lot in with the lethal cadres of suicide bombers. Most of them operated under the auspices of the Syrian regime and out of nationalist motives. Another example is the PKK, a separatist group that began to send suicide bombers on missions against Turkish targets in the mid-1990s. Members of the PKK are also of Muslim faith, but this is only of marginal importance; essentially, the PKK is a secular organization with a left-wing worldview and anti-colonialist ideas that justified the use of suicide terrorism.

In the Palestinian arena, which became one of the principal loci of suicide terrorism, a similar tendency can also be detected. Organizations that brought suicide terrorism to this area during the 1990s were the Palestinian Hamas and Palestinian Islamic Jihad, both of them Sunnite organizations holding a fundamentalist religious worldview. However, several years later, use of this tactic also spread to organizations with no outstanding religious element in their ideology. One of the latter groups was the PFLP (Popular Front for the Liberation of Palestine), a Palestinian organization with many Christian members, which over the years was marked by a fusion of Marxist and nationalist ideologies. Another organization is Fatah – the central faction in the PLO (Palestine Liberation Organization), which not only adopted this modus operandi but, during the course of the Al-Aqsa intifada, also became the group to send the greatest number of militants on suicide missions against Israeli targets, after Hamas.[5]

However, the primary setback in establishing a direct connection between radical Islam and suicide terrorism is the case of the Black Tigers suicide squad of the LTTE, which sought to achieve independence for the Tamil minority in Sri Lanka. In this case, as well, the prominence of a nationalist-ethnic element is much more evident than the religious element as a motive for mounting suicide operations. Furthermore, attacks by the Tigers, similar to those of many other organizations, were not directed at Western objectives but rather at governments in Asia and the Middle East that were of, or related to, the same culture as the terrorist organizations. This point detracts from the inference that this is a struggle between cultures or civilizations and indicates quite the opposite, that is, that this is an intra-cultural struggle.

After the group of culture-based researchers did not provide a sufficient explanation for the phenomenon of suicide terrorism, two novel approaches emerged, shedding light on aspects that, up to this point, had not attracted much attention. The advantage of these approaches is that they dispense with both the micro level, that is, the individual suicide attacker, and the macro level, that is, society and culture, and, instead, they focus on the intermediate level, namely, the organization. Whereas one approach underscores the rational processes in the decision-making of the organizational elite, ultimately leading the terrorist organization executive body to choose suicide bombers as the preferred alternative,[6] the second approach puts the emphasis on the various stages that take place in the frame of the organizational process. The latter refers to the recruitment of the individual into the organization and the socialization process he/she undergoes which transforms him/her into a 'live bomb' and eventually leads to his/her departure on the mission.[7]

In this chapter I shall review recent studies which tackle the phenomenon of suicide terrorism from different viewpoints. Despite my inclination to place special emphasis on the approaches which stress the organizational nature of the phenomenon, I will not neglect other approaches that have tried to explain it. The goal is to offer the following tri-stage model which has both the capacity to describe and explain the process that begins with strategic decision-making and concludes with the explosion of the suicide terrorist.

In the first stage, there is the rational process by which the heads of the terrorist organization, in view of considerations related to the struggle with a stronger enemy but also in view of internal political considerations, arrive at the conclusion that suicide terrorism is the most effective way of furthering their goals at a certain point in time. Nevertheless, the decision to mobilize suicide bombers cannot be implemented without a social environment that approves of this method of operation, for a terrorist organization acts on behalf of a social category and strives to advance its interests. If this same social group concurs with the organization's decision to deploy suicide bombers, then this support will most likely maximize the benefits of this strategy. To the extent that this social group, on the other hand, will have reservations regarding the use of suicide militants, the organization will be left with limited options. One option is to attempt to gain the community's support by portraying the idea of suicide terrorism as a noble act or, alternatively, to engage in completely different methods of action.

The second stage, after the organizational elite has decided on this mode of action, calls for the recruitment of suicide potentials. In contrast to research that focuses on the psychological problems of the individual which could lead him/her to commit such an act, I shall claim that the person who chooses this act is motivated by reasons anchored by his/her commitment to an ideology, a leader or a group of people. Alternative motivation could be a personal crisis he/she has suffered or feelings evoked by events undergone by the group to which they belong, and with whom they feel a deep sense of identification. This aspect, as well, cannot be analysed in isolation from the broader context, namely, the social endorsement of the committing of such an act. The social environment to which the individual belongs, whether it is a community or a more restricted organizational framework that insists on the idea of suicide, will significantly facilitate his or her enlistment to the mission.

The third stage consists of the process that takes place within the framework of the organization: it starts off with the definition of the individual as a potential suicide and concludes at the point when he/she is considered a 'live bomb'. After the candidate is recruited for the suicide action, he/she undergoes a process of training. Along with the necessity of operative training, the organization takes on the no less important challenge of training him/her mentally for the task. Despite the fact that, in many instances, this part involves only a short period of training, it must still be long enough to assess the personality of the candidate and his/her degree of willingness to perform the mission. There must also be time to remove any doubts that might be evolving in the candidate's mind. The objective is to bring him/her to a mental state which enables him/her to set out upon the operation fully reconciled with the purpose and thus reduce the chances that he/she will change his/her mind at the last minute. The preparation process is critical as far as the organization is concerned, and the organizations do not spare their efforts to persuade the candidate and strengthen his/her spirit.

In later parts of the chapter, I will elaborate upon each of the stages leading to the suicide action and, at the same time, present and sometimes raise questions with regard to different studies which aim at explaining the root causes of suicide terrorism.

Strategic-Rational Decision-Making

My basic assumption, therefore, is that suicide terrorism, like other types of terrorism, is a product of an organization's political strategy after it has defined its goals, clarified the options it has in order to realize these goals and checked the price label attached to each operational method.[8] The issue now is what has happened in the last two decades that has led so many terrorist organizations at such diverse and faraway places on the globe to learn and adopt this dramatic and brutal mode of operation and to favour it over more traditional methods of terrorism? It seems that the answer to this question should be divided into two dimensions: external and internal.

Suicide terrorism has made its appearance primarily in conflicts where the balance of power has been asymmetrical, meaning a relatively weak organization up against a strong state.[9] This method of action has succeeded, in many cases, in minimizing the advantages of the military superiority of the stronger side in the conflict. The explanation for this is straightforward. The great damage achieved by the suicide action, especially in terms of the number of victims, carries with it considerable psychological impact both on the citizens of the country under attack as well as on its policymakers. The anxiety that spreads through society in cases of a protracted campaign of suicide terrorism has the potential to reduce the faith citizens have in the government's ability to protect them, and the latter becomes subject to persistent pressures to concede to terrorists' demands.[10] Indeed, in the initial years following the deployment of suicide terrorists, this method earned itself a name as a 'winning strategy'.[11] By means of this strategy, terrorist organizations in different places in the world felt they were successful in advancing their goals in a very effective manner and with relatively low expenditure in comparison with strategies used in the past.[12]

However, the decision to adopt the method of dispatching suicide combatants is not only made on the basis of the benefits gained in the course of the organization's struggle against its opponent. Political considerations related to the organization's internal situation, and especially its affinity with the supporting population, may also have a considerable role in the decision on the choice of this strategy.[13] On several occasions, political scientists have in fact suggested that it is possible to detect similarities between terrorist organizations, particularly those operating within the borders of a certain country, and other political organizations, particularly political parties.[14] As with political parties, terrorist organizations are also dependent, to a great degree, upon the economic, organizational and moral backing of their potential public supporters, and they perceive the gratification of the public's demands as an important objective.

Furthermore, in national struggles, such as the Palestinian one, sometimes more than one terrorist organization will operate to further the interests of a single national group. Although these organizations are fighting against a common enemy, they are in effect also competing with one other. By adopting the suicide bomber tactic and fostering the culture of 'self-sacrifice', these organizations are endeavouring to show their total commitment to the community's struggle, while gaining that community's endorsement of their methods. In a situation where there is no strong socio-cultural resistance to the idea of self-sacrifice and where there is a feeling in the community that all other attempts to attain goals have not borne fruit, the organization featuring this tactic may gain points over rival organizations.[15] The more the organization is successful in adapting the fostered 'culture

of death' to the cultural elements of the society and sentiments of the public, the more the influence of the organization in the local political arena will increase and its standing
vis-à-vis the enemy will be reinforced.[16] The association that
is successful in preserving the grass-roots support of its
actions, and at the same time is able to make gains in the
struggle against the enemy, is thus able to translate this type
of struggle into a future political resource.

The Social-Cultural Aspect

If the decision of the organization's executive body to dispatch suicide bombers can be analysed in rational terms then,
in order to understand the widespread support for the phenomenon in various places in the world, explanations from
the other social sciences are necessary. As I maintained previously, in order to sustain suicide terrorism over a length of
time, the organization requires the legitimacy of the group or
groups in whose name it operates. In light of the fact that all
organizations dispatching suicide bombers until now have
originated in the Middle East and Asia, the inevitable question, already addressed above in part, is: are cultural factors
responsible for the widespread legitimacy accorded to suicide
terrorists? Or, alternatively, under certain political, economic
and social conditions, will certain societies reveal more of a
predisposition towards supporting this type of action?

I contend that while the answer to the first question is neg-
ative, the second question may be answered in the positive. In
order to substantiate my contention I will rely, at least
partially, on the thesis of the clash of civilizations, but not quite
in the way it has previously been used to provide explanations
for suicide terrorism. It stands to reason that Huntington
defined the various civilizations on the basis of historical,
lingual, religious and cultural features that evolved over hundreds of years. At the same time, he did not consider these
distinctions a sole immediate cause for confrontation, even
less, violent confrontation among the various civilizations.

So, what does in fact lead to violent clashes among civilizations? These conflicts, for the most part, result from the attempt to gain control of a certain territory or from the effort to add to the economic and military might of one force over another.[17] A review of the conflicts in which suicide attacks have been employed demonstrates, as shown above, that in most circumstances, there is a struggle over territory and an aspiration for self-determination of certain groups in a given territory. In other cases, especially that of Al-Qaeda, there is an effort to replace secular Arab regimes and to remove Western military, economic and political elements from Islamic areas, while the use of the rhetoric of a struggle between religions or cultures is in effect a veil for struggles of a more material nature.[18]

Having said that, it is hard to ignore the fact that suicide terrorism, originally from Iran and Lebanon, rapidly dispersed towards the east and south whereas, in the West, this phenomenon did not catch on. It is thus possible to assume that there apparently are societies and cultures that, under certain circumstances, will support suicide terrorism, whereas other societies will reject it out of hand. Durkheim's comparative research on suicide raised the first signs of this possibility. According to his view, the phenomenon of individualistic suicide was found to be prevalent at higher rates in Western culture compared with Eastern cultures. Social scientists who investigated the history of suicide in traditional societies backed up this claim. However, alongside relatively low rates of individualistic suicide in many Asian societies, they also found high rates of altruistic and fatalistic suicide types.[19]

The most prominent example of a surge of altruistic suicide in the twentieth century was that of Japanese kamikaze pilots near the end of World War II.[20] However, if the following contention is accurate, namely, that culture is the immediate factor responsible for altruistic suicide, then it is reasonable to assume that the kamikaze phenomenon would have accompanied the war from its first days and would not have made its appearance only towards the end, when Japanese military inferiority became clear. Another example of the transience of support for suicide operations among Eastern cultures is found in the idea of sacrifice which spread among Islamic insurgents in the Philippines hundreds of years earlier. The march to certain death received widespread social support and in fact became a pivotal cultural element, expressed in songs, recitations and texts, only when it was evident to insurgents that their other methods of action had failed.[21] Indeed, in much the same way that the kamikaze course of action disappeared at the end of World War II, the sacrifice phenomenon in the Philippines also reached its end when a new political reality emerged, providing hope for a better future for the Islamic community.[22]

Therefore, it appears that in a certain context, particularly in a state of real or perceived inferiority relative to an enemy that is not only hostile but also regarded as cruel, and following repeated failures in their attempts to fight it, certain societies will tend to support terrorist organizations that send recruits off to meet their deaths against this enemy.[23] The reason for this is rooted in, among other things, the attitude towards death in some cultures. If, in Western cultures, the threatening shadow of death hovers over the individual from the day of his birth and signifies termination and desolation, in other cultures death is accompanied by additional, different symbols, including honour and even sanctity.

In the relative deprivation approach, originally meant to explain group political violence, there are fundamentals that can also be instructive with regard to the conditions in which violence, no matter how brutal, can earn widespread social legitimacy. The source of violence, according to this orientation, is in the protracted sense of injustice which marks a certain group. As the disparity between the expectations and the practicable abilities of a group grows, the sense of deprivation also increases and with it a predisposition towards violence. One of the main pillars of this approach is how long the social group is subjected to feelings of deprivation and the extent to which it believes things might change. The longer that deprivation persists, combined with the subjective feeling that chances of change are small, the inclination to violence will grow.[24]

Although this approach was originally intended for explaining episodes of political violence within the context of the state, it is also possible to make use of it in different frameworks. The majority of organizations adopting suicide terrorism represent ethnic, national or religious groups. These groups feel that they are being, so to speak, trampled under the boots of other groups, thus barring them from the liberties and rights they deserve. In every one of these cases, one is speaking of feelings of deprivation and injustice that have developed over many years and occasionally even worsened in the event of a deterioration in the group's situation.

The galvanization of social support for activating suicide bombers is contingent upon a three-phase process. In the first phase, feelings of discrimination and despair spread to large parts of the society. These feelings are also accompanied by a fierce hostility towards the oppressive factor and sometimes even lead to a dehumanization of it.[25] In the next phase, the terrorist organization will attempt to mobilize these feelings for its own ends. It will supply the group with heroes and symbols that give meaning to an existence in a hopeless reality.[26] The organization will also offer a strategy that will cause the enemy much pain and sometimes even force it to change its policy and thus provide the group in whose name it acts with a feeling of accomplishment. The third phase depends on the reactions from the side subjected to the suicide attacks. If the enemy reacts with great force to the suicides and harms innocent civilians, there is a possibility that public legitimacy for suicide actions will only increase. A change for the better in group conditions is liable to bring with it a decrease in the support for this type of action. Another possibility is that the enemy will respond in a more sophisticated manner, for instance it will effect changes in policy for the benefit of the community in whose name the organization acts, without rewarding the organization itself. This kind of situation will lead to a breach between the organization and its supporters and sometimes even to sanctions applied by the community against the organization, if the community feels that any gains achieved are being jeopardized.

In sum, a supportive social environment has a decisive influence, both on the organization's decision to adopt suicide terrorism and to continue to pursue this strategy, as well as on the individual who decides to join the organization in order to take part in the suicide mission.

Recruitment of the Potential Suicide Bomber

The appropriate question at this point, other than the supportive environment discussed above and the organizational process to be discussed later on, is whether it is possible to compile a list of the distinctive features of those individuals who join the ranks of suicide legions?

A short while after the events of 11 September 2001, the President of the United States, George W. Bush, called the plane hijackers 'evil cowards'. Senator John Warner went even further and stated that those who performed suicide aggressions are not rational people and therefore there is no possibility of deterring them with rational countermeasures.[27]

These statements well reflect the tendency that was popular among many social scientists following the contemporary flare-up of suicide terrorism. These same scholars, for the most part Western, found it hard to understand what compelled a person to carry out a suicide attack and assumed that the cause must stem from some type of mental pathology. At the same time, they disregarded the fact that most suicides were on a mission, groomed and dispatched by active terrorist organizations, and were not individuals often termed, in the jargon of students of terrorism, 'lone wolves'. Therefore, it was easier for them to claim that embarking on a suicide action was an expression of an individual's mental disturbance rather than a rational tactical strategy.[28]

The great interest sparked by suicide terrorists in the imagination of researchers led to the emergence of two principal psychological approaches which sought to assess the factors leading a person to engage in such an action. The first approach, deriving from the psychology of personality, put an emphasis on the personality traits that could indicate suicide potentials, while the second approach, based on a more social–psychological orientation, attempted to detect the specific circumstances that drive someone to embark on a suicide action. I must admit that both schools left me with many unanswered questions. This may be due to the fact that these approaches make it very difficult to offer convincing explanations that can be put to empirical tests. Nevertheless, I believe that the different psychological schools should be discussed, and I will devote the following paragraphs to that purpose.

One of the conclusions drawn from the attempts to fathom the personality of the suicide terrorist was that not one single personality trait common (as demonstrated by the literature) among suicides – including affective disorder, alcohol or drug addiction or severe childhood disturbances – was found to be prevalent among suicide terrorists.[29] Therefore, it comes as no surprise that attempts to use conventional psychoanalytical theories to explain suicides in the realm of suicidal terrorism have produced only partial results. For example, Shneidman's theory, perceiving suicide to be consequent upon feelings of hopelessness and helplessness deriving from ungratified psychological needs, may in fact shed light on certain aspects related to suicide terrorists. Suicides, according to this approach, choose the path of taking their own lives when they perceive this option as the only possible way to put an end to the pain they are enduring.[30] Having said that, the main problem in trying to put this theory into practice when explaining suicide terrorism is that it was primarily intended to account for suicide on an individualistic basis and in the case of suicide terrorists, while many of them have been found to suffer from despair on a community or nationalist level, very few of them were in fact subject to despondency due to purely individualistic causes. Furthermore, in contrast to individualistic suicides, suicide terrorists do not have a history of attempts to harm themselves. And the act of suicide was not committed following a harsh quarrel with members of their families or friends and they did not report in their videotaped or written last testaments a sense of exasperation with their existence as often found in the letters of those who take their own lives. Furthermore, unlike other suicides, the primary goal of suicide bombers is to kill others; their own death only serves the purpose of attaining this goal.

Nonetheless, researchers in the field of psychology have not yet thrown in the towel. Recent years have seen the surfacing of an assumption – not yet empirically confirmed – whereby many suicides suffer from a borderline personality disorder. According to this point of view, these people suffer from defective bonding and dependency needs, fear of abandonment and existential anxiety. They are plagued by feelings of shame and use defence mechanisms that enable them to cast blame on others. Due to their disturbed sense of judgement, they are apt to distort reality, perceive it in a defective manner and act impulsively under the influence of this sentiment.[31]

The origins of this disorder, according to researchers, are rooted in childhood experiences. In many traditional societies, the father fills the role of the central figure in the education of his sons. However, these fathers are often removed from their children so that the greater part of the burden of educating children falls on the mother, who is an oppressed figure in patriarchal and conservative societies. In many cases, the mothers transfer a great deal of the pain they feel onto their sons and create much frustration in them. These childhood experiences cause these young boys to become introverted and shy in comparison to their peers and foster in them the tendency to be attracted to charismatic figures.[32] These are the type of youths that recruiters from terrorist organizations are looking for, according to some researchers. After spotting a youth who exhibits these characteristics, they present him with the most exalted myths and fantasies of the society in which he lives and offer him the ultimate way of channelling the aggressions and frustration he carries with him. The act of suicide, his handlers assiduously maintain, will transform him into a mythological hero and secure him a place in the fantasies of his people. This argument is corroborated by the videotaped last testaments of many of the suicide attackers, who refer to the suicide as a heroic act performed for the sake of the collective. In these same recordings, there also seem to be no signs of feelings of hopelessness or helplessness on the personal level.[33]

Another group of scholars who investigated the personality features of suicide attackers put forward the concept of the authoritarian personality. As with their colleagues who focused on the borderline personality disorder, these researchers also detected the seeds of the suicidal act in the socialization process of a conservative society. In their view, education in conservative and – in most cases, Islamic – societies is founded on an imperative towards obedience and an indoctrination of perceptions and beliefs. This is in contrast to the strong emphasis on providing skills for rational assessment among alternatives in educational systems in other societies. Furthermore, traditional societies imbue the youth with political and religious authorities which absolve him from internal reservations and clearly define for him who is friend and who is foe and in this way reinforce the internal cohesion of the society. The family institution in these societies does not serve as a counterbalance to the messages the youth picks up in the education system, because familial relations are also rooted in clear-cut definitions of roles and dictates of obedience.

Consequently, in his childhood and youth, the individual is subject to harsh discipline, which demands from him submission and also precludes the option of acquiring critical tools to deal with reality. The result is an authoritarian personality structure, where a deep hatred of the other and a willingness to harm him in order to defend his own society are basic constituents of one's personality.[34]

The conclusion from the above is that theories trying to explain suicide terrorism by means of personality factors do not indicate an organic flaw and neither do they attribute the suicidal tendency to an innate cause. Conversely, they call attention to the socialization process of the individual and point to the society where he grew up as a decidedly primary factor in shaping the personality into a potential suicide terrorist. One of the significant stumbling blocks associated with these approaches pertains, as already noted, to the fact that they have not undergone empirical testing and it appears doubtful that they will in the near future.

The numerous problems inherent in the approaches which sought to indicate the personality features of the individual or the long-term social processes he undergoes as central principles for explaining suicide terrorism led a different group of scholars, many of them social psychologists, to focus their attention on more immediate factors. In this case, too, the task of discovering the causes which transform a human being into a suicide terrorist was no mean feat. Already, as in earlier cases, a simple perusal of their articles leaves the reader with the impression that it is not possible to identify a dominant single factor responsible for the individual becoming a perpetrator. Apparently, it takes a number of factors at the same time in order to reach the critical juncture that compels the individual to develop into a potential suicide terrorist.

Three studies that adopted this approach as their premise indicated the individual's rational deliberation within a certain social context as a factor that has influence on the choice of the suicide option. In the first place, a review of Muslim suicide terrorists shows that several elected to participate in the mission as a means of purification or self-cleansing from sins committed in this world and with the aim of guaranteeing for themselves life in a next-world paradise.[35] A direct parallel can be drawn with the Muslim martyrs who operated in the Philippines, where also many of them were branded sinners.[36] In this particular context, it is important again to elaborate on the dominance of the afterlife concept for the religious person. In many religions, the present life is defined as a narrow corridor ultimately leading to eternal life. Consequently, the fear is that, due to his/her sins in this world, a person will be forced to spend his/her next life in hell, and this may in fact bring the believer to seek out every possible means of atoning for sin, including self-sacrifice.[37] Second, in some episodes of suicidal martyrdom, the suicide bomber and his family are rewarded with a change in social status. A person who ended up on the margins of society, and thus might have caused much shame to him-/herself and his/her family, will become a hero after death and will entitle those close to him/her to much honour.[38] In the third place, the change in the social status of the suicide bomber's family members is often complemented with a change in their material status. Testimonies, particularly from the Palestinian arena, provide evidence that many families of suicide bombers received monetary compensation from the organization that dispatched their son or daughter on the suicide mission and occasionally from other sources, foremost among them Saddam Hussein. Material compensation that might amount to a few thousand dollars is considered to be a genuine incentive for people who have been living for many years in the squalor of a refugee camp and may ensure a significant change in the quality of life for their remaining kin.[39]

Then again, social psychologists claim that it is not always possible to consider an act of suicide as a culmination of rational deliberations. This argument is based on the many episodes where cause for the suicidal act turned out to be the individual's desire to take revenge on an enemy considered, in his view, to be responsible for a historical injustice, as well as for the oppression and humiliation of the social group to which he belongs.[40] In other cases, the wish to avenge comes from the experience of losing a family member or close friend who was harmed by the enemy, and sometimes the source of the motive to vengeance is physical harm or humiliation to which the 'suicide' person was subjected.[41]

Due to the complexities cited above, it is possible to conclude that the discussion of the factors leading an individual to commit the suicidal act is still in its early stages and will apparently also serve as a basis for additional academic discussion in the future. In chapter 6, I will elaborate on my own observations on the individual causes for suicide terrorism.

The fact that my perspective is not psychological led me to look into macro and micro social experiences and dynamics that may lead a person to make such a decision. As mentioned earlier, I will specifically focus on the concept of crisis that is associated with personal and communal experiences to which the individual was exposed in the period prior to the attack and the concept of commitment to ideas, leaders and above all to comrades as key terms in exploring individual motivation for the perpetration of suicide attacks.

The Organizational Procedure

The organizational procedure of devising the suicide operation and training the suicide potential is performed in a number of parallel and distinct steps. Planning the operation is vested in the hands of the higher echelons of the organization. They design the strategic guidelines and engage in a continuous process of raising economic, organizational and tactical resources, thus enabling the organization to maintain an unbroken succession of suicide actions over time. Concurrently, the tactical levels are at work gathering intelligence, scouting for targets and on the lookout for ways to enhance the impact of the attack. Additionally, there are trainers or handlers, part of a group of organization activists responsible for the recruitment of potential suicides, training and then dispatching them to their final operation.[42] The discussion below will focus on this process.

The first step in the process is the recruitment of the potential suicide bomber. Whether it is someone who approached the organization on his/her own accord or someone who was contacted by organization activists, the degree of suitability for the task must be assessed. Despite the tactical advantages in dispatching older men or women to suicide operations, organizations generally prefer to recruit young adults and youths who are not attached to family or have other commitments.[43] On some occasions, the work will be made easier for recruiters. These are the cases where the potential suicide bomber makes first contact with them. The reasons that lead someone to offer himself as a candidate for a suicide operation, as we have already seen, are diverse and may range from a hunger for revenge to commitment to a group or a community. Nonetheless, the more he/she is determined on carrying out the action, the shorter the training phase, which may decrease from a number of days and even weeks to a matter of hours.

The reason for the great importance ascribed to the training period of the suicide is associated with the need to bring a human being, within a short period of time, to engage in a mission whose psychological intricacy is significantly greater than its tactical and technical challenges. In the past, it was customary to believe that suicide bombers were veteran members of the organization and their decision to undertake the suicide operation had crystallized over a long period so that over the years they were gradually able to assume the mental fortitude and operative abilities necessary to engage in the operation.[44] In recent years, the reality has altered. Many suicide bombers are recruited to the various organizations or are approached for only one purpose, that is, the suicide act, and this demands prompt and efficient training.[45]

The most important phase of the training process is the indoctrination, or under its more popular name, brainwashing.[46] This alludes to the process that aims to bring about change in a whole set of attitudes, opinions and beliefs of a person by means of mental and occasionally even physical persuasion. In most of the cases of suicide terrorists, the process is somewhat different because operatives are 'preaching to the converted', in that recruits are already well aware of the purpose for which they were enlisted in the first place and the goal of indoctrination is not to change their behaviour but rather to reinforce an existing inclination within a short period of time.[47] The indoctrination process is two-pronged: presenting the recruit with persuasive thematic material and exploiting charismatic images to help internalize these materials. When the combination of the two is successful, a special dynamic is created, during which the feeling of a calling wells up in the prospective suicide, followed by a decreased fear of death.[48] Matters reach such a point that in the last phase of training, when the suicide prospect is asked to write a farewell letter and leave behind a videotaped testament to his/her loved ones, he/she is already in a mental state where all his/her hopes are pinned on the suicide action. These same recorded testimonies reveal that some of the living martyrs in fact express an eagerness to perform the action and a great joy on this occasion.[49] From this point on, the chances that the suicide will go back on his decision are relatively small because such a step would give rise to condemnation on the part of his friends in the organization and sometimes even on the part of the community at large, as well as grave harm to his/her self-esteem.

In many cases, the indoctrination process is complemented by the organization's efforts to create a strong sense of commitment among the suicide candidates themselves, if such a commitment has not already been established within their social network prior to their recruitment for the suicide mission. By the nature of things, this process does not take place in all organizations and is completely absent on occasions where the individual approaches organization representatives on his own initiative and is sent on the operation shortly thereafter. However, research that tracked religious Palestinian groups and also the Tamil Tigers for a period of years discovered a similar process of preparation of suicide potentials in group forms called martyrdom cells *(haliya istishhadiya)* in the case of Hamas and Palestinian Islamic Jihad, and in units called Black Tigers for men and Birds of Freedom for women in the case of the LTTE. The purpose of this group cohesion is essentially to create a sense of unity whereby members of each cell reinforce each other and establish a sort of contractual framework binding them to the mission.[50]

This technique which is utilized by the leaders of the terrorist organization relies on past experience and on an understanding of the group dynamic that occurs in army units as well as other organizations.[51] Time and again, the question has been raised, what compels soldiers in armies all over the world to meet smoking barrels head-on on the battlefield?[52] The answer is found in the profound sense of commitment the soldier feels towards fellow members of his unit.[53] Evidence of this commitment can already be found in the mass suicide carried out by the besieged group of Jews in the fortress of Masada, who, rather than surrender to the Romans in 73 AD, took each other's lives out of a strong sense of common destiny and mutual assurance.[54] Another example from more recent history is the consecutive suicides of IRA prisoners in the early 1980s who starved themselves and died one after the other. This sequence of suicides was explained by a group pact that none of the group members was willing to break. The fervour of their commitment to the contract only increased from the moment the first hunger striker died.[55]

Summary

From all of the above, it is possible to conclude that the bulk of studies that have attempted to explain suicide terrorism have focused on specific aspects of the phenomenon. This could be, for example, either the decisions taken by an organizational elite or the personal and environmental circumstances that led the individual to take part in this action or the training process that the suicide recruit undergoes within the organizational framework. Every one of these approaches has revealed an important piece of the mosaic of the complex of suicide terrorism, but until now, an integrated explanation of the phenomenon has yet to be presented. In the following chapters, I will try to clarify the picture.

3
Turning to Suicide Terrorism: Hezbollah and the Palestinian Organizations

I have chosen to present in three separate parts a discussion of the factors which led the various organizations to adopt and occasionally discard the use of suicide terrorism. In practical terms, this will facilitate the reading of this subject, but this is not the only or most important reason for breaking up the discussion into smaller segments. While investigating the respective cases, I discovered that a single comprehensive study of *all* the organizations could perhaps shed light on a number of key factors responsible for compelling organization elites to either adopt or abandon suicide terrorism. However, this type of discussion would also obscure features that are no less important and which become particularly prominent when the comparison focuses on a smaller number of organizations similar in nature to one another and operating under similar circumstances. Therefore, in this chapter, I will focus on Hezbollah and the Palestinian organizations. The next chapter will be devoted to a comparison of the Liberation Tigers of Tamil Eelam (LTTE) in Sri Lanka and the Kurdistan Workers' Party (PKK) in Turkey and, finally, chapter 5 will concentrate on Al-Qaeda and local groups related to Al-Qaeda which have also deployed suicide terrorists as well as to the cases of the Chechen and Iraqi insurgents.

The basic assumption of this chapter, and, to a large extent, the following two chapters as well, is that the preference for suicide terrorism on the part of terrorist organizations is a consequence of advance planning and informed assessment of other alternatives, as each one of the organizations calculates how it can further its goals vis-à-vis a number of targeted publics. These three publics are: the stronger opponent,[1] the public the organization seeks to represent, and the local political rivals.[2]

To elaborate, in this chapter I will demonstrate that the principal factor explaining the decision to adopt and apply suicide terrorism over a period of time – as well as its ultimate suspension – is associated with the benefits for the organization in its struggle with a stronger state and the costs of using this method. Suicide terrorism was adopted by Lebanese and Palestinian organizations as a psychological and strategic device. In psychological terms, the reason why organizations use suicide terrorists is to signal to the countries where they are fighting, and to their own citizens, their great determination to engage in an uncompromising battle in the name of their people and a certain ideology. On a strategic level, most suicide campaigns are meant to bring about political and military changes.

However, both the Lebanese and Palestinian cases show that despite the fact that the principal factor for activating suicide terrorists is linked to the conflict with an external and powerful force, additional considerations related to the *internal* political situation in which organizations operate cannot be treated lightly, in particular competition among rival organizations battling one other for the public's support.[3] But why should terrorist organizations compete among themselves when they are in effect fighting for a common cause? The answer is quite simple, especially if we rely on the assumption that the majority of organizations act in the name of a certain nationality and are committed to establishing an autonomous political entity. History shows that a significant number of terrorist organizations using violence in their efforts to achieve national liberation indeed later strove to become political parties in the national sovereign entity that emerged at the end of the struggle. Political parties, by their very definition, are organized groups, holding a common worldview, which seek to rule the government. This rule depends on the degree of public legitimacy the party enjoys and the political support it is able to muster.[4]

The discretion displayed by the leadership of terrorist organizations in internal politics is analogous to the rationality they show towards their enemy. If they sense that the public whose support they are seeking perceives activation of suicide bombers in a positive light, and this public also shows support for other organizations in the same arena that make use of suicide attackers, the chances are they will also adopt this tactic and invest in the 'marketing' and glorification of their actions.[5] Decisions about whether to increase or reduce the number and magnitude of operations, or whether to change the targets of suicide attacks will also, to a great extent, be a direct consequence of the support that organization steersmen sense they are receiving from their 'constituency'.

In this chapter, I will also try to confirm the contention that the use of suicide bombers will be suspended under the following three conditions. First, if the goals of the organization have been attained. Second, if the side that is being attacked finds effective ways of containing this phenomenon and the organization leadership becomes aware that this strategy is no longer beneficial. Third, if the public which the organization seeks to represent makes it apparent that it no longer sanctions the use of this method.

Founding Fathers of Modern-Day Suicide Terrorism: Hezbollah in Lebanon

During the course of the 1980s, the term 'suicide terrorism' was virtually synonymous with the Hezbollah organization in Lebanon. With more than twenty years' hindsight, it is still not easy to believe that the organization which today controls vast areas of southern Lebanon – in both military and civilian terms – and is represented in the Lebanese parliament, is that same fledgling movement that was founded by a group of Shiite Muslims who adopted the Koran as their programme and announced the founding of the Party of Allah (the meaning of 'Hezbollah' in English) in 1982. Hezbollah was established at the time that civil war was raging in Lebanon and foreign countries were increasing their involvement and direct influence on events in the country. The primary goal of the organization was to bring an end to the presence of foreign military forces in Lebanon and the principal target was Israel. Israeli forces invaded Lebanon in June 1982 with the aim of deterring Palestinian terrorist organizations. Despite committing to a withdrawal of its forces within a short time frame, Israel's stay in Lebanon persisted and its hold on large areas of the country became entrenched. This presence provoked much agitation among the citizens of the country in general and also among the broader Shiite population, the supportive base of the Hezbollah organization. The position which opposed the Israeli presence in the country gained the endorsement of Syria, Lebanon's neighbour to the east, and also Iran, the patron and main benefactor of the organization.[6]

However, the first suicide attack to be associated with Hezbollah was carried out against a non-Israeli target. On the 18 April 1983, a stolen commercial vehicle laden with about 400 kg of dynamite drove up to the American embassy in Beirut and exploded in its vicinity. From the impact of the blast, an entire wing of the seven-storey building collapsed; 63 people were killed and another 120 were wounded. Many of the dead and the wounded were employees of the American embassy and CIA representatives in the Lebanese capital. Subsequently, it turned out that the vehicle had been driven by a suicide bomber.

Suicide terrorism – a winning strategy

A reasonable question at this point is why does a small and juvenile organization such as Hezbollah inaugurate its operations, of all ways, in such a fashion? The Iranian influence on the organization evidently plays a central part in the attempt to find an answer. Hezbollah grew up in the lap of a theocratic leadership headed by the Ayatollah Khomeini, which became well established in Iran in the early 1980s. The Iranian influence on the Lebanese movement was not limited solely to religious and cultural aspects. To a large degree, the Hezbollah organization served as an Iranian offshoot in the Middle East, and confirmation of this can be found in the fact that delegates from Tehran were involved up to the very last detail in determining organizational goals. They were also responsible for developing methods of operation.[7] Tangible evidence is also the fact that more than a thousand troops of the Iranian Revolutionary Guard (the Pasdaran) were sent by Khomeini to Lebanon with the aim of erecting an additional base for the Islamic revolution.[8]

In the period prior to the establishment of Hezbollah, relations between Iran and the United States reached an unprecedented low point, and actions taken against American objectives, especially by indirect means, were perceived as extremely important by the authorities in Tehran.[9] Moreover, an impressive assault on an American target by means of a terrorist tactic rarely seen before in Lebanon had the potential of placing Hezbollah in the top category of resistance organizations in Lebanon.[10]

The immediate American response to the attack on the embassy in Beirut was its relocation to a new site in Aukar, north of the capital.[11] For Hezbollah, this was a highly significant accomplishment. Not only had the operation been successful in tactical terms, that is, a direct hit on a well-protected installation, it also had considerable symbolic implications. In the very first suicide operation to be executed, the organization had already brought the strongest power in the region to its knees, causing it to react in a defensive way and to withdraw its embassy from the capital to a distant town.

Borne along on the wave of success, Hezbollah steersmen proceeded to plan their next attacks. Early in the morning of 23 October 1983, a Mercedes truck filled with more than 100 kg of TNT infiltrated the American Marines' barracks

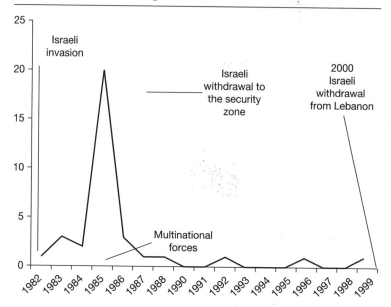

Figure 3.1 *Suicide campaigns of Hezbollah and other Lebanese organizations*

and exploded in the yard there. As a result of the impact of the explosion, the four-storey building collapsed. Out of more than 300 casualties, 241 people were killed and 80 were injured, mostly Marines serving in the multinational force sent to keep order in Lebanon. Two minutes later, another truck blew up, this time in the compound of the French forces, which was about three kilometres distant from the American Marine quarters. Fifty-eight people, most of them French troops who were part of the same force, were killed.[12] Less than two weeks later, on 3 November 1983, a booby-trapped truck exploded adjacent to the Israeli forces' head-quarters in the city of Tyre. Twenty-eight Israeli soldiers and thirty Lebanese citizens were killed in the blast.

These attacks by Hezbollah suicide bombers were executed at short intervals, directed at strategic targets associated with foreign armed forces stationed in Lebanon, and were carried out in such a way as to result in many casualties. This strategy proved to be highly effective as far as the organization was concerned. As a result of the high number of military casualties and the inability of the Lebanese army to regain control over parts of Beirut, and contrary to the original plans of President Reagan, the United States government decided to immediately withdraw all its troops from the Lebanese capital. And, in fact, on 26 February 1984, the last of the American Marines left the country.[13]

Spurred on by its successes, Hezbollah intensified its use of suicide attacks against the remaining Israeli forces in Lebanon. The tactic used against the Americans was now tailored to the properties of the new enemy. Trucks that were rigged with dynamite in order to pierce the well-shielded barracks of the multinational force were replaced by lighter vehicles, mostly cars, that were exploded in close proximity to Israeli army posts and those of the SLA (South Lebanese Army). In other cases, explosives-laden cars driven by suicide operatives were detonated near convoys of vehicles as they moved along the roads in the southern parts of the country. These attacks led to many casualties among Israeli soldiers.

On 14 January 1985, the Israeli Minister of Defence, Yitzhak Rabin, announced Israel's intention to withdraw its forces from the more central part of Lebanon and redeploy them in the security zone in the south. This signified substantial realignment of Israeli forces in Lebanon and, in practice, partial capitulation in face of the pressure applied by Hezbollah suicide bombers. Israel, which had sustained heavy losses in these suicide actions, elected to reposition its forces in close proximity to the international border while maintaining control of certain regions in southern Lebanon with the intention of safeguarding settlements inside northern Israel from the range of Katyusha rockets.

The Israeli decision only reinforced Hezbollah's resolve. Their leadership now felt that the winning strategy they had adopted could not fail them. Evidence of this was seen in the sharp rise in the number of suicide attacks perpetrated against Israeli forces in the period of time between the declaration of the intention to retreat and the actual completion of the withdrawal.[14] However, directly following Israel's redeployment in southern Lebanon, suicide attacks against IDF soldiers almost completely ceased. Concomitantly, suicide assaults on the SLA, which acted in collaboration with Israel, actually increased.[15] However, the intense suicide offensive against SLA soldiers was apparently meant to serve additional purposes other than an assault on the Israeli army. By attacking SLA troops, Hezbollah was establishing its position as corresponding to that of the Lebanese populace, which perceived members of the SLA as traitors. At the same time, it indicated to the soldiers themselves that they should reconsider their alliance with Israel because, if they refused, they would have to pay a heavy price.[16] All the same, a short while after the retreat of the Israeli forces to the security zone, suicide attacks against SLA troops did in fact cease. The reason for the change in Hezbollah's position vis-à-vis a strategy which had served it so well is apparently related to the reduced rate of benefit they stood to gain from suicide attacks in light of the new emergent reality.[17] IDF troops, backed up by SLA troops, were deployed at forty-five well-protected military outposts that were situated at strategic locations.[18] Moreover, the distances IDF supply convoys had to cover were reduced and vehicles were better armour-reinforced. Under these conditions, it seemed that dispatching suicide bombers utilizing conventional Hezbollah operational methods lost some of its effectiveness.[19]

In actual fact, over the course of the fourteen years in which the IDF controlled the security zone in southern Lebanon, the Hezbollah organization altered its modus operandi significantly. Its members, who in the past belonged to groups of suicide attackers, were reassigned to sophisticated guerrilla training that included, among other techniques, launching missiles and mortars against outposts and discharging concealed roadside bombs at passing armoured Israeli convoys. The organization's strategic versatility, manifested in the adaptation of its operational methods to changing conditions, proved to be quite effective. A multitude of guerrilla attacks that took the lives of many IDF soldiers radically changed the Israeli public's position on continued deployment in the security zone in south Lebanon. In effect, Ehud Barak's victory at the Israeli polls in May 1999 owed more than just a small part to his pledge to the Israeli public that, during the first year of his incumbency, he would withdraw the Israeli military forces from Lebanon.

Suicide terrorism as a tool for gaining power in political arenas in Lebanon and the Middle East

Despite the fact that, above all, suicide bombers have been used by Hezbollah as a tool in its struggle against Israel, they have also operated in Lebanese internal politics and the wider Middle East arena as well. Lebanon is a country that is deeply fissured, ethnically and religiously. Although the Shiite ethnicity is the largest in the country and comprises 41 per cent of the population, members do not necessarily all have the same political leanings. For a long time, the Amal movement, headed by Nabih Berri, united many of the Shiite factions and became the dominant voice of the Shiite population in Lebanon. Since its establishment, Hezbollah has tried to propose a completely different political agenda to this population.

The strong will of the Shiite elites in ridding Lebanon of foreign forces in the early 1980s is a result, to a great extent, of the Shiite leaders' supposition that Western forces supported the Maronite Christian minority and have always acted in tandem with Israel. The different Shiite factions had a collective interest at that time in preventing both the increase of Israeli influence and the upset of the political balance among ethnic and religious groups in favour of the Christians.[20] Hezbollah's suicide attacks signalled to the Shiite population that the organization was a very determined actor in this struggle. They also utilized the notion of self-sacrifice, which has remained prominent in the mythology of Shiite Islam since the death of Ali, the prophet's son-in-law.[21] The heroic image ascribed to Hezbollah led to a surprising swell of support also far beyond the limits of the Shiite population in the country.[22]

The leaders of the organization's elite were shrewd enough to exploit the popularity it had gained. From the early days of Hezbollah, they did not settle for military actions alone. As both part of their religious worldview and an appreciation of the political benefits thereof, they invested great effort in constructing an education, welfare and religious network that provided services to the Shiite population in the country.[23] In the late 1980s, they realized it was time to cash in and convert the organization's military and social status into political currency. They announced the founding of a political party and, beginning in the 1990s, made sure to compete in the elections for parliament in Beirut as well as local elections. Evidence of their success is the high rate of support Hezbollah receives on a consistent basis in Shiite regions. An additional indication is how the Lebanese Shiites' concern over the possible dilution of their votes among Hezbollah, Amal and other Shiite bodies led to the establishment of joint lists consisting of a number of organizations in which Hezbollah played a dominant role.[24] So, in effect, the use of suicide bombers in the 1980s and the strong-willed determination exhibited by the organization in its struggle against Israel in the following years had a considerable influence on its transition into a dominant political institution among the Shiite populace in Lebanon in particular and into a central actor on the Lebanese political scene in general.[25]

However, Hezbollah was not satisfied with a significant standing only in Lebanese politics. Despite the fact that it had ceased its suicide attacks some time previously, it continued to flaunt its status as the founding father of this method and encouraged terrorist organizations all over the world to follow the path it had carved out. As I will elaborate later, a great number of terrorist organizations that decided to deploy suicide bombers relied on Hezbollah's experience and learned from it. Still, the region where Hezbollah longed to gain a foothold and genuine leverage was in the Middle East and, in particular, the scene of the Palestinian struggle. During the course of the 1990s, and especially after the outbreak of the Al-Aqsa intifada, Hezbollah was significantly involved in providing both spiritual inspiration and operative support to Palestinian organizations in their struggle against the Israeli enemy. This was a factor that transformed it, over the years, into an actor with genuine clout in Palestinian politics.

A significant part of the speech delivered by the secretary general of Hezbollah, Hassan Nasrallah, on 14 December 2001, was dedicated to bolstering the spirit of the various Palestinian factions and encouraging them to increase the use of suicide terrorists in their assault on the Israeli 'home front'.

After opening his oration with a religious justification for committing suicide, Nasrallah proceeded to a tactical line of reasoning: '. . . sacrificing life in the holy name of Allah is the weapon entrusted by Allah into the hands of this nation and which no person can take away from us. They can take away [our] cannons or tanks or planes but they cannot take away our spirit that yearns for Allah and our resolve to surrender life in the sanctification of the name of Allah.'[26] Clearly evident in these words is the profound identification of the Hezbollah organization with the Palestinian struggle. Nasrallah would like the Palestinian public to understand that by means of suicide bombers, they could achieve results similar to those of Hezbollah in its struggle against its enemies.

As previously noted, Hezbollah support for Palestinian suicide terrorism was not only restricted to a declamatory aspect.[27] Despite the theological gap between the Shiite Hezbollah and the Palestinian organizations – the latter comprising Muslims of the Sunnite faith – Nasrallah and his people took steps to increase their involvement in the Al Aqsa intifada and, in particular, to promote suicide actions. To this end, they transferred technological know-how and even military weaponry to Fatah's Al-Aqsa Martyrs Brigades and other Palestinian organizations.[28] Due to the crisis it suffered in the beginning of the year 2004, Hamas improved its ties with Hezbollah, which provided money and infrastructure for operations. The affinity between the two organizations grew to such a point that following the Israeli attack on the Hamas leader, Sheikh Ahmed Yassin, his replacement, Abd el-Aziz Rantisi, approached Hezbollah for

assistance in launching an operation in revenge for the liqui-
dation of the sheikh.

In summary, it appears that the mobilization of suicide
attackers proved itself quite beneficial in serving all of
Hezbollah's major goals. With this method of terrorism, the
organization was successful strategically in forcing countries
with greater military capabilities to accept its conditions
and change their policy accordingly. In internal and regional
political terms, Hezbollah's determination, reflected in its
willingness to make frequent use of suicide attacks, turned it
into a leading force among the Shiite populace in particular
and Lebanese politics in general. Furthermore, many terrorist
organizations in the world saw in Hezbollah's tactics a
winning model for their own campaigns. While organizations
such as the LTTE, the PKK and Al-Qaeda imitated the organization's modus operandi, Palestinian factions in recent years
have became genuinely dependent on it and consequently
have transformed Hezbollah into a powerful actor in the
Israeli–Palestinian conflict and the Middle Eastern theatre in
general.

External or Internal Struggle? Suicide Terrorism in the Palestinian Arena

Despite Hezbollah's considerable contribution to the initiation of many suicide attacks on the Palestinian scene since the
outbreak of the Al-Aqsa intifada, in the first years of Palestinian
suicide operations, Hezbollah was an important inspiration but
did not yet take a significant part in their campaigns.

The first suicide mission performed by a Palestinian organization took place on 16 April 1993. In the late hours of
a Friday afternoon, a car driven by Sahar Tama Nabulsi, a
Hamas operative, slowly rolled into the parking lot of a
restaurant run by members of the nearby Mechola settlement
in the Jordan valley. This restaurant was known as a meeting
place for soldiers who regularly dined there when going
home on leave or returning to base. Nabulsi parked the car

loaded with explosives between two buses and then detonated the explosive device. The number of casualties caused
by the explosion was relatively reduced owing to the fact that
most of the soldiers destined to travel on these buses were in
the restaurant at the time. Still, this operation carried the
seeds of a dramatic change that was about to overtake the
scene of the Palestinian struggle.

Among policymakers in Israel, the first Palestinian incident
was received with great astonishment. This was because until
that same day, the phenomenon of suicide terrorism was
mostly limited to the Lebanon region. However, the basis for
their reaction was not entirely founded. Hamas had already
adopted 'in principle' the idea of using self-immolating
terrorists four years previously. In leaflet no. 68 of the organization, distributed in the wake of a wave of arrests of its
top-ranking officials in 1989, there was a summons to the
movement's loyalists to begin engaging in suicide missions
against Israeli targets.[29]

Suicide terrorism – a strategy for advancing the peace process?

The question is why did the Hamas wait four years from the
day of their appeal for suicide operations until the actual
implementation? The answer can be found in the same rational approach that in general guides the organization's leadership. In their view, violence is a means and not an end and the
decision whether to use violence or not and, if so, which tactic
should be chosen, is an outcome of the anticipated benefits
inherent to each method of operation.[30] Therefore, what
specifically *did* lead the Hamas executive body to begin dispatching suicide bombers to the cities of Israel in 1993?
Despite the fact that the research of suicide terrorism in
general, and the study of the Palestinian case in particular, is
still in its early stages, the question of the objectives Hamas
had in mind by initiating suicide attacks piqued the interest
of many scholars and has led to the emergence of two polar-
ized academic views. Despite the disagreement between the
approaches, they equally rely on a common basic assumption,

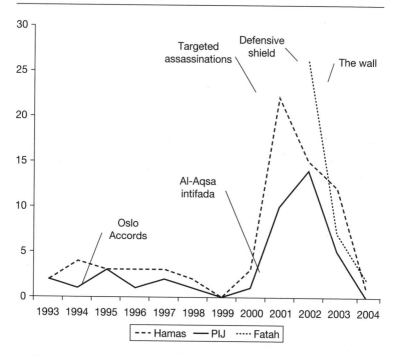

Figure 3.2 *Suicide campaigns of the Palestinian organizations*

that is, they both accept the doctrine of controlled violence. In other words, this is an assumption according to which the decision to initiate suicide missions is a rational choice among a number of several options.[31]

The first approach holds the view that the aim of Hamas suicide attacks was to coerce Israel into fulfilling its part of the Oslo Accords, which it signed with the Palestinian Authority in September 1993. This view is based on the complications that evolved in the implementation of the Accords a short while after Israel and the Palestinians signed them. For example, according to the Accords, Israel was required to withdraw from Gaza and Jericho between 13 December 1993 and 13 April 1994, but it did not comply with this timetable. Furthermore, Israel and the Palestinian Authority became involved in disputes regarding the size of the Palestinian police force to be stationed in evacuated cities and also regarding the question about Israel's right to 'hot pursuit' after terrorist suspects in these territories. When talks on these issues reached an impasse, Hamas executed two suicide attacks; the first on 6 April and the second on 13 April 1994. Several days later, on 18 April, the Knesset approved the decision to draw back its forces and, according to this approach, in this fashion gave in to force applied by Hamas suicide terrorism; withdrawal itself began on 4 May 1994.[32]

Confirmation of this approach, according to which suicide attacks were used as leverage against Israel with the intention of imposing implementation of the agreements, was evident in the next wave of suicide attacks near the end of 1994 and the beginning of 1995. This time, the actions were putatively in response to the delays in the implementation of the second stage of the agreements, that is, the withdrawal of Israel from highly populated areas in the West Bank. Between October 1994 and April 1995, Hamas, together with the Islamic Jihad organization, launched seven suicide strikes. The attacks ceased only after the Palestinian Authority explicitly requested Hamas and Islamic Jihad to discontinue their operations and, in the wake of these events, Israel reached a target date for withdrawal, that is, 1 July 1995. Unexpected delays on the part of Israel, linked to the need to pave secure bypass roads for Israeli vehicles in order to avoid evacuated territories, led to the renewal of suicide attacks by these two organizations. On 24 July and 21 August 1995, two suicide attacks occurred which took the lives of eleven Israelis. Less than two months later, Israel agreed to pull back from West Bank cities and this was *before* the construction of bypass roads, a demand that it had previously and forcefully insisted upon. The withdrawal itself began on 12 December 1995.[33]

On the face of it, the explanation provided by the first approach seems to have merit. It is in fact supported by statements made by the Israeli Prime Minister at the time, Yitzhak Rabin, who, as early as 18 April 1994, maintained that the only way to cope with the great losses inflicted by suicide terror was to pull back from Palestinian territories.[34]

However, the basic assumption of this first approach appears to be somewhat flawed. According to this assumption, the goals of the heads of Hamas and Palestinian Islamic Jihad were identical to those of the leaders of the Palestinian Authority, who sought to expedite the implementation of the Oslo Accords. The problem with this reasoning is that it does not account for the vehement rivalry between these two organizations on one hand and the Fatah-controlled Palestinian Authority on the other, and therefore the idea of some type of cooperation at that time is not entirely persuasive.

The second approach analysing the Palestinian organization's use of suicide terrorism accounts for this rivalry and also does not overlook the influence of internal Palestinian political considerations on the espousal of the suicide terrorist strategy.

Suicide terrorism as a strategy in the contemporaneous struggle against both Israel and the Palestinian Authority

If the argument of the first approach was that the aim of Hamas and Palestinian Islamic Jihad in dispatching suicide bombers was to speed up implementation of the Oslo Accords then, according to the second approach, their aim was to sabotage implementation of the Accords and undermine the legitimacy of the Palestinian Authority. From the moment they were signed, the Oslo Accords were problematic for Hamas and Palestinian Islamic Jihad, for two reasons. First, the Accords would bring an end to their lofty vision of the establishment of an Islamic state on all Palestinian-Israeli territory. Second, and no less important, the Accords granted Fatah a dominant status in the institutions of the Palestinian Authority and excluded Islamic organizations – which enjoyed widespread popular support – from the process of making and executing policy in the Authority.

The tension among religious and national political currents in the Palestinian arena therefore is not surprising. With the establishment of the Hamas movement in the last months of

1987, it was already clear that there were more differences than common ground between it and Fatah. Both movements in fact agreed upon the importance of the 'armed struggle doctrine' forged by Fatah in the 1960s, putting forward the notion that fulfilment of Palestinian aspirations would become possible only by means of violent struggle. However, while Fatah aimed mainly at national aspirations, Hamas ideology integrated both national and religious elements. The Hamas position was that establishing a Palestinian state on the lands of Judea, Samaria and Gaza was not enough. Their claim was that all of Palestine as well as the territories of the State of Israel comprised the holy land *(wakf)* of the entire Islamic world and hence must be liberated from the possession of infidels.[35] Moreover, opposing ideological worldviews were not the only source of strain among the movements. The heads of Hamas felt that the gradually increasing legitimacy accorded to Fatah, coupled with the considerable power amassed by the United National Headquarters of the Intifada, jeopardized the political viability of Islamic movements in Judea, Samaria and Gaza.[36] This new reality was not at all welcomed by the movement and its leadership decided to fight against it.

Hamas at that time had an advantage over Fatah in two primary respects. First, before the signing of the Oslo Accords, the preponderance of the veteran Fatah leadership had been in exile in Tunisia and other Arab countries, whereas the Hamas leadership operated from its central base in Gaza. Second, together with the vehement rhetoric voiced against Israel in order to drum up the Palestinian masses, Hamas was wise enough to rely on the traditions of the Muslim Brotherhood and Hezbollah and founded a network of charitable and welfare institutions that granted aid to the needy Palestinian populace.[37] Yasser Arafat, leader of Fatah, shortly after the institution of Hamas, already understood the ominous potential of the organization and began to work against it. Hamas responded by intensifying its military actions against Israeli targets, actions that earned the organization growing public support.[38]

Although the first suicide attack mounted by Hamas took place a short while prior to the signing of the Oslo Accords, the beginning of organized Hamas suicide campaigns was highly evident in the months following the signing of the Accords. Among both Hamas and Palestinian Islamic Jihad, there was full concurrence regarding the policy that multi-casualty suicide attacks would ultimately dash the hopes of Israelis who thought the Accords would put an end to terrorism and would gain security for the Israeli 'home front'.[39] Erosion of the support of the Israeli public for the agreements was henceforth meant to cause serious hindrance in their implementation, accompanied by the undermining of Fatah's status as both the Israeli leadership and the Palestinian public perceived it.

Three concentrated campaigns of suicide attacks launched against Israeli targets did not further the goals of these organizations, nor did they lead to the collapse of the Oslo process. However, the campaign that began in February 1996 did have significant results.[40] The four attacks carried out by Hamas in the cities of Jerusalem, Ashkelon and Tel Aviv in the months of February and March 1996 were labelled by the organization as acts avenging the assassination of Yehiya Ayyash ('the Engineer') the man who developed and enhanced the organization's method of suicide attack and who had been eliminated by Israel not long before. However, the leaderships of terrorist organizations generally do not engage in retribution. Reprisals for actions perpetrated against them are first and foremost prescribed by their goals. In the case of this campaign, Hamas sought to realize two goals. First, it wanted to signal to Israel that the elimination of the person most responsible for dispatching suicide attackers would not put an end to the phenomenon, and, second, the suicide campaign was also an attempt to halt the progress of negotiations between Israelis and Palestinians.

To further these goals, they actively hoped for the election of Binyamin Netanyahu, then leader of the right-wing Likud Party, in the elections scheduled for May 1996. In contrast to the incumbent Prime Minister at the time, Shimon Peres, who was committed to the Oslo process, Netanyahu made no secret of his hawkish orientation and expressed reservations regarding his willingness to implement the agreements in the future.

It seems that Hamas was able to accomplish these two goals that it set for itself. Even after the death of Ayyash, the organization was able to accomplish extremely lethal suicide actions that claimed a very high price and in this fashion made it obvious to Israel that its capabilities were intact. More important, Binyamin Netanyahu won the elections, albeit with only a slight majority, but it must be remembered that he managed to defeat his opponent in Labour (Peres) just a little more than six months after the assassination of Prime Minister Yitzhak Rabin, leader of the Labour Party. That murder, which stunned Israeli society, was supposed to have been converted into sweeping support for Rabin's party, as surveys at that time in fact indicated.[41] However, the suicide attacks led to an erosion of support for the Labour Party, and the gap between Labour and the right-wing Likud Party gradually diminished until it completely vanished on election day.

Hamas and Palestinian Islamic Jihad racked up a victory in another sense. Suicide actions perpetrated in those years conformed to the general feelings of the Palestinian people at the time. A survey conducted in February 1995, a short while after the double suicide attack by Palestinian Islamic Jihad at a roadside bus stop for soldiers at Beit-Lid, demonstrated the support of 46 per cent of Palestinians for persisting in attacks against Israeli targets, whereas only 34 per cent were opposed.[42] Hence, in terms of internal Palestinian policy, the execution of suicide attacks proved to be an important political tool. It allowed Islamic organizations to appear more determined and daring than Fatah and led to higher rates of support for the former.

Suicide terrorism as a tool in inter-organizational rivalry – the case of the Al-Aqsa intifada

Towards the end of the 1990s, following a short period of decline in Palestinian support for carrying out suicides, there was a discernible change in public opinion. A survey conducted in 1998 showed that, for the first time, the number of supporters for attacks against Israeli targets had risen to 50 per cent.[43] The operative manifestation of this shift became apparent only two years later, when the Al-Aqsa intifada erupted in late September 2000. At the outbreak of the intifada, the number of suicide terrorist actions multiplied a hundredfold, and at the vanguard of the actions stood the Hamas movement. Khaled Mishal, chief of the movement's political bureau, claimed that, in contrast to the first intifada, which had assumed a more popular nature and was marked by demonstrations and acts of sporadic violence, it was now time to resort to an organized mobilization of military hardware and suicide bombers and that the standard of reference was now the Lebanese model of armed resistance.[44] The strategic directive that guided Hezbollah action over the years was highly prominent in Mishal's oration. According to him, the present balance of power between Israel and the Palestinians would preclude Hamas from being victorious over Israel. Acts of resistance (and especially suicides) performed by the movement were to grant it cumulative advantages by virtue of its endurance and the determination of the public it represented.[45] Mishal's words certainly did not fall upon deaf ears. At that time, more than 60 per cent of the Palestinian people supported the continuation of violent attacks on Israel and 63 per cent maintained that Palestinian resistance organizations should adopt Hezbollah methods.[46]

Indeed, the Hamas suicide campaign that began shortly after the onset of the Al-Aqsa intifada had far-reaching implications for the fate of the agreements between Israel and the Palestinian Authority.[47] Sending suicide bombers into the streets of Israel at that time wore away the little hope that still remained among the Israeli public regarding the peace process. The fact that suicide attacks were a Hamas initiative did not have much importance for the majority of Israelis, who had lost faith in the Palestinian leadership and its will and capacity to cope with terrorism. The results of this crisis of faith were not slow in finding expression. In February

2001, the head of Likud, Ariel Sharon, one of the leading voices in the opposition to the peace process with the Palestinians, was elected Prime Minister of Israel with a sweeping majority unprecedented in Israeli politics.

Once again, the Palestinian organizations' accomplishments were twofold. Not only were they able to bring about the ultimate downfall of the Oslo Accords and create a strategic balance of terror with Israel although its power was far greater than theirs, for the first time in their brief history these organizations were also able to hold sway over the political agenda of the Palestinian street. The broad support for suicide attacks among Palestinian public opinion, as well as the increase in support for Hamas, did not fail to make a strong impression on the other organizations. A fear of an erosion of their own public standing created a sobering sense of pressure which led to a change in their line of action. Soon enough, organizations that in the past may have condemned the idea of suicide bombers – including factions from the leftist front such as the Popular Front for the Liberation of Palestine – also joined the vicious cycle of suicide-dispatchers.[48]

However, the culmination of these developments was Fatah's decision to adopt suicide terrorism. For the Fatah organization, this was indeed a real revolution.[49] Prior to the eruption of the Al-Aqsa intifada, members of Fatah, many of whom had served in the security forces of the Palestinian Authority, had refrained from any direct involvement in terrorist activities, let alone suicide actions. In fact, many of them had been put in charge of preventing exactly these types of action. Even in the first weeks of the Al-Aqsa intifada, it seemed that the heads of Fatah could not decide what steps they should take. Confusion in the organization's ranks was demonstrated in the first period of these events, when veteran activists restricted themselves to shooting incidents aimed at Israeli civilian and military targets and younger members took part in heavy riots and lynchings of Israeli citizens. However, these 'small noises' of the Fatah actions got lost in the mayhem of the multitude of suicide attacks perpetrated by Hamas and Islamic Jihad.

A survey conducted in July 2001 revealed that the degree of Palestinian approval for attacks against civilians inside Israel had increased to 58 per cent. Seventy percent of respondents in fact felt that attacks on Israel rather than a pursuit of the political process were more likely to further Palestinian goals. This same survey shows an additional important finding which explains why Fatah also chose the path of suicide violence. While Arafat's and Fatah's popularity had plummeted between July 2000 and July 2001, at the same time, support for Islamic organizations rose in almost identical proportion.[50]

The Fatah leadership could not remain indifferent to these developments. As events of the intifada escalated, Fatah set up the Al-Aqsa Martyrs Brigades which relied on the Tanzim infrastructure – a network of local organizations uniting the younger members of Fatah among them.[51] The goal of the Al-Aqsa Martyrs Brigades was to serve as a counterweight to the suicide arms of Hamas and Palestinian Islamic Jihad, the brigades of Iz a-Din al-Kassam and the Al-Quds Brigades. The new Fatah suicide squads, endorsed by the highest echelons of Fatah and the Palestinian Authority,[52] performed their duty to the full. On 18 February 2002, Fatah's first suicide attack was carried out and, in the following months, Al-Aqsa Martyrs Brigades became the most active group in the initiation of suicide actions. The number of actions perpetrated by Fatah at the time exceeded those of Palestinian Islamic Jihad and almost reached the number of attacks for which Hamas was responsible.[53]

About halfway through the year 2002, Israel defined suicide terrorism as a first-degree strategic threat and began to take great pains in dealing with it. Among other things, it increased its 'targeted assassinations' policies, regained control of the majority of Palestinian territories and hastened the erection of the fence separating the territories of the Palestinian Authority from its own lands. These steps made it very difficult for organizations to initiate suicide actions aimed at the Israeli 'home front'. At this point, Hezbollah's involvement in the Palestinian arena was deep-seated, and the logic that directed the Hezbollah leadership to abandon suicide terrorism when Israel withdrew to the security zone in southern Lebanon in 1985 was also somewhat noticeable in the actions of Palestinian factions affiliated with the organization. Although it was evident that they had not given up their efforts to dispatch suicide bombers, the organizations vigorously engaged in other types of warfare. One method was launching more Qassam rockets from the Gaza Strip to Israeli settlements in the area. Another measure, and no less important, was to adopt tactics of guerrilla warfare inside the Palestinian territories themselves. The first indication of this was the remote-controlled explosion of two IDF armoured personnel carriers in Gaza on 11 and 12 May 2004, by means of highly powerful roadside bombs and anti-tank missiles. The transition to warfare of this type was indicative of the considerable strategic logic underlying actions of Hamas and other Palestinian organizations and their capability to adjust the logistics of their struggle to a changing reality.

In conclusion, the crucial question is: to what extent did suicide actions help Palestinian organizations further their goals? It is hard not to agree with the contention above, according to which Hamas-instigated suicide campaigns contributed to the acceleration of the Israeli withdrawal from cities in the West Bank at the time of the implementation of the Oslo Accords, something that perhaps indirectly served the interests of the Palestinian Authority.[54] However, the major significance of suicide missions is in fact rooted in their cumulative influence. Although I do not have at my disposal the tools necessary to prove a causal relationship between the two, it nonetheless appears that since the intense suicide campaigns of the Al-Aqsa intifada, there has been a genuine change in the attitudes of the Israeli public and elites regarding the question of whether or not to maintain control of the Palestinian territories. If the architects of the Oslo Accords hoped that the Israeli public would approve the relinquishing of Israeli control over Judea, Samaria and Gaza on the basis of a belief in a vision of peace and cooperation between Israelis and Palestinians, well then, these particular hopes were now scattered to the winds.

Throughout the whole period during which Israelis and Palestinians pressed ahead on their way to a peace agreement, the Jewish population in Israel remained divided with regard to the question of the withdrawal from the territories and the evacuation of settlements. This change in public opinion happened in fact during the years of the intifada. Israelis gradually reconciled themselves to the notion that in order to live a normal life in their country, there was no alternative but to disengage from the Palestinians. In plain words, suicide attacks had succeeded where a vision of peace had failed. These attacks had brought about a substantial increase in Israeli public support for withdrawal from the territories – but this was out of a sense of resignation and not from a feeling that it was possible for Israelis and Palestinians to coexist peaceably, at least not in the near future. Therefore, it can be inferred that both Hamas and Palestinian Islamic Jihad, groups that from the very beginning objected to the Oslo Accords, had realized their goals. The Israeli public was fed up with the Accords and, at the same time, was willing to accept the idea of secession from the territories without a Palestinian commitment to peace or even an end to terror. The change in the Israeli public attitude was so dramatic that even Prime Minister Ariel Sharon, chief architect of the settlements in Judea, Samaria and Gaza, is now struggling in his efforts to promote a political plan based on an Israeli unilateral disengagement from the Gaza Strip and evacuation of settlements in northern Samaria.

At this juncture, it is necessary to verify if indeed there has been genuine progress for the Palestinian struggle in general. The answer is not so obvious, for a number of reasons. First, in the short term, the erection of the separation fence and Israel's renewed takeover of extensive territories belonging to the Palestinian Authority have made the lives of many Palestinians quite unbearable and also led to the point where there are serious doubts regarding the accomplishments of the armed struggle. Second, with respect to long-term consequences, Ariel Sharon has sought, in exchange for the disengagement from Gaza, to shore up settlements deep in the territories of

Judea and Samaria, a fact that will significantly reduce the size of a Palestinian state and will create a situation where there are Palestinian enclaves surrounded by territories under Israeli control. The persistence of an Israeli military presence in Palestinian territories will make it difficult to improve the quality of life of the population in the area and will perpetuate the sources of conflict.

The third point addresses the effect of the use of suicide bombers on the internal Palestinian state of affairs. During the course of the last few years, there has gradually been growth in the popularity of the Islamic bloc. Representing about one-quarter of the Palestinian public, it has become a political power to be reckoned with. Concurrently, Fatah's status as a dominant force has steadily eroded. Once again, it will be hard to prove a causal effect of violent struggle in general, and the use of suicide bombers in particular, on the change in the constellation of political power in the Palestinian theatre. However, an in-depth review of surveys conducted among Palestinians in the last decade indicates an affinity between the struggle of Islamic currents against Israel and the surge in public support for them. Conceivably, it would seem that, much like other political bodies, Islamic terrorist organizations, too, will seek to convert public support into political influence and will become a central actor in the institutional politics of the Palestinian state.

Summary

A comparison of Hezbollah and the Palestinian organizations in their use of suicide terrorism indicates that this strategy has had a considerable influence on political processes in the Middle East. An attempt to try and assess which one of the various organizations has benefited most from the application of this method will place Hezbollah at the top of the list. Not only has the organization been able to realize its strategic goals and bring about the withdrawal of various foreign forces from Lebanon, but activating suicide terrorists has also earned it great popularity and substantial influence on the Lebanese political scene and, at a later stage, on more extensive areas in the Middle East conflict. Despite no longer utilizing suicide bombers after the strategy had more or less exhausted itself in southern Lebanon, Hezbollah continues to 'spread the news' on this subject throughout the world.

Among the Palestinian organizations, the great winner from the use of this method was Hamas and the loser was Fatah. Nonetheless, the Palestinian case is more complex than the Lebanese one. Hamas was successful in significantly damaging the Oslo Accords process and tipping the scales of Israeli public opinion in favour of support for the withdrawal from the lands of Judea, Samaria and Gaza during the Al-Aqsa intifada. It forced Israel to be inclined to pull out of Palestinian territories that were not part of the peace agreements and without requiring the Palestinians to yield to any of its original demands. Moreover, Hamas and Palestinian Islamic Jihad have become significant forces in the Palestinian political arena and they will have to be accounted for in any future situation that will include a division of political goods. At the same time, Israeli determination to wage war on suicide terrorism has landed a strong blow on the Hamas leadership, which became a major objective of the policy of 'targeted assassinations'. This has left Hamas in the position of a strong popular movement seeking institutionalization and aspiring to receive a slice of the authority over lands to be evacuated by Israel, yet, at the same time, the backbone of its senior leadership has been eliminated. Grooming a new generation of leaders could take a long time. Furthermore, it was Israel's effective foiling policy that forced Hamas and Islamic Jihad to downgrade their suicide bombing campaigns, rather than any other factor.

A concluding word about Fatah: it is more apparent now that this organization was drawn into the use of suicide bombing rather than actually being a spearheading model of it. In the case of Fatah, this tactic was not a vehicle used to promote strategic or political interests but rather a necessary means of political survival. In effect, Fatah's use of suicide terrorism during the time of the Al-Aqsa intifada was the last nail in the coffin of the Oslo Accords – the same Accords the organization had signed approximately one decade earlier. Furthermore, it is reasonable to assume that the majority of the accomplishments brought about by Palestinian suicide terrorism will be attributed in the future to Hamas and Palestinian Islamic Jihad whereas Fatah's role in this context will probably be made light of. As for *internal* Palestinian politics, it is hard to suppose that Fatah's perpetration of suicide bombings was or will be the magic bullet that could help the organizational elite protect or revive its former, higher standing. Over the years, the image of the Palestinian Authority has gradually worn away in the Palestinian public eye due to leadership failures and corruption. If the public remains loyal to the movement, it will apparently be due more to the long-lasting commitment to this institution as the flag-bearer of Palestinian liberation rather than on account of its activation of suicide bombers.

4
Turning to Suicide Terrorism: the LTTE and the PKK

The decision to present the cases of the LTTE (Liberation Tigers of Tamil Eelam) and the Kurdistan Workers' Party (PKK – Partiya Karkeren Kurdistan) immediately on the heels of the analyses of the Hezbollah and Palestinian organizations is not just a matter of coincidence. A study of the factors that led these organizations to launch and in some cases eventually terminate campaigns of suicide terrorism will be helpful in understanding whether the aspects relevant to explaining the phenomenon are universal or, on the other hand, particularistic and location-dependent.

Moreover, linking the LTTE of Sri Lanka and the PKK of Turkey as the focus of this chapter is also deliberate. The LTTE and the PKK are two organizations operating in countries quite remote from each other yet, despite the geographical distance between them, they share many common features. Both of them became active in the 1970s and were raised on the tenets of a radical left-wing ideology. Both of them represented or aspired to represent large ethnic groups struggling to achieve independence and sovereignty in a given territory. Furthermore, both the PKK and the LTTE have consistently endeavoured to recruit support from the diasporas of the ethnic group they sought to represent, principally from western Europe, but at the same time, they also applied mechanisms of control and oppression against that same ethnic group in the territory where they operated. These two organizations were also determined to gain international legitimacy for their causes but, at the same time, financed a great deal of their actions by criminal means, including smuggling drugs into different countries around the world.

However, the most striking similarity between the LTTE and the PKK was the fact that both were headed by charismatic leaders who were responsible for the sect-like features of their organizations. Above and beyond the commitment made by organization members to a certain ideology or interest, their primary duty was to their leader. The leadership style of the commanders of the LTTE and the PKK, Vellupillai Prabhakaran and Abdullah Ocalan, respectively, was almost identical. Neither tolerated resistance or disagreement and reacted very aggressively to any signs of challenge. They also were not lenient, to say the least, towards political personages outside the ranks of the organization who did not fully agree with their policies. Finally, in both cases, these organization leaders were the ones responsible for adopting the idea of suicide attacks, devising strategic guidelines for activating bombers, and they also served as the principal source of inspiration for the suicides themselves.

Overall Strategy or Specific Tactic? Suicide Terrorism of the LTTE in Sri Lanka

Before elaborating on the factors that led the LTTE to resort to suicide terrorism, it seems appropriate to address the group's instrumental-tactical orientation towards this method of operation. In regard to organizations discussed in the preceding chapter and those that will be presented later on, the decision to adopt suicide terrorism was in effect a quantum leap and once this method had been chosen, they placed it at the very forefront of their operations. In the case of the LTTE, on the other hand, it was evident that the use of suicide attackers was not a radical change in the organization's central strategy and it was perceived first and foremost as a highly useful tactic in situations where other methods seemed less effective.

Many terrorist organizations in the world are known for their limited organizational and military capabilities. In such cases, suicide attacks may serve as a strategic tool, enabling them to upgrade their operational capacities and thus creating a 'balance of terror' when up against powerful states (also known as 'asymmetrical warfare'). In comparison with these groups, the LTTE is an exception. It is an example of a highly efficient guerrilla organization, suggestive in its structure of a small army, principally specializing in sophisticated small-scale operations. In fact, its achievements using this mode of warfare did not fall far behind those of many armies.[1] Even before adopting the suicide bombing method, LTTE commanders were not afraid of engaging in major confrontations with the Sri Lankan army in their efforts to gain control over areas considered to be of strategic significance.

The decision to set up suicide squads was made by Prabhakaran after he had carefully studied the many benefits of this method on the basis of the Hezbollah experience in Lebanon.[2] However, he was also aware that it was necessary to adapt this mode of action to the particular requirements of his organization. In contrast to Palestinian organizations, which regarded suicide terrorism as a means for attaining an effect of mass casualty terrorism with the intention of shocking Israeli society, Prabhakaran saw the potential benefits of this method specifically in carrying out targeted assassinations in situations where it was difficult or impossible to attack a certain public figure or group of people using other methods.[3] The assassinations themselves, and not the element of suicide, were the strategic objective for the organization; they could possibly be used as a vehicle for changing political reality in the country. A review of a chronology of the actions of the LTTE reveals that nearly a quarter of the suicide attacks attributed to the organization were assassinations of political figures. In other cases, suicide attacks were employed by the LTTE as an effective battering ram in order to pierce well-defended army installations otherwise virtually impenetrable by the organization's guerrilla squads. In addition to the LTTE's tactical use of suicide squads, the picture would be incomplete if the other advantages of this method were not mentioned. These benefits are particularly evident when the organization was in a tight spot. In these cases, suicide attacks provided the LTTE with the ability to signal to the government in Colombo, as well as the Tamil population, that the organization was not easily to be defeated. Even under heavy pressure, it was still very determined and in fact capable of inflicting considerable damage on the enemy.[4]

Suicide terrorism as a tool in the Tamil minority's struggle for independence

The LTTE's first suicide action took place on 5 July 1987. Captain Millar, who eventually was to become one of the most revered persons in the organization, blew himself up inside a vehicle loaded with explosives in the centre of a Tamil university taken over by the army. Hezbollah's influences on Prabhakaran were highly manifest in this operation, which culminated in the deaths of seventy-five people. The trademark features of this operation were almost completely identical to those of the Hezbollah attack on the US Marine headquarters in Beirut.[5] The assault on the university was the opening chord in a long line of suicide attacks perpetrated by the LTTE throughout most of the 1990s and the early years of the new millennium. Indeed, this was the only organization whose suicide attacks almost reached the numbers of those committed by Palestinian organizations.

Despite the many differences between the Palestinian and Tamil situations, there are still a number of similarities that may help shed light on the factors responsible for the extreme violence of these two conflicts. A comparison may also help explain why both the Palestinian and the Tamil communities were so understanding and receptive towards the organization's deployment of suicides. In both cases,

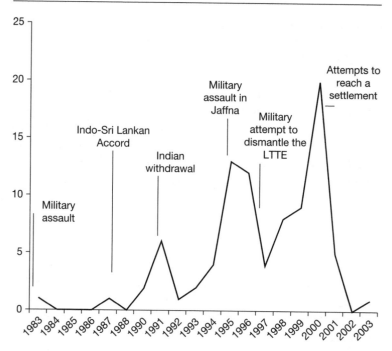

Figure 4.1 *Suicide campaigns of the LTTE*

suicide terrorism emerged after years of the oppression of aspirations towards sovereignty in a given, contentious territory and a violent and protracted struggle that did not further the goals of these groups in the way they hoped it would. One of the key aspects of the Palestinian–Israeli conflict, like the Tamil–Sinhalese struggle, was the end of British rule over these divisive territories in 1948.

A short while after the British began to cede control over Ceylon (Sri Lanka), the Sinhalese majority, which comprises about 74 per cent of the country's population, embarked on a process of ethnocratization that gradually wore away the civil rights of the Tamil people.[6] The process of excluding the Tamils from political and public life in Ceylon persisted for several decades and reached its peak after the British severed the last remaining strands of their control over the island in 1971.[7]

During the course of the 1970s, the political scene in the country continued to bubble and simmer and the tension between the two communities increased until it reached a violent boiling point in 1983. In July of that year, the LTTE carried out its first large-scale guerrilla operation. In a well-planned ambush, thirteen soldiers of the Sri Lankan army were killed in the Jaffna region, where there are large concentrations of Tamils.[8] The reaction of the Sinhalese community was fierce and swift in coming. For the next seventy-two hours, Tamil-owned houses and businesses were pillaged, burned and destroyed. Tamil women were raped and 360 Tamil citizens were killed. Although the extent of the active part of the defence forces in these events is not exactly clear, testimonies from on-the-spot witnesses indicate that many army officers chose to turn a blind eye and did not prevent harm to innocent citizens. In the following days, the riots continued to spread as bands of Tamils began to confront the rioters. In response, the government authorized the army to attack Tamil concentrations in Jaffna and quash the resistance. Ultimately, the Tamil United Liberation Front was banned and ousted from parliament in Colombo. This step closed off the last little political recourse left to the battered Tamil minority, which consequently had no means of promoting its interests by means of legitimate political action.[9]

Between the years 1983 and 1986, members of the LTTE intensified their attacks in the streets of Sri Lanka with the use of sophisticated guerrilla tactics. Prabhakaran's goal was to keep the Tamil problem on the country's political agenda and apply constant pressure in order to further the organization's demands for independence. In the beginning of 1986, while under continuous attack by the LTTE, the government yielded and began to engage in negotiations with the hope of reaching some kind of agreement. However, talks were not conducted with Tamil representatives but rather with Indian authorities. The aim of negotiations was to try and find a resolution that would provide a partial autonomy for the Tamils while receiving support and Indian guarantees for the agreements.[10] Unfortunately, things took a turn for the worse.

An explosion at a busy bus station in Colombo caused 113 fatalities, which prompted the government to mount a wide-scale military operation in the Jaffna area. Once again, Tamil residents of this region were hit very hard. The Indian government stepped up its efforts to put an end to this violent stand-off and, following a concentrated effort, an agreement (the Indo-Sri Lankan Accord) was signed between Sri Lanka and India in July 1987. The Accord guaranteed partial rights to the Tamils while India pledged that it would provide assurances to the government in Colombo. At the same time, there were also clauses protecting the interests of both countries.[11]

However, instead of advancing a compromise in this region, the Accord led to an escalation of tensions. Radical Sinhalese movements, which had reservations about the Indian role in Sri Lankan internal affairs, began to knuckle down and work hard to torpedo the agreements, a fact that led once more to a worsening of relations between the two ethnic groups. Moreover, Prabhakaran and his people had doubts about the deployment of an Indian peacekeeping force in the Tamil areas of the country, and so now Indian soldiers, as well as Sri Lankan ones, became a target for hostilities. At this stage, LTTE guerrilla attacks – always marked by great daring and sophistication – were complemented in the months after the signing of the agreements by a systematic use of suicide attacks. In many cases, suicide bombers functioned as force multipliers that compounded the destructive effect of the actions.[12]

Similar to the Lebanese case, the intense and protracted assaults on peacekeeping forces had a coercive effect on the Indian government. In March 1990, India withdrew its forces from the country and President Premadasa of Sri Lanka announced his readiness to engage in negotiations with representatives of the Tamil factions. Three months later, the talks ran aground, which once again led to an escalation of the situation in the country. Members of the LTTE exploited the new conditions and took forcible control of the Jaffna region in what was termed Elam War II. The anticipated and severe response of the Sri Lankan army to the takeover of

Jaffna, like the events of 1983, including the rape of women and the 'disappearance' of many men, served the interests of the LTTE well. Support for the organization swelled and with it the reserves of potential recruits.[13]

In 1991, there was once again an upsurge in LTTE actions. The organization mounted a wide-ranging campaign including a wave of suicide attacks that reached its climax in 1994. As noted before, one of the main features of LTTE violent operations was the use of suicide bombers in the assassination of prominent political figures with the aim of changing the region's political reality. In May 1991, a woman suicide bomber from the organization took the life of the Prime Minister of India, Rajiv Gandhi, together with her own, as she blew herself up during one of his election rallies. About two years later, it was the President of Sri Lanka, Premadasa, who was killed by a suicide assassin. The assassin had become a member of the President's house maintenance staff and detonated himself at the President's side on the way to a press conference. Another elimination, which took place in November 1994, had a decisive influence on the country's political system. This time, the target was Gamini Dissanayake, the presidential candidate of the Sinhalese United National Party. In addition to Dissanayake, fifty of the party's directorate were killed and, in effect, the entire leadership sector of the party was wiped out. In the wake of this mass killing, the People's Alliance Party, headed by Chandrika Bandaranaike Kumaratunga, took over the government helm in Colombo.

The new government adopted a mixed approach in relation to the Tamil issue. On one hand, there were attempts at making contact with representatives of moderate Tamil organizations and, on the other, the LTTE was politically excluded. Militarily, the pursuit of organization operatives continued. In April 1994, one of the first manifestations of this approach was the massive air force bombardment of LTTE bases located in the Batticaloa region of the island. Not long after this, in July 1995, the government of Sri Lanka submitted a proposal that put forward a political compromise to Tamil representatives. The crux of the proposal was the idea of establishing a federal republic consisting of eight autonomous districts, each with limited independence and all subordinate to the central government. The LTTE rejected the offer outright, compelling the entire Tamil population to decline it as well.

The government's response to the LTTE's position was not long in coming. The army launched an extensive operation aimed at weakening the organization's muscle and its ability to force its attitudes on the Tamil population. In an operation termed 'Riviresa', which began on 3 December 1995, Sri Lankan military forces were able to restore control of Jaffna to the government. Encouraged by their success, the forces continued to apply considerable military pressure on the LTTE so that its fighters retreated into the jungle regions. The second Riviresa operation got under way only a short time later with the aim of overpowering the organization and bringing about its collapse. For a while it appeared that the government was about to accomplish its goals. However, the LTTE was able to regroup its forces and wage battle yet again. This turn of events led the army in 1996 to set out on operation Riviresa number three. The outcome of this operation was already less promising for the government of Sri Lanka. Members of the LTTE had taken advantage of the interim period between operations to rebuild the organization's military infrastructures and subsequently retaliated against the third operation with the most severe campaign of suicide attacks since the commencement of operations.[14] In this particular case, suicide operatives were exploited by the organization as a balancing factor in view of the other advantages held by the Sri Lankan army at that time and were able to inflict great harm to the larger opponent.

In the beginning of 1999, following another period of reorganization, LTTE forces launched their own extensive military campaign, which included the incorporation of suicide attacks. Their goal was the attrition of Sri Lankan military gains in the past four years with the ultimate objective being the reconquest of Jaffna. The fighting continued for three months and Prabhakaran's people made substantial gains. The most crucial was the takeover of Elephant Path, a road of major strategic significance because it connects Jaffna with the rest of Sri Lanka. The LTTE sought to make the most of this advance in order to build up momentum for continuing their attack; however, their progress towards the takeover of Jaffna was slower than they anticipated.

Disillusioned with their inability to realize the goal they had set for themselves, the LTTE submitted an official ceasefire proposal to the Sri Lankan government at the beginning of May. In exchange for a cessation of hostilities in the region, Prabhakaran and his people called for the withdrawal of army forces from Jaffna. The government, which sensed the organization's distress, rejected the proposal and violence in the region resumed. The conflict reached one of its low points in December 1999 when, during an election rally, a suicide terrorist blew herself up right next to President Kumaratunga and injured her in the eye. As before, the goal of the LTTE was to alter the political *status quo* by means of a campaign of assassinations in the attempt to bring about a replacement of the country's leadership.

The above account supports the assumption that the LTTE's use of suicide attackers was highly sophisticated. The organization singled out goals whose aim was to further the interests of the Tamil population as perceived by the organization leadership. For a great part of the operations, suicide actions were a tactical device designed to bring about strategic changes. In other words, they made it feasible for the LTTE to cause serious damage to the country's political leadership and in this fashion reshuffle the political deck of cards in the hope that this change would serve the organization's aims. In other cases, suicide missions were an effective tool for attacking security forces when other organizational methods proved to be less effective. From the events described above, it appears that the importance of suicide attacks for the LTTE leadership progressively increased in circumstances where the organization suffered from military inferiority and was in need of military gains in order to renew a balance of deterrence. At this point, it seems appropriate to ask the question that was relevant to the Hezbollah and Palestinian campaigns: did suicide assaults have a role in the organization's attempt to muster the support of the population it sought to represent as well as in its competition with other Tamil groups?

Suicide terrorism and the Tamil political arena

A study of developments in the Tamil theatre during the years when the LTTE made use of suicide terrorism confirms that, for this organization, deploying suicide bombers had less significance than in the Palestinian and Lebanese cases. This reinforces the assumption presented before. Initiating suicide attacks was regarded by Prabhakaran as a case-specific tactic more than an overall strategy; he did not seem to be making a consistent attempt to utilize suicide terrorism as a vehicle for achieving political gains in the internal affairs of the country.

The reason for avoiding the use of suicide terrorism as domestic political propaganda is not because the LTTE lacked rivals in the Tamil political arena. In fact, the opposite is true. Over the course of time, dozens of organizations emerged on the scene, some of them violent while others elected to keep their actions within the limits of the law. All these organizations sought to gain the confidence of the Tamil minority and to represent its interests. However, the reason why the LTTE did not require suicide terrorism in order to enhance its reputation was much simpler. Over the years, the organization systematically and violently eliminated the majority of competing organizations until it was left almost completely on its own.

To elaborate, in the 1970s, the Tamil National Tigers – the group which eventually was to become the Liberation Tigers of Tamil Eelam – was only one in a long list of political organizations in the volatile Tamil political arena. Even at its beginnings, this group turned out to be much more militant in comparison with the others. It started out as part of the Tamil

United Front, but withdrew in the year 1978 due to ideological disputes. The source of these disputes was related to the Tigers' call for more forcible measures in the struggle for Tamil independence and its marked dissatisfaction with the actions of veteran organizations.[15]

The hostility displayed towards other Tamil organizations by the LTTE did not just amount to a lack of cooperation. Unlike Palestinian organizations which, despite considerable differences among them, attempted to maintain over the years, at least on the face of it, a certain degree of cooperation and worked together to prevent the outbreak of civil war, the Tigers opted to deal with rival Tamil organizations in aggressive ways. Signs of this were already evident in the organization's early years. In contrast to what might be expected from a guerrilla or a terrorist organization whose goals were national liberation, the first violent actions initiated by the Tigers were not aimed at army forces or Sinhalese politicians but rather at moderate politicians and Tamil civilians in Jaffna suspected of collaborating with the government.[16]

Throughout the 1980s, this tendency grew. In those years, many organizations, both nationalist and local, continued to operate in the Tamil arena. The Tigers, who had maintained their status as the most extreme Tamil organization and increased their numbers in the wake of the 1983 events, mounted a campaign about two years later to remove these organizations. Following Prabhakaran's orders and applying brutal force, his people systematically liquidated leaders and sometimes activists of other organizations. On several occasions, the targets of these eliminations included former allies of the LTTE who were regarded as a threatening factor.[17]

Things reached such a point that, in May 1986, the Tigers carried out a full-scale massacre of members of the Tamil Eelam Liberation Organization and their leader Sri Sabaratnam.[18] The elimination campaign at the time was so aggressive that associations such as the People's Liberation Organization of Tamil Eelam, which had already lost most of its combat potential and was quite subservient in any case, continued to be a target for Prabhakaran devotees, who sought to bring about the complete immobilization of some of these groups.[19]

In the years subsequent to the Tigers' systematic campaign of terror against rival groups, they remained the single most dominant organization in the Tamil arena. Therefore, the idea that, as a political organization, the Tigers employed the suicide method in order to gain public sympathy in its contest with rival groups – a factor which, in the Palestinian case, was highly germane – is basically of no consequence in this case. The LTTE simply did not allow any other organization to be of relevance, let alone be in direct competition with them.

It is also difficult to prove that suicide terrorism was committed in order to gain Tamil public approval. It is hard to make an unequivocal connection between suicide terrorism and increases in the organization's public approval ratings at the beginning of the 1980s. As mentioned earlier, in contrast to other cases, where the introduction of suicide tactics often indicated a new stage in the battle waged by the particular organization, for the Tigers this method was just one link in a chain of an assortment of warfare tactics employed over the years. Therefore, it would be a very difficult task to isolate the effects of suicides from other conflict-related events, especially the aggressive actions of the army and Sinhalese groups which were often enough to propel the Tamil population into the arms of the LTTE.

In general, two principal types of affinities evolved between the LTTE and the Tamil community: voluntary mobilization and coercion. The mobilization of public support was often facilitated by the harsh attitude of the government in Colombo towards the Tamil minority. For example, while the number of LTTE members in 1983 was around 600, a short while after the large-scale operation against the Tamils, these numbers increased into the tens of thousands.[20] Persistence of the government's iron-fisted policy towards the Tamils played into the hands of the LTTE in another respect. During the 1970s, and especially during the 1980s, support for the organization spread to the Tamil populace all over Sri Lanka as well as to Tamils abroad. Support from the diaspora was important for the Tigers because it formed a strong base for recruiting a significant part of the organization's resources.[21]

Another opportunity for marshalling Tamil support took place in September 1990 when the LTTE took over the Jaffna region. When the government retaliated with severe military measures, rioting broke out among the Tamil population. These events not only led to a broadening of support for the Tigers, they also inspired scores of men, women and even youths of both sexes to want to join the organization's ranks and engage in combat against army forces.[22] The Tigers knew how to take advantage of these circumstances and enlisted many of these volunteers for military action, including, not surprisingly, suicide missions.

Many recruits to the Tigers organization at that time were young, below the age of eighteen. Frequently, elements of coercion and intimidation were applied by the LTTE when picking potentials from among the Tamil population. Taking on children for military operations would often elicit the dismay of parents, who expressed their reservations to organization representatives regarding the use of children in the battlefield. But as far as the LTTE was concerned, acknowledging these attitudes or even negotiating with local representatives on the question of the children was not up for debate. Organization operatives simply demanded from each family that at least one of their children join the ranks of the warriors. If refused, children were snatched from the streets or even taken from schools.

The Tamil population's reverence for – as well as fear of – the Tigers was demonstrated in Mia Bloom's attempt to conduct a public survey among it. Before the survey was even attempted, many of the potential subjects expressed their reluctance to participate, fearing for their well-being. They agreed to answer survey questions only after receiving explicit permission from LTTE operatives. Survey findings well reflected the feelings of admiration accompanied by trepidation. In the first place, approval for the LTTE was very high.

Respondents even expressed reservations about the founding of other Tamil organizations that might turn out to be competition for the LTTE. In the second place, all of the LTTE's methods of operation, including activation of suicides, garnered high rates of support. Survey participants did not find any ethical problem in the committing of suicide attacks against military targets. In fact, the opposite was true. They saw this as a fully legitimate method of operation with the potential of forcing authorities into solving the Tamil problem at the negotiations table.[23] At the same time, using suicide attackers against civilian targets received significantly lower rates of support. This corresponded with the LTTE's official position, which consistently expressed reservations regarding the use of this method against civilians and denied any responsibility for actions that were aimed at civilian targets.[24]

Factors leading to the LTTE's suspension of suicide attacks

The question, at this juncture, is what brought about the dramatic decrease in LTTE-instigated suicide attacks subsequent to the year 2000? The question is especially relevant in view of the fact that this operational method rendered the organization such good service over the years. The answer can be found in changes that took place in three frameworks that were of critical importance for the LTTE. These were the struggle with the government, the international context and the internal Tamil arena.

With respect to the struggle against the government in Colombo, it appeared that discontinuing the use of suicides was, to a great degree, in direct consequence of a conclusion reached by the organization leadership: specifically, that the benefits of this tactic had been exploited to the full, at least for the time being. Furthermore, it seemed that both the authorities in Colombo as well as the LTTE had reached a state of sobering fatigue due to protracted and mutual attrition. As a result, following years of violent confrontation, both sides exhibited considerable flexibility at the negotiation table. The LTTE shelved its demands for independence in exchange for a Tamil autonomy in a federal system. The government, on its side, was forthcoming in its very willingness to negotiate with LTTE representatives and by regarding them as formal representatives of the Tamil minority.[25]

Another explanation, and one no less important, for suspending the use of suicides, is related to the changes that occurred in the international arena. According to Puleedevan, one of the organization's spokespersons, the events of 11 September 2001 transformed suicide attacks into a method of operation that was subject to widespread condemnation by the international community. The LTTE, which throughout the years was fairly concerned about its image in the international arena, was not interested in being put in the same category as organizations such as Al-Qaeda.[26]

In terms of Tamil internal politics, the ongoing violence that characterized the LTTE's struggle, including the use of suicide actions, made it increasingly difficult for the population and not only because of pressure applied by the army. At a certain stage, in the late 1990s, when insurmountable obstacles began to appear in recruiting funds for the organization's activities from the Tamil diaspora in North America, Australia and Africa, the LTTE shifted the focus of its money-raising efforts to Sri Lanka. The consequence of this step was the considerable financial exhaustion of the Tamil population, whose economic situation was unsatisfactory even prior to the LTTE's fresh appeals. As a result, the organization began to be concerned that if it were to increase pressure on the local population, support for the organization and its operational methods would gradually decrease and, by the same token, there would be a greater disposition to a resolution of the Tamil problem at the negotiation table.[27]

In conclusion, while the factors that led the LTTE to engage in violent struggle have a resemblance to the Palestinian case, the reasons for incorporating the suicide method were considerably different. In respect to the battle with the government and army, suicide terrorism for the LTTE was just one tactical weapon among several others that were employed during the course of the conflict. The effectiveness of the suicide method was primarily apparent in assassination operations aimed at undermining the political system and in penetrating fortified military installations in order to create a balance of terror and prove to the army the organization's imposing capabilities. Using suicide bombers as a vehicle designed to influence public opinion and in this way put pressure on policymakers did not seem of central importance for the organization. Also, with regard to the country's internal political affairs, the use of the suicide method by the LTTE differs, to a certain extent, from the circumstances of organizations described earlier.

It would indeed be hard to argue with the fact that the determination demonstrated by the organization's readiness to send its members on certain-death missions helped it win the sympathy of certain parts of the population. Nevertheless, there seemed to be no intentional use of suicide terrorism as a tool for mobilizing political support, let alone as a factor in the competition with other Tamil organizations.

Suicide Terrorism as a Means of Organizational Survival: the PKK in Turkey

It is hard not to be struck by the many similarities between the LTTE and the PKK. All the same, these are not identical organizations. In fact, the differences between them seem to be the main reason why the LTTE was successful in advancing a significant number of its goals and was able to survive while the PKK failed to last and eventually folded. The Kurdistan Workers' Party was established on 27 November 1978 and was one of a number of radical left-wing organizations that emerged in Turkey in the 1960s and 1970s. However, in contrast to other organizations which sought at the time to promote different strains of a communist worldview, Abdullah Ocalan, the organization's founder, regarded the integration of a Marxist revolution with the Kurds' struggle for independence as a central objective.

The PKK's involvement in violent action against Turkey began only six years after the organization's formal institution. Ocalan, who received substantial assistance from the Syrian authorities, took advantage of this interim period to create an organizational infrastructure for guerrilla actions and to train groups of fighters.[28] As with all the organizations discussed above, the PKK's decision to opt for suicide terrorism was eventually made only after long years of involvement in a wide diversity of guerrilla operations and other types of terrorism.

Before going into the factors that led the PKK to adopt suicide terrorism, a certain critical question, long associated with the organization, should be asked. Researchers who have followed the PKK during the course of its operation are divided in their opinion regarding the question of the organization's objectives. Was the Kurdish ethno-national interest in fact so close to Ocalan's heart as it appeared in his messages, or were most of his gestures made with the aim of promoting a Marxist revolutionary ideology?[29]

Halfway through the 1980s, a short while after deciding to take the path of violence, the PKK formed two military organizations. The first one was ERNK (National Liberation Front of Kurdistan), established in 1984.[30] As already evident in the group's sporadic acts of terrorism, it is possible to provide a partial answer for this question and at the same time learn about one of the PKK's most crucial problems over the years: the organization's only partial ability to convince the Kurdish population about the sincerity of its intentions in respect of the promotion of its interests and, in consequence, the difficulties it has always had in drumming up support for its cause.[31] The minor effectiveness of ERNK's activities in terms of the struggle against Turkey and the indifference with which the organization was received among Kurds mainly in the urban centres led Ocalan to institute ARGK (People's Liberation Army of Kurdistan) in 1986. Somewhat wiser from his bitter experience, this time Ocalan sought to assemble Kurds into guerrilla units that would form a people's army and in this fashion gain the support of the Kurdish population.[32]

However, the organization's actions to a large extent gave lie to its goals. Over the years, ARGK was responsible for the deaths of more than ten thousand people, most of them Kurds. The systematic and grave injury sustained by precisely the same population which the organization claimed to represent was justified by the organization as efforts to demonstrate to the Kurdish public its ominous power and to deter it from collaborating with the Turkish authorities. In general, it appeared that despite its declared intention to represent the Kurds, the PKK did not pass over any opportunity to threaten them and alienate them from the organization. Even when it was necessary to recruit new fighters to its ranks, the PKK preferred in many cases either to abduct young Kurds from their houses or to depend on the recruiting abilities of the organization's envoys in Kurdish centres in western Europe – where the PKK had more success – rather than approach Kurds in southeast Turkey directly in the effort to gain their confidence.[33] The sporadic attempts to muster support among the Kurds were quite crude. For example, in the mid-1990s, Ocalan who, throughout the years championed a Marxist worldview tried, ironically, to link up with the Islamic Welfare Party. His purpose was to capture the hearts of those Kurds known for their tendency to exhibit sympathy for Islam-affiliated organizations.[34]

Popular support, member morale or strategic interest?
The PKK's opting for suicide terrorism

The PKK launched its first campaign of suicide terrorism in June 1996 and suspended it soon afterwards; the second campaign was launched in 1998 and stopped in August 1999. Unlike other organizations where the decision to dispatch suicides was reached by the higher ranks of leadership, in the case of the PKK, the subject was, at least formally, debated and the action eventually authorized by representatives who participated in the organization's congress.[35] And yet, in comparison with the LTTE, the number of suicide operations was quite trifling. While the LTTE conducted

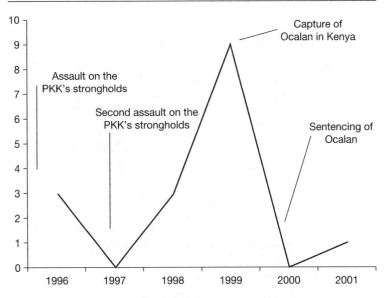

Figure 4.2 *The suicide campaign of the PKK*

more than 170 suicide actions during the course of its five campaigns between the years 1987 and 2003, the number of PKK-activated suicides between the years 1996 and 1999 added up to no more than fifteen operations that reached their target and seven that failed. These attacks were part of two campaigns, the major one (1998–9), peaking in 1999 following the capture of Abdullah Ocalan in Kenya. The key question that I will try to answer in the following paragraphs is what were the factors that led the organization to opt for suicide terrorism at the time?

As noted above, prior to the first suicide attack, it was possible to describe the PKK as an organization whose direction was ambiguous. On one hand, it wished to be an authentic representative of Kurdish national aspirations and, on the other, the tough attitude displayed towards this population over the years and the considerable ideological gap between the organization's leadership and majority of Kurds did not exactly help the former to win the latter's confidence. The very decision to use suicide terrorism – until then, identified in the Middle East with religious Islamic organizations – can be interpreted as an attempt by Ocalan and his people, who were deeply influenced by the success of the religious organizations, to signal to the Kurdish population that their organization was not significantly different from those same religious organizations that had gained the support of the Kurdish population. Another possible explanation why the PKK chose the path of suicide terrorism is related to the low morale of the organization rank and file due to the tough obstacles encountered in its attempts to advance its goals.[36] Dispatching suicides injected new blood into the organization's veins and raised, if only for a short time, the morale among its members.

Yet, the pivotal factor which led the organization to set out on a campaign of suicide terrorism was strategic. From 1992 on, the Turkish army launched a salvo of hard and consecutive blows at the PKK.[37] In March 1995, large army forces set out on 'Operation Steel'. About thirty-five thousand soldiers accompanied by air and artillery support crossed the Iraqi border and began to operate in the Kurdish enclave in northern Iraq with the aim of halting PKK operations and establishing stability along the border.[38] After seven weeks of intensive military action, the authorities in Ankara announced that they had attained their goals and had decided to draw back most of their forces to Turkey. Army sources claimed that they had killed 555 PKK fighters and had seriously damaged the organization's assorted infrastructures.[39] The first suicide operation initiated by the PKK took place not long after these attacks on the organization's strongholds. A female suicide terrorist, who was hiding the explosive device under her clothes, killed nine soldiers who were marching in a military parade in the city of Tunceli.[40] This incident signalled to Ankara that, despite the widespread army operations that had seriously damaged the organization's military capabilities, they still possessed ways of inflicting severe damage on the Turkish 'home front'.

In May 1997, the Turkish army crossed its border into Iraq once again. This time, the extent of the military operation was downgraded. About ten thousand troops, accompanied by tanks, artillery and air support, penetrated Kurdish enclaves with the intention of striking at PKK bases. Despite the smaller forces, reports from news agencies stated that 1,300 PKK fighters were killed and 200 more were captured. The pressure on the PKK was so intense that Ocalan was forced to approach the Turkish authorities in an appeal for ceasefire. His petition was emphatically rejected.[41] In the period following the operation, the organization's activities were almost completely neutralized aside from one aspect, that is, the dispatching of suicides.[42] It is possible to assume that the PKK's ensuing and obvious strategic inferiority was a significant factor in Ocalan's decision appreciably to increase the number of suicide operations. In the absence of other effective devices and in view of Ankara's refusal to arrive at some compromise with the organization, Ocalan was trying to show the authorities that, even in a state of battlefield inferiority, the organization still had the capability of striking back at strategic targets in the heart of Turkey. Ocalan's message was clearly understood by Ankara. The Turkish government at the time was acutely aware of the fact that PKK suicide operations in the country's tourist centres could lead to serious economic losses.[43] Still, the PKK was not successful in its attempt to force the government to concede to its demands and to let up in its iron-fisted efforts to stamp out the organization's suicide terrorism campaign.

The role of Turkish policy in thwarting further PKK suicide actions

For countries that are struggling with similar types of terrorism warfare, many lessons can be learnt from Turkey's battle against the PKK. Unlike the cases reviewed above and those which will be discussed below, Turkey was able to suppress the PKK suicide campaign and overpower the organization before it could benefit from the advantages inherent to this method of operation. Nevertheless, Turkish policy also demonstrates that success in such a struggle is often accompanied by heavy losses, and it is questionable whether many democratic countries – particularly those where human rights are an essential foundation – could afford to pay this price. One of the main elements responsible for thrusting Turkey into an uncompromising struggle with the PKK was the Turkish army, which traditionally had served as a significant force in the country's political system. While political echelons found it difficult to assess the degree of the organization's threat to the Turkish polity and therefore were also hesitant in their selection of tools to fight it, as far as the army was concerned, there were no doubts. The PKK was considered a genuine threat, and higher-ranking army officers applied heavy pressure on the political system to persuade the politicians to invest greater resources in the fight against the organization. In effect, the army assumed the role of spearhead and leading light in this battle. Its forces tenaciously laboured against PKK contingents in southeast Turkey and did not hesitate to invade Kurdish enclaves in northern Iraq when the higher echelons found this necessary.[44] It would be erroneous to maintain that army leaders purposely endeavoured to harm those sectors of the Kurdish population uninvolved in organization activities. Their principal goal was, for the most part, to harm the PKK in such a critical way that its military operational capabilities would be neutralized. However, in situations where Ocalan's fighters operated from within Kurdish villages, army units did not think twice about entering these villages and engaging in actions that were in serious violation of human rights.[45]

In principle, political factors in Ankara accepted the army's position, according to which it was necessary to put a stop to the organization's activities. At the same time, they tried to prevent a situation in which the general Kurdish public would be severely harmed because this was also liable to drive the latter straight into the arms of the PKK. Therefore, they adopted a policy of 'divide and rule' with the aim of driving a wedge between the organization and its potential 'constituency'. One of the first steps taken by Ankara was to acknowledge the Kurdish minority's cultural uniqueness. Although an initial and small step, it should be emphasized that this was a significant change in the policy of Turkey, which for many long years had obstinately refused to recognize Kurdish claims and made it particularly difficult for Kurds to engage in political action.[46]

The divide and rule policy lasted throughout the years of armed conflict between Turkey and the PKK. It relied on a number of measures and among them was an attempt to shore up Kurdish groups that opposed the PKK. In addition, governmental financial assistance was awarded to Kurdish regions in southeast Turkey suffering from serious economic destitution. At the same time, Kurdish political elements considered to be militant were excluded from both the political system and public life. Finally, the army received political cover for persisting in its struggle against the PKK.

The army's actions were also distinguished by features of this same two-pronged policy. On one hand, aggressive operations were mounted against PKK strongholds which led to serious casualties among residents in that area. On the other hand, the army's generals indicated to residents that they had no intention of harming them and that one of their main goals was actually to protect them from the organization itself. In light of the difficult history of relations between the PKK and many of the Kurds in the area, it comes as no surprise that many residents chose to cluster in villages that the army constructed for them. The military and financial support provided to residents of these villages allowed them to cope with PKK attacks in a better way. As for the army, in return, it used these villages as frontline outposts in Kurdish regions. In this fashion, it was able to increase its intelligence-gathering abilities and also could be ready to attack at much shorter notice when urgent operations against the organization were necessary.

The uncompromising military pressure on the PKK and the state's success in winning over a considerable part of Kurdish public opinion ultimately led to Ocalan's flight, together with some of his associates, to Syria and Lebanon. However, the Turkish authorities did not relent at this stage. Ankara applied considerable diplomatic pressure on Syria and this eventually led to the deportation of the PKK followers from the region.[47] Ocalan was now continuously on the run, unable to find a place where the long arm of the

Turkish security authorities could not reach him. During the course of his flight, he even made his way to Kenya where, due primarily to the newly enhanced intelligence capabilities of the Turkish security services, he was finally caught.

The ramifications of Ocalan's capture and his prosecution are very interesting, especially when compared to Israel's policy of assassinating Palestinian organization leaders responsible for dispatching suicide attackers. It seems that the Israeli policy of targeting leaders leads to a short-term confusion among the organizations and some degree of erosion in their operational capabilities but ultimately does not unsettle their motivation to continue to dispatch suicides. In Ocalan's case, on the other hand, his apprehension caused an intensification of the suicide attacks in the short run, yet the events that followed brought the attacks to a halt and later led to the virtual dissolution of the PKK.[48]

During the course of Ocalan's trial, and perhaps due to the intense pressure he was under, he denied responsibility for the suicide attacks and expressed reservations regarding fundamental premises of the PKK's ideology. The death sentence served on Ocalan on 26 June 1999 more or less put the last nail in the coffin with respect to the activities of the PKK.[49] It is difficult to speculate what exactly were the reasons that led Ocalan to implore his people to cease their aggression and focus only on defensive actions,[50] but it is reasonable to believe that a major reason was the assumption that, in exchange for the cessation of PKK's violent actions, his death sentence would be commuted to imprisonment.[51] Ocalan's dominant status in the organization led to the almost unreserved compliance of his people. The threat of dispatching suicide bombers was removed and other planned violent actions were also discontinued. However, this was not the last of his capitulations. Ocalan's call also obliged the PKK leadership to abolish the Free Women's Union of Kurdistan (YAJK – Yekitiya Azadiya Jinen Kurdistan), which had served as the principal military arm of the organization for mounting suicide actions. This act essentially wrapped up the last chapter in the organization's history.[52] Furthermore, in the

PKK congress that was held in the year 2000, the organization revised its ideology and announced that it was relinquishing its ambition of establishing a socialist Kurdish state.

In conclusion, from the early years of its founding, the PKK could be identified as an organization whose goals were not entirely unambiguous, a fact that at times encumbered its operations. Ocalan's leadership might have been indisputable among the organization's rank and file, but not among different segments of the Kurdish people, who were ideologically more remote from the organization and were more likely to suffer from its strong-arm tactics. Under these circumstances, the PKK was left with a relatively narrow backbone of support, especially in the rural areas. This fact also made it easier for the government of Turkey to prise open the existing fissure between Ocalan and his followers on one hand and the Kurdish people on the other, and then isolate the organization and strike at it. The group's decision to incorporate suicide attacks as a feature of its terrorist tactics was evidently an attempt to preserve some kind of element of deterrence in view of the unrelenting pressure from the Turkish army. However, Ocalan failed to read correctly the Turkish determination to clamp down categorically on his group's activities and therefore it is difficult to point out any genuine achievements that this sole suicide campaign actually brought him. The most important lesson to be drawn from the case study of the PKK is the fact that, under certain conditions, a resolute counter-policy applied by a government contending with suicide terrorism may actually bring an end to the phenomenon.

Summary

Despite the many similarities between the LTTE and the PKK, it is in fact the *distinctions* between the two that shed light on the circumstances leading these organizations to commence and eventually to cease carrying out suicide attacks. As shown above, the LTTE regarded this method as more a specific tactic than an overall strategy. Having said that, in a number of episodes, both organizations committed suicide attacks in situations where they felt powerless or were pushed into a corner, most often as a result of protracted military pressure. Dispatching suicide bombers under these conditions was meant to demonstrate to the state and army that these insurgent groups were not to be suppressed. These organizations were in fact signalling that they still had the capacity to cause substantial harm to sensitive targets on the 'home front' of the other, dominant side, while also trying to dissuade the authorities from bringing the stand-off to a critical, decisive point. The very fact that the LTTE was able to survive and even accomplish several goals (to a great extent, on account of suicide terrorist campaigns), whereas the PKK failed in its endeavours and was eventually overpowered, is largely rooted in the circumstances where, despite the intricate relations between the LTTE and the Tamil public, the LTTE was able to create for itself significant bases of support among a population that believed the organization was completely committed to its interests. Therefore, the hard-hitting attacks of the Sri Lankan army only fuelled support for the organization among major segments of the Tamil people and enabled it, time and time again, to recover and recommence its operations. In the case of the PKK, the reality was exactly the opposite. The organization was ideologically remote from large segments of the public it sought to represent. It had abused the Kurds in one way or another over the years so that, ultimately, it became hard for it to mobilize extensive popular support. For that reason, being subject to formidable offensives on the part of the Turkish army did not endear the organization to the locals nor help it draw support from them in order to recoup for counter-attack. Unlike Prabhakaran, Ocalan was forced to flee for his life to another country. Even after he was captured and prosecuted, his organization did not have the strength to force the Turkish authorities to release him nor commute his sentence and therefore Ocalan was obliged to instruct his people to end all hostilities and, in effect, cease from any and all activities.

5

The Transition to Suicide Terrorism: Al-Qaeda and the Network of the Islamic Fundamentalist Groups

One of the main reasons for the recent growth of academic interest in suicide terrorism has been the actions of Al-Qaeda and in particular the 11 September 2001 suicide attack on the World Trade Center in New York and the Pentagon building in Washington. Before investigating the reasons which led Al-Qaeda to launch its campaign of suicide terrorism, two important matters should be clarified about this organization. First, despite the ostentatious nature of Al-Qaeda suicide operations, in comparison with organizations discussed previously, Bin Laden and his group have in effect made little use of suicide terrorists. Second, many acts of terrorism, including suicide attacks which have taken place in the last few years all over the world, have been credited to Al-Qaeda. Although there may be a fair degree of truth in some of these allegations, there is probably at the same time an equal amount of fallacy.

The meaning of the word Al-Qaeda in Arabic is 'the base' and this name is already an indication of its nature. Al-Qaeda is an umbrella organization which involves, with various degrees of affinity, affiliated terrorist groups in more than forty-five countries in the world, including Pakistan, Iraq, Turkey, Saudi Arabia, Morocco and Indonesia, as well as many other countries in the Middle East, Asia and Europe. Many of these groups consider Bin Laden and his organization a prime example and model for simulation and in fact tend to gather under the banner of a jihad rhetoric against the West. At the same time, it should not be presumed that the reasons for dispatching suicide bombers by one organization will necessarily be relevant to the others. In fact, Al-Qaeda is not a 'unitary actor' and to approach it in this fashion would hamper our efforts in elucidating the factors that led its numerous affiliates to undertake suicide campaigns throughout the world.[1]

The critical questions at this point are: what are the goals of the Al-Qaeda organization? Why has Bin Laden adopted the method of suicide terrorism? And what are the reasons that led organizations associated with Al-Qaeda to initiate suicide attacks following the events of 11 September and the American invasion of Afghanistan? The task of finding answers to these questions is not an easy one so that, understandably, it is often a source of impassioned dispute among scholars involved in the study of this organization.[2]

The Strategy of Ostentatious Suicide Terrorism: the Al-Qaeda Organization

The stated goal of Bin Laden and his adherents, according to a religious ruling (*fatwa*) made public by the organization in August 1996 and February 1998, was the Muslim duty to engage in a worldwide, violent and uncompromising struggle in defence of the holy places and sanctity of Islam. In this ruling, Bin Laden determined that Muslims must avow that Allah will be the only god of their worship and, given the above, a violent 'war to the end' must be fought against all infidels. He also lamented over the heretic takeover of Arabic wealth in the Arab peninsula and regarded this as part of a sweeping global assault on all of Islam. In conclusion, Bin Laden stressed in this ruling the necessity of joining in battle, especially against the Americans and their allies, and further declared that they must be killed without discriminating between civilians and soldiers.[3] These goals are not surprising, given the fact that Al-Qaeda's ideology is based on the Salafi interpretation of Wahhabism.[4] This is a revivalist school which promotes violent rebellion against secular regimes in the Muslim world and the establishment of states that follow the laws of Islam.[5] As maintained in a more elaborate version of Bin Laden's ruling, Al-Qaeda aspires to transform the Western world into a part of the Islamic caliphate. In the view put forward by organization ideologues, the world can be divided into two: *Dar al-Islam* (the house or domain of Islam) – the lands where Islamic reign already exists – and *Dar al-Harb* – the domain or lands controlled by infidels which must be liberated by 'virtue of the sword'. Terrorism is the modern-day sword brandished by members of the organization.[6]

Nevertheless, a quick glance at Bin Laden's personal history will suffice in order to cast doubt on the assumption that the central motive for the organization's terrorism is the decision to set out on a holy war meant to overthrow the West. In essence, Al-Qaeda's ideological roots are embedded in the radical Sunni (Wahhabi) Islamic perspective, according to which the worship of any god other than Allah is blasphemous and anyone who believes in a god other than Allah deserves to die.[7] It is therefore imperative upon Muslims to engage in armed struggle (jihad) against the enemies of Islam and anyone who is not a believer in Allah's singularity.[8] However, Bin Laden fought for goals that were far more concrete. In the late 1970s, the nationalist-territorial conflict between the Soviet Empire and Afghan fighters was a breeding ground for the recruitment of many Islamic fighters. It also formed a fertile basis for creating a connection between the struggle for liberation from the yoke of the foreign conqueror and the radical approach of the Islamic Jihad.[9]

By the 1990s, Bin Laden had already set his sights on a different enemy in order to fire up his warriors for battle. In the beginning of 1998, Bin Laden announced the formation of 'The International Islamic Front for Jihad against Jews and Crusaders'. During that same year, the first two suicide actions were carried out by the organization. On the morning of 7 August, United States embassies in Kenya and Tanzania were attacked within a five-minute interval of each other. As in the cases of the early operations of Hezbollah and the LTTE, operatives driving trucks loaded with explosives hurtled into embassy complexes. In attacks that *post factum* turned out to have been meticulously planned for many years, 224 people were killed and more than 5000 were wounded. The organization's second offensive took place on 12 October 2000, targeting the American destroyer *USS Cole*, which was anchored for fuelling and taking on provisions in the port of Aden in Yemen. This attack was also based on the experience of other organizations, in this case, the LTTE, which had instituted a marine division (divers, etc.) in order to carry out actions at sea or underwater.[10] This operation was directed by two suicide bombers who rammed a boat full of explosives into the destroyer, blasting a hole in its hull.[11]

This time, too, Bin Laden's goals in founding the Front and in launching attacks were much more concrete than the abstract idea of a religious war. Worth mentioning *inter alia*, are the organization's aspirations to depose secular Arab regimes that Bin Laden considered to be corrupt, the desire to remove foreign army forces that had ensconced themselves in Saudi Arabia and the Persian Gulf during the first war in Iraq, concern for Palestinian interests in the conflict with Israel and the ambition to protect the economic interests of Arab nations with an eye on the price of oil exported by their countries.[12] All these objectives had one common denominator: the American connection. The United States was the one with its forces dispersed throughout the Middle East; it was a major supporter of secular Arab regimes as well as Israel; and it also had a vested interest in bringing down oil prices. Hence, as far as Al-Qaeda was concerned, the road to the achievement of organization goals was paved with murderous hostility towards the United States.[13]

From the above, it is also clear why Bin Laden chose to engineer his struggle in the United States by adopting a strategy of suicide terrorism, specifically, grandiose suicide attacks. Al-Qaeda is a small organization that had embarked on a war against a hegemonic power in a unipolar world. The asymmetry in the balance of power is remarkably prominent in this case. Hezbollah's earlier experience made it evident to Bin Laden that in order to strike the United States in such a way as to lead to policy revision, it would be necessary to perpetrate attacks at a high level of sophistication with the potential of producing the greatest number of casualties and most severe damage. Subsequently, the effect would have to be enough truly to shock the American people and to change public opinion in a way that would ultimately sway the government to instigate new policies or courses of action. The attacks on the US embassies in Africa and on *USS Cole* apparently did not bring about the anticipated results in terms of organizational goals and so the Al-Qaeda leader opted for more drastic measures.

The attacks on 11 September 2001 consisted of hijacking four passenger planes and crashing them into the Twin Towers of the World Trade Center in New York, the Pentagon building in Washington, DC, and a third target in the Washington, DC, area. The third attempt failed and the plane crashed in an open field in Pennsylvania. On the whole, this coordinated terrorist attack was unprecedented in the history of global terrorism. The terrorists demonstrated very high levels of daring and planning that almost enabled them to realize their goals completely. They inflicted massive damage to life and property and, furthermore, assaulted the very heart and core of the targeted country and struck a blow to its economic symbols and security establishment.

The principal aim of these attacks, as noted earlier, was to disrupt the American political system and make it clear to public and political elites in the United States that they were up against an enemy that was perhaps strategically not as strong but with enough audacity and determination to compensate for this inferiority. It is reasonable to assume that Bin Laden did not believe the United States would in fact capitulate in the wake of this attack and subsequently revise its policy in the Middle East. It is more likely that he anticipated an escalation in American military involvement in the Middle

East and Asia. This would increase the alienation many
Muslims felt towards the United States and so help the
Al-Qaeda leader to galvanize a united Islamic Arab front
against the conqueror.[14]

At the same time, other, more internal factors must be
accounted for when specifying the motives responsible for
the mega-terrorist attacks in the United States. Bin Laden was
interested in positioning his organization at the forefront of
Islamic terrorist groups. His advantage over other organizations was rooted in the fact that Al-Qaeda was a supranational movement that included members from different
countries, all ready to fight for the cause even in places that
were far away from their country of origin. The organization's
international character and the willingness of its members to
fight for Islamic interests wherever necessary provided Bin
Laden with a very convenient base for mobilizing support
among radical political groups throughout the Muslim world.
A direct assault on the economic, military and political
symbols of the United States served as an ideal catalyst for
recruiting this kind of support.[15] An additional and somewhat surprising explanation for the mega-attacks was found
in the computers left behind by high-level Al-Qaeda
members in Afghanistan following the American operation.
According to Alan Cullison's analysis of these documents, the
aim of the attack, *inter alia*, was to close the ranks of the organization and reduce tensions that had evolved between the
leadership in Kabul and Al-Qaeda cells dispersed at different
locations all over the world.[16]

The results of the 11 September attack were mixed from
the perspective of Bin Laden and his people. The organization was indeed successful in striking at the very heart of the
United States, especially a blow to the morale of the
American people; however, its strategic objectives were only
partially realized. As expected, the response of the American
government to the attack was in fact the intensification of its
military involvement in the Middle East. Yet, Arab and
Muslim mobilization for the war against the United States
was late in coming. On the contrary, until the beginning of the

war in Iraq, the strengthening of ties between the American government and friendly Arab regimes, and of course Israel, in fact led to an increase in the region's stability. Furthermore, the direct attack on the Al-Qaeda organization and its benefactor, the Taliban regime in Afghanistan, caused great damage to the organization's infrastructure and severely impaired its military capabilities.

On the face of it, this was a major defeat for the organization. Over a number of months, it was transformed from an institution that held bases in Afghanistan, where it had enjoyed total freedom of movement, into a relatively small group that found itself in a defensive stance against a superior power. In practice, however, the picture was not so clearcut. Al-Qaeda had achieved two major accomplishments. The first was the preservation, to a certain degree, of the operational capacities of local groups that identified with Al-Qaeda and whose goals were partially shared by the Bin Laden organization. The second, within relatively few years and mostly following the American invasion of Iraq and efforts to supplant the Saddam Hussein regime, was how organization ideology became a magnet for Arabs and Muslims who began to identify with Bin Laden's notions regarding the 'nature of American imperialism' and the 'evilness' of the United States.[17] While its leadership did not directly enjoy the fruit of its efforts, Al-Qaeda-affiliated organizations in various places all over the world certainly did.

Suicide Terrorism of the Islamic Fundamentalist Groups

Before going into the factors that prompted groups associated with the idea of jihad to embark upon campaigns of suicide terrorism, it is necessary to explain and set the record straight regarding a number of facts. First, suicide operations linked to some of the jihad organizations had been under way and in certain cases already suspended a long time before Al-Qaeda dispatched its first suicide bombers. Second, aside from the Iraqi and Chechen cases, which were both marked by a

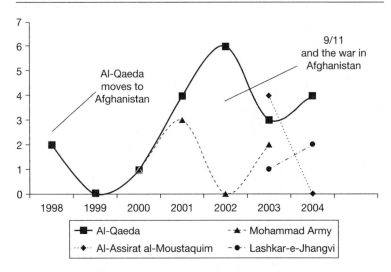

Figure 5.1 *Suicide campaigns of Al-Qaeda and its global jihad affiliates*

succession of suicide actions, in most other situations, suicide episodes were either sporadic or consisted of several incidents at the most. Third, in both the Iraqi and Chechen cases – to be discussed in more detail later on – it has been very hard to verify the identity of the perpetrators of each incident, thus making it difficult to analyse the factors responsible for attacks. The reasons for this had to do with both the restrictions on the media coverage of many of these events, as well as the difficulties involved in deciphering with certainty the organizational structure underlying attacks in these two cases.

One of the first jihad organizations to make use of suicide missions was the Egyptian Al-Gama'a al-Islamiya. This organization dispatched one of its operatives to the city of Rijeka in Croatia as early as October 1995. The operative detonated a car bomb at the entrance to the city's police station. The purpose of this action apparently was to deter Croatian authorities from cooperating with Egyptian officials in the pursuit of organization members in Croatia. About a month later, another Egyptian organization, the Egyptian Jihad, executed a suicide action at the Egyptian embassy in Pakistan.

In an attack that, in certain ways, was reminiscent of Hezbollah methods, a suicide bomber blew himself up in the centre of the embassy compound. Once again, the aim of the operation was to discourage local authorities from pooling resources with Egyptian security forces in their efforts to apprehend organization activists.[18]

Another association that began to utilize the suicide tactic even prior to the commencement of Al-Qaeda operations was the Armed Islamic Group in Algeria (GIA). Most of the hundreds of GIA members were Afghanistan war veterans and some of them even trained at *mujahidin* camps in the early 1980s. The Group was the most prominent among a number of armed movements founded under the patronage of the Islamic Salvation Front (FIS) following the annulment of the latter's victory in the Algerian 1991 elections. Initially, the organization mounted attacks against the Algerian regime but later it also included civilian targets in its use of the suicide tactic.[19] Among the more significant attacks initiated by this group was the explosion of a car bomb driven by three suicide operatives in January 1995, in the town of Boufarik. Seven months later, a suicide-driven explosives-laden truck was detonated amidst a crowd of civilians in the capital city of Algiers. In these two attacks, more than fifty people were killed and more than a hundred injured.[20] It also should be noted that above and beyond the organization's pivotal role in the devastating civil war that transpired in Algeria in the early 1990s, it also initiated terrorist attacks in the mid-1990s directed at French targets in general and French Jews in particular.

However, the principal inspiration for suicide actions by radical Islamic movements sprang from the events of 11 September 2001. For many years, and before his involvement in his own terrorist operations, Bin Laden began disseminating his ideas among Islamic organizations in different locations in the world and helping them construct the infrastructure for terrorist activities. His success was helped in no small measure by the fact that in the late 1980s and early 1990s, many of these organizations lost the sponsorship they had received in the past from various other sources.

Al-Qaeda's penetration into countries in Southeast Asia, Indonesia, Malaysia, Singapore, Thailand, Myanmar and the Philippines was made possible principally by the cessation of economic support from Libya in the early 1990s.[21] But first contacts had been made even earlier in Afghanistan, when Muslims from different countries geared themselves up for the *mujahidin* and underwent military training.[22] In western European countries as well, Bin Laden's operatives were successful in forming networks of cells that were based on first- and second-generation immigrants who lived in these countries, but who also displayed tendencies towards fundamentalist Islam. Although many of these cells underwent a spontaneous process of radicalization whereby members would progressively and mutually influence each other to adopt a more violent course of action, they were in need of the direction and infrastructures that Al-Qaeda could provide.[23]

The events of 11 September were a sort of catharsis for many jihad cells. On one hand, they were an inspiration and encouraged members to join Bin Laden's battle, and, on the other, they created a sense of urgency as the siege closed in on Bin Laden and the operational capacities of cells linked to the leadership in Afghanistan gradually dwindled. Still, the immediate factors for terrorist actions perpetrated by most of these cells remained local.

The first major terrorist operation that took place after 11 September occurred on 12 October 2002, in the nightlife hub of the tourist island of Bali in Indonesia. This incident was an example of the complex connections between Al-Qaeda and organizations in Southeast Asia as well as the considerable importance of local interests in the motivation for terror. The group responsible for the calamity in which 187 people were killed and 300 more were wounded was the Jemaah Islamiyah (JI), which was not an Al-Qaeda cell and was not directly controlled by Bin Laden and his people. This was a relatively experienced organization, already established in 1993, and its aim was entirely local: to supplant the regime in Indonesia with a theocratic one.

The affiliation of JI members to Al-Qaeda initially stemmed from a common worldview. Over the years, relations gradually grew closer between the two organizations as well as their elites, and JI fighters began to frequent training camps in Afghanistan and receive information from Bin Laden activists. As time passed, the influence of Al-Qaeda on the JI increased all the more. This was particularly evident when the organization adopted the global jihad agenda as its own and established cells in Malaysia, the Philippines, Singapore and Indonesia. Each of these cells functions in a self-contained manner, that is, according to the conditions and range of operation in that specific country. However, it seems that in exchange for the dissemination of Al-Qaeda's ideas in their own countries and the erection of local infrastructures for recruiting new members and launching attacks, these organizations receive intelligence and military know-how, as well as equipment and economic resources, in order to promote their local interests.[24]

The same can be said for Indonesia and the Philippines. The MILF (Philippines Moro Islamic Liberation Front), a local Islamic organization dedicated to an ethnic-religious struggle in the Philippines, had already sent off members in the early 1990s to train in Al-Qaeda camps in Afghanistan. The reason for this was the cutback in financial support it had previously received from Libya and its need for a steady flow of funding in order to sustain its activities. The only suicide attack perpetrated by the MILF was in fact aimed at a Philippine military installation and was carried out by two local activists. However, closer investigation of the incident reveals that the suicide attackers had been assisted by two foreign trainers: Mohammed Gharib Ibrahimi from Egypt and Al Maki Ragab from Saudi Arabia.[25]

Another Philippine organization likewise drawn into collaboration with Al-Qaeda was the Abu Sayyaf Group. A relatively veteran organization, it was founded in 1991 and its main goal was the establishment of an Islamic theocracy in the Mindanao region in the southern Philippine islands.[26] Already in the 1990s, Bin Laden had estimated that the

Group – whose worldview was not that far from his own – could serve as a convenient base for operations in the Philippines. For that reason, he approached their leader and offered him economic and logistic aid. This offer was readily welcomed by the organization. The support he received from Bin Laden enabled Abu Sayyaf to start a campaign of formidable terrorism against the government in Manila. In exchange for Al-Qaeda sponsorship, organization members granted refuge to Bin Laden's cohorts. In the first half of the 1990s, they were even partners in devising a number of ostentatious operations orchestrated by Bin Laden; however, these were ultimately not carried out.[27]

The suicide bombings that took place in May 2003, in Riyadh, Saudi Arabia and Casablanca in Morocco, once again proved Al-Qaeda's capacity to grant support and inspiration to Islamic organizations striving to promote local objectives. On 12 May, nine operatives blew themselves up adjacent to residential buildings inhabited by foreign citizens in Riyadh. This attack, masterminded by Ali Abd al-Rahman al-Faqasi al-Ghamdi, who had fought in the service of Al-Qaeda in Afghanistan and was among the highest-ranking officials of the organization,[28] led to the deaths of twenty-five people. Four days later, in an even more sophisticated operation, twelve suicide bombers belonging to the Salafist Jihad organization, based in Casablanca, detonated themselves at various locations. Five separate details from the organization, which sought to remove Americans and Jews from the kingdom,[29] attacked the Belgian embassy, a Spanish culture club and restaurant and a Jewish recreation club and cemetery. In these attacks, forty-three people were killed and more than a hundred wounded.[30] The organization engaged in armed resistance against local regimes that approved of the Western presence and sought to eliminate this presence in their countries by targeting these sites. A communiqué issued by Bin Laden's deputy, Ayman al-Zawahiri, and tape-recordings that the suicide bombers left behind, provided evidence of the close affinity between the interests of local cells and the Al-Qaeda global jihad.[31]

The double suicide attacks in Istanbul in late 2003 carried the hallmarks of a campaign sponsored by Al-Qaeda, which had seemed to be absent in this region until this incident.[32] Three of the attackers came from the city of Bingol in eastern Turkey and were members of the Turkish Hezbollah.[33] That same organization had in the past received support from the Turkish government as part of its battle against the PKK, but it was deprived of this backing in 1999 and therefore in need of alternative financial resources to sustain its activities. Furthermore, its members required military instruction in the perpetration of guerrilla and terrorist acts.[34] In line with his principles, Bin Laden was willing to grant the necessary assistance to the organization. An investigation of the events in Istanbul revealed that at least two of the suicide bombers took part in military training programmes in Al-Qaeda camps in Pakistan and Afghanistan and, after completing their training, they returned to their home city. After reaching a decision to conduct the operation in protest against the collaboration of the United States, Britain and Turkey,[35] Al-Qaeda activists arrived in the region to provide aid in constructing explosive devices and in the tactical planning of the mission. In addition, they taught local operatives how to exchange enciphered information and instructions on the Internet after Al-Qaeda advisers had left the country. Indeed, in the period preceding the operation, the suicide attackers communicated with Al-Qaeda operatives in an Internet café owned by one of them.[36]

From the above, we can conclude that, for the most part, suicide actions performed under the flag of the jihad and attributed to Al-Qaeda were, in effect, local initiatives stemming from Islamic organizational interests operating within the borders of a given country and whose aspirations principally amounted to a change of rule in that same country. In order to advance these goals, they availed themselves of Al-Qaeda's assistance. From the organizations' perspective, Al-Qaeda services were a convenient platform from which they were able to operate. From an Al-Qaeda standpoint, these local offensives were a powerful propaganda tool that sent a message both to the organization's constituency and to the countries it was up against. The gist of this message was that the long arm of Al-Qaeda could reach numerous and sundry points all over the globe. The routing of the Taliban reign in Afghanistan had many assuming that the organization had suffered a fatal blow and that its operational capabilities were severely impaired. Therefore, the message conveyed by these renewed offensives was of particular importance.

However, as mentioned above, in respect to the two principal foci of suicide terrorism in recent years, Chechnya and Iraq, it has been in fact difficult to find the tell-tale marks of Al-Qaeda sponsorship. Although information from these regions regarding actions and perpetrators is inconsistent as well as incomplete, and despite the fact that, in both cases, the organizational base or bases responsible for dispatching suicide bombers have not been clearly identified, it is still possible to venture that, as in the cases discussed above, the principal reasons for sending off suicide attackers into the streets of Russia and Iraq stem from local conflicts. In the Chechen case, activists seek independence from Russia and their struggle is nationalist-ethnic in nature, whereas in Iraq the struggle is conducted directly against the American occupation of the country. In Iraq, suicide dispatchers attempt to create chaotic conditions that will enable them to gain more influence and reap political benefits once the occupation is over.

Chechnya is an autonomous republic in the Russian Federation and the majority of its residents are Muslim. Despite relatively loose ties with Moscow, the Chechen Republic has been and is subject to the control and occasionally even military containment of the central government. After the break-up of the USSR, many separatist groups appeared in the country, inspired by the mythology of the Chechen struggles for independence. Like their predecessors, the new separatist groups also wished Chechnya to secede from Russia and declare independence. While the majority of the members of these groups were Sunnite Muslims, their fight, at least at the beginning of their campaign, was painted

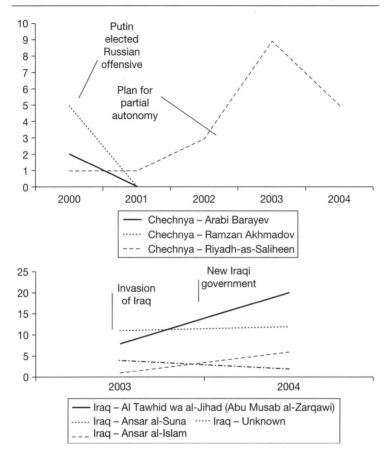

Figure 5.2 *Suicide campaigns in Chechnya and Iraq*

in strong ethnic colours and religion had only a marginal role. However, during the course of the 1990s, ties were forged between Al-Qaeda and several of these groups, and they all began to steep their struggles in jihad rhetoric.

As in the other cases, suicide terrorism was first introduced in Chechnya at a relatively late stage of the conflict. Suicide operations commenced only after two episodes of intense battles in the years 1994 and 1996 and a terrorist campaign in the streets of Moscow in 1999 followed by a harsh Russian response.[37] Eventually, the first Chechen suicide offensives were carried out in July 2000. Again, attacks were suggestive of Hezbollah methods of operation. Two suicide operatives, a woman and a man, drove a booby-trapped truck and blew it up near the barracks of a Russian army base at Alkhan-Yurt. A week later, another Chechen suicide bomber detonated a car bomb at a Russian checkpoint near Alkhan Kala. In the ensuing months, this operational pattern gradually spread to the streets of Chechnya, while suicides from rebel ranks repeatedly attacked military and civilian Russian targets.[38]

As time passed, it became evident that, like the Palestinian organizations, the Chechen use of suicide bombers became increasingly sophisticated and also began to focus more on civilian targets. A prominent example of this tendency took place in July 2003, when two female suicide bombers, who belonged to the Riyad Us-Saliheyn organization headed by Shamil Basayev, detonated themselves near a stadium in the suburbs of Moscow where the Krilya rock festival took place. The two suicides activated their explosives within a quarter-hour interval, one next to the ticket office and the other at a nearby market. In this incident, sixteen persons were killed.[39] Another example is the explosion of a Chechen woman suicide bomber on the underground train in Moscow on 6 February 2004, during the morning rush hour. In consequence of that operation, originally committed in order to avenge the massacre perpetrated by the Russian army in Chechen villages in February 2000, thirty-nine civilians were killed and more than 130 were injured.[40] Additional examples are the takeover of a theatre in Moscow in October 2002, the exploding of a passenger train in Russia by a single woman suicide terrorist in January 2004, the explosion of two passenger planes in September 2004, and the ambush and takeover of the school in Beslan, also in September 2004, that concluded in a very tragic and large-scale bloodbath. In addition to the incident at the stadium, Basayev's Riyadh-as-Saliheen faction took responsibility for the last two of these incidents as well.

It would be no mean feat to assess what were the goals of each one of the factions in initiating these actions. However, it is possible to assume that the unifying goal of the majority was the desire to liberate themselves from Russian control and to achieve independence, whether as a Chechen state or Islamic theocracy. The force of the rebels' struggle had been fuelled to a large extent by the severe reaction of authorities in Moscow to events and the widespread harm caused to the civilian population during efforts to crack down on rebel pockets of resistance. In the same context, it is important to clarify that the Chechen political arena was marked by a number of rival factions. This raises the supposition that the use of suicide terrorism, at least as employed by the Basayev group, was intended to signal to the population its fervent adherence to the struggle.

Iraqi suicide terrorism in fact appeared a short while prior to the American invasion in early 2003. The first suicide incidents in this country were somewhat characteristic of the difficulty in isolating factors responsible for suicide actions, including motives. The first Iraqi suicide happened to be of Kurdish origin. The attacker exploded a car bomb near a structure inhabited by Kurdish forces about one month before the outbreak of fighting. The second attack occurred immediately upon the beginning of American army activities in the country and before the invasion of Baghdad. An Iraqi army officer behind the wheel of a car full of explosives detonated it at an American army road barrier. Four soldiers were killed. Four days later, two Iraqi women, one of them seemingly pregnant, blew themselves up in front of an American road barrier in the northern part of Baghdad. The video left behind showed both of them wearing explosives belts in the style of Palestinian suicide bombers. At about the same time, the Iraqi Information Minister, Mohammed Saeed al-Sahaf, announced that the Saddam Hussein regime had at its disposal four thousand suicide bombers ready to act at any given moment. Saddam Hussein's intention of using suicide attackers was later corroborated, as hundreds of sophisticated explosives belts were found in various ammunition caches of the Ba'ath regime. However, suicide operations were suspended a short time after the concluding stages of the American invasion and were not renewed until August 2003.[41]

When operations recommenced, they were already of a completely different nature, and apparently Saddam Hussein's regime had no connection to them whatsoever. The suicide operations that took place were similar in style to the Hezbollah method and included the use of massive explosive charges planted or concealed in cars, ambulances and trucks. One of the more prominent terrorist operations during this wave of attacks took place on 27 October, and greatly resembled the coordinated offensive in Riyadh, which occurred three months earlier. Five suicide bombers drove vehicles laden with explosives into the vicinity of Iraqi police stations and detonated all of them almost simultaneously. Unlike most incidents where it was not possible to identify suicides after the explosions, in this case, one of them was caught and identified as a Syrian volunteer who had crossed the border in order to fight in Iraq, a fact that indicated a possible connection with Al-Qaeda.[42]

This series of attacks escalated in the following months. Targets of suicide attacks were mostly coalition forces as well as Iraqi security forces, with an emphasis on recruitment centres. The principal names mentioned in the context of these operations were those of the organizations Ansar al-Islam, Ansar al-Suna and Al-Qaeda while, in the background, the name of the Jordanian terrorist Abu Musab al-Zarqawi – known for his connections with Al-Qaeda but also with Saddam Hussein's regime and even Iranian authorities – repeatedly appeared.[43] Bombers in this campaign would commonly make sure to conceal their identity and were even capable of shaving themselves and wearing a mask before setting out on their mission. This made the detection of perpetrators a tough job. It was equally hard to uncover who the dispatchers were, so that, ultimately, the assessment of the precise nature of their goals also became complicated. However, one can cautiously postulate that, despite the abundance of factions fighting in Iraq, Sunnite groups have a higher profile in the initiation of suicide attacks.[44]

It is easier to assume that the objective of local Sunnite factions in Iraq was to prevent the establishment of a new government under American patronage which would also be detrimental to the preferred status enjoyed by Sunnites during the years of Saddam Hussein's reign. But, then what *are* Zarqawi's goals, if he is in fact the one responsible for suicide operations and if the estimation (often subject to doubts) is correct that he worked in close affinity with Al-Qaeda people? For those Islamic organizations coming from outside Iraq, direct battle with American forces and countries under their sponsorship in the Middle East was an opportunity to try to replicate the accomplishments of Hezbollah in Lebanon about two decades earlier; or, in other words, to cause the greatest power in the world to withdraw its forces from the country. Unlike Hezbollah, a local organization which, following its success in the campaigns against the multinational force and Israel, converted its new status into political clout, it is plausible to assume that the immediate goal of Islamic organizations operating in Iraq was actually to mobilize the endorsement of Arabs and Muslims from other countries. The assault on American forces therefore served as a highly effective tool in the recruitment of such support. In the future, this backing could be converted into the destabilization of US-friendly Arab regimes and an attempt to try and institute theocratic republics in their place.

Summary

Osama Bin Laden launched the ostentatious Al-Qaeda suicide-attack campaign from both political and organizational motives. Borne along on the wave of a Wahhabist credo, Bin Laden saw himself as a supranational leader. He believed in the liberation of the Middle East and Muslim world from the control or influence of the West and its allies. Notwithstanding, it is difficult to accept the assumption that his solitary goal was to try and spread the control of Islam to other regions in the world. Therefore, the depiction of Al-Qaeda actions in general, and the organization's suicide

operations in particular, in terms of a clash of religions or civilizations goes a bit too far. Bin Laden's decision to mount
large-scale suicide offensives principally against American
targets was meant to signal to the United States that it was
dealing with a highly determined organization that was not
deterred by the necessity of engaging in brutal warfare even
if it suffered from strategic inferiority. Moreover, Bin Laden
wanted to provoke the Americans into an aggressive
response against himself, and paradoxically also to intensify
its military involvement in the Middle East. His aim was to
demonstrate to Arabs and Muslims the predatory nature and
cruelty of the United States on one hand, and his devotion
to their interests on the other. As noted above, organizational
concerns were also included in his designs. He sought to
close ranks around his leadership and to indicate to the
various Al-Qaeda cells that he was the leader and mainstay
of a struggle that was not possible without him. Although the
central leadership backbone of Al-Qaeda in Afghanistan was
severely weakened by the American invasion, it would still
be difficult to disagree with the inference that the organization's grandiose operations had strengthened Bin Laden's
status and even transformed him into a major symbol of the
global jihad.

The factors that led Islamic cells with only loose connections to Al-Qaeda to initiate suicide attacks were, for the
most part, local ones. Prior to the events of 11 September,
these were sporadic episodes. Suicide attackers were a convenient and effective weapon in the hands of organizations
that generally did not possess large-scale military options in
their fight against the regimes pursuing them. Even after the
attacks in New York and Washington, the motives for dispatching suicide bombers remained largely local. However,
the increase in suicide operations also stemmed, to a large
degree, from the fact that cells in assorted places drew their
inspiration from 11 September. An additional reason for
the rise in the number of suicide attacks was the desire of
the Al-Qaeda leadership to prove to the world that the
organization still existed in full force. Islamic cells scattered

in different countries, which identified with the organization's ideology and were indebted to its leadership on account of the material support they received over the years, served as an ideal vehicle for showing that the organization was still very active.

Finally, two principal foci where campaigns of suicide terrorism still persist must be addressed: Chechnya and Iraq. In both these cases, it is hard to gauge precisely to what degree local motives or external interests are involved. Nevertheless, it still seems evident that in Chechnya the principal emphasis is local, so that revisions of Russian policy towards this region are liable to reduce substantially the incentive to send suicides off into the streets of Moscow. In the Iraqi case, on the other hand, it seems that the use of suicide tactics is conducted both by local insurgents and non-local factors, thus transforming the country into a battleground in their struggle with the United States. After a short period of rivalry between the local and foreign insurgent groups, it seems that the level of cooperation between them has increased.[45] American withdrawal from the country will be perceived by these organizations, as well as other Islamic radical elements, as a significant accomplishment directly in line with Bin Laden's vision, and therefore it seems that the end of suicide terrorism in Iraq is still some way off.

6
Who Becomes a Suicide Terrorist?

One of the remarkable facts that come to mind when reading the life stories of suicide bombers is how commonplace they are. For example, Ahmad Qasir, who drove a vehicle loaded with explosives into the Israeli military compound in the city of Tyre on 11 November 1982,[1] was no different from many other fifteen-year-old boys who lived in countries subjected to protracted violent conflicts. He was not a very happy individual, but at the same time he was definitely not miserable. Qasir had a loving and supporting family and was described as a kind young man. He was forced to drop out of school when he was only eleven years old due to financial difficulties in the family. He joined his father and helped him sell fruit and vegetables. Later, Qasir left Lebanon to work as a janitor in a Saudi-Arabian hospital; his purpose was to save some money and send it to his family.[2] Upon his return to Lebanon, Qasir, like many of his peers, began to perform minor errands for Hezbollah. He found it very exciting and was proud to be assigned on logistic missions such as smuggling equipment for the organization's fighters and spying on Israeli convoys for gathering intelligence. Yet, despite his involvement in these underground operations, he also found time to spend with his friends. They were mostly interested in Qasir's two favourite activities, camping and hunting.

One morning, Qasir took his father's passport, transferred ownership of the family truck and disappeared. His concerned family had no idea what had happened to him. Two and a half years later, when Hezbollah exhibited Qasir's pictures as a heroic figure in the fight against Israel, his stunned family members received the devastating news that he had been sent on a suicide mission. They had never even considered this possibility and were left with many unanswered questions. In fact, until this day, no one really knows what led Qasir to sacrifice his life.[3]

Exactly twenty-one years later, on 15 November 2003, Gokhan Elaltuntas, a young man from the Turkish city of Bingol, was one of two suicide bombers who exploded their trucks in front of the Neveh Shalom and Beth Israel synagogues in Istanbul.[4] Again, as far as could be seen, nothing in Elaltuntas's childhood and youth suggested that by the age of twenty-two he would become a suicide terrorist.[5] Elaltuntas was the second of six children.[6] His parents were involved in real estate and electricity projects and were considered rather affluent in the impoverished city of Bingol.[7] Like many members of his community, Elaltuntas was raised as a religious Muslim but he was never closely involved in radical Islamism, neither did he join a radical Muslim movement.[8] Actually, his real passions in life were soccer and video games.[9]

After failing university admission exams,[10] Elaltuntas began to work at his father's Internet café, where he met a group of new friends, some of whom were later described as radical Muslims.[11] Their influence on Elaltuntas became evident when he began to express radical political views and started praying five times a day.[12] The real turning point occurred after an earthquake caused enough damage to destroy the family store. In the wake of this blow, his parents sent Elaltuntas to Istanbul. They wanted him to have the opportunity of starting his own business somewhere else and were hoping that the move to the big city would loosen the ties with his new friends.[13] They were especially concerned about one figure, Azad Ekinci, a charismatic twenty-seven-year-old who had been educated in the *madrasahs* of Pakistan and who had even taken part in the wars of Chechnya and Bosnia.[14] Ekinci appeared to be the group's leader and was admired by its members.

However, Elaltuntas's move to Istanbul did not help much in this respect. Ekinci decided to move together with him and the bonds between them only grew closer.[15] Still, despite Ekinci's sway over him, nothing in Elaltuntas's plans or deeds indicated any intention of sacrificing his life. On the contrary, he opened a new shop for cellphones, redecorated his house in a Western style and even told his uncle that he was seriously thinking of marrying his fiancée.[16] Yet, four months after moving to Istanbul, Elaltuntas blew himself up inside a truck along with his victims in the Neveh Shalom synagogue. As in Qasir's case, Elaltuntas's family refused to believe he was involved in the attack and was left with many perplexing questions regarding his motivation.[17]

Four months prior to the attack in Istanbul, on July 9, Zarema Muzhakhoeva, a twenty-three-year-old Chechen woman, carried a bomb to *Mon Café* in the heart of Moscow. Minutes before she was supposed to detonate the bomb, she handed herself over to police officers who were on the premises. Like Qasir and Elaltuntas, Muzhakhoeva was Muslim. However, she never really practised Islam and, furthermore, the Chechen nationalistic cause was not really important to her. She was much more preoccupied with her own personal problems.[18]

Four years earlier, her husband had been killed during the course of a business dispute. Shortly afterwards, the dead husband's family took away Muzhakhoeva's newborn baby girl and she was prevented from seeing her child. All she could think of was how much she wanted her daughter back. Driven by her distress, Muzhakhoeva stole her grandmother's jewels, sold them for $600 and made her way to her mother-in-law's house. She asked for permission to spend some time with her daughter, yet her real plan was to run away with the baby to Moscow. Members of her late husband's family kept a close watch on her the whole time and when Muzhakhoeva tried boarding an aircraft, they took her child away and left her beaten and humiliated at the airport. Muzhakhoeva was absolutely heartbroken; not only had she stolen her grandmother's jewels, she had also lost her daughter.[19]

It took her a few days to recover a little from these blows, and then she joined the Shamil Basayev faction of the Chechen rebel movement Riyadh-as-Saliheen Martyrs Brigades. Her only incentive in doing so was financial. She heard that the family of a suicide bomber received $1000 for carrying out a mission for this faction. Muzhakhoeva, who did not see much point in continuing life without her daughter, thought that if she died for this faction, at least her grandmother would be compensated for the stolen jewels. When she met Basayev at the rebel camp, he was not very enthusiastic with regard to her motivation. He told her that a person should not set out on a suicide mission just on the basis of financial distress. He even offered to let her stay and marry one of the rebels, but Muzhakhoeva refused even to discuss this possibility. Her only thought was to put an end to her problems.

However, a little while before the day of the planned attack, she started having second thoughts. She concluded that her problems did not justify sacrificing her life for a cause which was still quite alien to her and she looked for a way out of the mission, but at this stage it was far too late. She was locked in an apartment with other women who were assigned to suicide missions and all of them were under constant observation by Basayev's men. Therefore, she decided to embark upon the mission and surrender herself once her handlers could no longer watch her. Tragically, the explosives belt which she carried was ready to be activated and when one of the police officers tried to defuse it, the bomb exploded and killed him.[20] Muzhakhoeva remained unscathed and was arrested.

The descriptions above reinforce the conclusions of many studies that have investigated the characteristics and motiv-ations of suicide terrorists. The majority of suicide bombers are not crazy.[21] Furthermore, they generally are not forced into perpetrating the suicide act.[22] In effect, most suicide terrorists can be described as ordinary people. Studies have shown that they exhibited no suicidal tendencies prior to the act and lived normal lives, although many of them came from conflict-ridden areas where a 'normal life' is a relative concept. Most of them were not leading figures in their communities or organizations but they also did not come from the fringes of society. Suicide attackers were generally not highly educated, but also not illiterate. They were not very successful, but, at the same time, not complete failures. Attackers were both men and women; some were very religious while others were completely secular. Some were politically active for many years and others became active only in the perpetration of their suicide mission.

So who, indeed, are the suicide terrorists? And what drives them to take their lives and the lives of so many others? In this chapter, I will attempt to portray the characteristics of a sample of suicide bombers from different parts of the world and I will study the motivations which led them to turn themselves into live bombs. Yet it is not my intention to offer a psychological or any other type of profile.

Looking into the personal motivations of suicide terrorists is a highly complicated task, mainly due to the fact that perpetrators are no longer alive and their stories are therefore derived from secondary sources. However, other factors may also raise difficulties in the undertaking of such a study.[23] First, many organizations are not interested in exposing the identities of individuals they have sent on suicide missions. In some cases, even the governments of countries that have been victims of suicide bombers have refrained from exposing the identities of perpetrators, mostly in order not to jeopardize their counter-terrorism efforts. Hence, we know a great deal about Lebanese and Palestinian suicide terrorists whose acts were publicized and praised by their respective organizations. We have also heard a lot about the hijackers responsible for the events of 11 September 2001 in the United States. The magnitude of these events drew the attention of many reporters and scholars who made extensive efforts to get their stories across and track down the motivations of terrorists. However, our knowledge about the characteristics and motivations of suicide bombers from the LTTE, the PKK and Chechnya is far more limited. With regard to perpetrators of suicide attacks in Iraq, information is almost impossible to obtain because of the meticulous attempts by the terrorists to remove all signs that might lead to their identification.

Second, even if we are able to uncover the identity of perpetrators, how can we learn about their motivations? Some scholars chose to interview family members and the friends of suicide bombers.[24] Such an approach is very useful in obtaining background information about the particular person. However, many suicide bombers, such as the three described at the beginning of this chapter, left their families a long while before they committed the act. In other cases, families may have their own agenda when describing their loved ones who were responsible for the attacks. For example, they may embrace their son or daughter and portray them as heroes in order to gain respect from their community or even financial support. In other instances, family members may do everything possible to dissociate themselves from the suicide bomber, mainly in order to signal to authorities that they had nothing to do with the act.

Another group of scholars have chosen to focus on the diaries and videotapes left behind by perpetrators.[25] Again, such information is highly valuable. Yet, there is also a good chance that a lot of the information obtained from these sources was meant to serve the propaganda purposes of the organization, and thus the question of whether these data actually reflect the thoughts and feelings of the terrorists still remains unresolved. A third group of researchers decided to interview those who had failed in their attempts at suicide bombing.[26] Admittedly, these scholars got hold of information which could not have been obtained in any other way. Yet, they profiled the 'losers', that is, those who did not complete their missions. The question of whether these profiles are identical to the ones of the 'successful' suicide bombers remains unresolved.

It is important to address these methodological problems since they have the potential to bias research. Yet I strongly believe that this bias is marginal. Despite the various problems involved in the study of suicide terrorists, most scholars have been able to offer valuable analyses of the characteristics of individual bombers. As mentioned earlier, many have come to similar conclusions. Personality and psychological traits play only a secondary role in the make-up of a suicide terrorist. In order to find the reasons for an individual's decision to turn him- or herself into a live bomb, there is a need for a broader approach which will focus on the different experiences this person has undergone during the years and months preceding the event.

To examine this approach, I rely on two main sources. The first is the life stories of suicide terrorists from different corners of the world as documented by the media. These reports do not cover the whole population of suicide terrorists and sometimes offer only limited information about them. Thus, as mentioned earlier, I will not engage in ambitious attempts to outline the profiles of terrorists and instead I will limit my efforts to a search of the common motivations of these perpetrators. The second source of research is a dataset of the whole population of Palestinian suicide bombers. In the Palestinian case, organizations had an interest in revealing the identities of *shahids* and advertising their stories for the purpose of portraying them as heroes. In this fashion, legitimacy was gained from the community, which in turn influenced many others to volunteer for such missions. The process of collecting data took more than three years. In order to be as accurate as possible, we studied and cross-checked facts obtained from both Israeli and Palestinian publicly accessible sources, most prominently, newspaper reports and websites devoted to *shahids*.[27] In the first part of this chapter, the dataset is drawn on for the purpose of telling the stories of some suicide bombers; in the second part, it provides the numerical basis for the changing features of Palestinian suicide bombers.

Preconditions for the Emergence of Suicide Terrorism

Suicide terrorism is a political phenomenon orchestrated by an organization; this has been a major guiding assumption throughout this book. Any attempt to look into the personal motivations behind the decision to become a suicide bomber without taking this fact into consideration would generate only partial results. Suicidal behaviour is a common phenomenon in almost every society. Usually, people decide to take their own lives when suffering from one or a variety of problems. There is nothing unique or novel about this. However, people who kill themselves as a means of killing others are a different story. Are there specific conditions which may serve as a breeding ground for this phenomenon?

A careful scrutiny of the data on suicide attackers in different parts of the world led to the following conclusion. Suicide bombers can be roughly classified into two main groups: (1) members of an organization or social network, and (2) individuals who were recruited – or volunteered – specifically for the suicide mission. The precipitating factors compelling individuals to embark on such missions in the two groups are different, yet they are not mutually exclusive.

For the first group, the key word would be *commitment*. This could be commitment to a cause, an ideology, to one's comrades or leader or to all of these combined. Like soldiers, members of such organizations or networks become increasingly dedicated to the framework to which they belong, to what it stands for and especially to their comrades, sometimes even to the degree that they are willing to sacrifice their lives on the basis of this commitment.

The precipitating factors motivating individuals who belong to the second category are different. Here the key word should be *crisis*. This can be a real or perceived crisis situation and it can be on either the personal or community level or both. In some cases, the decision to embark on a suicide mission is the direct result of a specific crisis and takes place shortly after the crisis has occurred. In other cases, the potential suicide bomber might be predisposed towards the mission as a result of an accumulation of crises that has eventually overwhelmed him or her.[28]

On the personal level, both financial and individual-emotional crises seem to be fair predictors of the willingness to become a suicide bomber. Yet, while financial motivations appear to be relatively weak in predicting the successful completion of suicide missions, crises that involve the loss of a loved one seem to be a much stronger predicting factor. In the majority of cases, an individual crisis might be a direct consequence of painful acts inflicted by an oppressor, and the person's main motivation in perpetrating the act would be revenge. On the community level, the decision would most likely be a result of a sense of hopelessness and frustration with a static or even deteriorating situation.[29] In the following sections, I will demonstrate these different motivating factors.

Commitment as a Motivation for Suicide Attacks

Not many leaders of terrorist organizations elect to send well-trained warriors and long-time members of the organization on suicide missions. Except for the LTTE, Al-Qaeda and the religious Palestinian organizations (for example, Hamas and the Palestinian Islamic Jihad) in their early years, all other organizations have preferred to dispatch individuals recruited specifically for these assignments. In other cases, suicide bombers were individuals who were recruited to the organizations for more general purposes, but during the initial training phase displayed no qualities which could have been useful for the organizations and hence were perceived as 'expendable' by the leaders. So, in effect, leaders of organizations utilizing the suicide tactic acted quite rationally. They did not want to send valuable operatives, who could have served them in many different ways, on a deadly mission which in actual fact required very little sophistication and few combative skills.

Yet, in some cases, strongly integrated members of an organization who felt a deep commitment to the group or cause persuaded their leaders to send them on suicide operations. The story of Salah Ghandour is highly illustrative of this phenomenon. On 25 April 1995, when he was twenty-six years old, Ghandour (also known as the 'Angel' – *Malaak*), a veteran member of Hezbollah, rammed a car laden with explosives into an Israeli military convoy near Bint Jbeil. Ghandour's attack took place long after the Hezbollah leadership had decided to stop deploying suicide bombers. Actually, his commanders did everything they could to prevent him from embarking on this mission. One of them later spoke of the long discussions with Ghandour when they tried to convince him it would be wrong to sacrifice himself and leave behind a young wife and three babies. Even Hassan Nasrallah, Secretary General of Hezbollah, took part in the efforts to prevent Ghandour from setting out on this irrevocable operation. The source reported that Ghandour had tried to persuade his commanders to dispatch him on a suicide mission for over three years and they had always managed to stop him. Yet his belief in the organization's ideology was so profound that ultimately his only aspiration was to die as a *shahid*. At a certain stage, however, Ghandour's commanders understood he was utterly determined and that there was no way to talk him out of his resolve. So they gave him the explosives and their blessing. In the videotape that he left behind, Ghandour seemed happy and confident. He stated that he was leaving to fight the oppressors in the most honourable way.[30]

Ghandour's story exemplifies the power of the organization in reinforcing commitment. People who spend long periods of time within organizational frameworks, especially those that offer a compelling ideology accompanied by symbolism and ritualism, identify more and more with the group and its goals. In most cases, this ideology serves the organizational needs. However, in Ghandour's case, it became dysfunctional. While his commanders valued his skills and wanted to keep him in the ranks of Hezbollah, he became so devoted to the cause that he could think of no other way of expressing his commitment.

The LTTE is another example of a movement where a strong commitment gradually developed. Over the course of years, the association of members with each other, as well as with their leaders, had a strong influence on their organizational allegiance.

Prem, for example, was the first suicide bomber who managed successfully to take the life of a political figure in the government of Sri Lanka. A long-time member of the LTTE, he blew up his car on 2 March 1991, when the convoy of the Sri Lankan Minister of Defence, Ranjan Wijeratne, passed close by.[31] For many years, Prem had served as the personal driver of one of the organization's leaders. His strong commitment to this specific leader and the LTTE's cause in general led him to volunteer for the suicide mission. Previous attempts to assassinate Wijeratne, including remote-control bombs with radio connections, had been unsuccessful. Due to the complicated nature of the operation, in which Prem himself had to activate the bomb, and as a result of several previous and unsuccessful attempts on Wijeratne's life, Prem had to go through a long training period. In the attack, nineteen people were killed, including the Minister of Defence and his bodyguards.[32]

Maybe the most striking example of the role of commitment as an incentive to become a suicide bomber was that of Yogarajah Koneswaran aka Major Kantharuban from the village of Valvettithurai. He became an orphan at a very early age and joined the LTTE in 1987. While he was serving as a guard at the LTTE camp at Thondamannaru, the site came under attack by Sri Lankan army forces and he swallowed a cyanide capsule in order to avoid capture. He survived the poisoning but remained physically weak. Because of his bravery, he was adopted by the revered leader of the LTTE, Velupillai Prabhakaran. After several years, he felt that he was strong enough to set out on his own and volunteered for a suicide mission. On 7 July 1990, he drove a boat full of explosives and crashed it into the *Edithara*, a military ship of the Sri Lankan navy.[33]

In the case of Hamas and Palestinian Islamic Jihad, commitment to the organization, its ideology and its members was forged in many instances during the long periods members of these groups spent incarcerated together. Israeli prisons in effect replaced the institution of the army boot camp where rites of passage into group members and identification with the cause are more commonly performed. The reason for this is that, unlike other organizations which turned out suicide terrorists, the Palestinian factions operating in the West Bank and Gaza never had camps where they could isolate members from the rest of the community and train them. Israel monitored these organizations very closely and prevented the establishment of such camps; however, Israeli authorities failed to see that, in the meantime, this same solidarity process was taking place directly under their very noses.[34]

The story of Yusef Ali Mohammed Zughayar and Suleiman Musa Dahayneh illustrates the power of this commitment. Zughayar was an activist in Palestinian Islamic Jihad and an inhabitant of Anata, a village near Jerusalem. The twenty-three-year-old Dahayneh came from Silat al-Harithiya, close to Jenin, and also was a member of Palestinian Islamic Jihad. These two villages are quite distant from one another, and since these two young men were not related the likelihood of their getting acquainted was quite slim. However, both were prosecuted and sentenced for lengthy periods in prison on charges of being active members of the local chapters of Palestinian Islamic Jihad.

Like many other Palestinian prisoners, Zughayar and Dahayneh became very close while in prison and reinforced each other's ideological commitment. Suleiman even became acquainted with Zughayar's sister and married her after he was released.[35] Once they were both out of prison, they became inseparable.[36] They were staunchly dedicated to one thing: expressing their devotion to the cause through the act of self-sacrifice. On 6 November 1998, the two friends embarked upon a double suicide attack at the Mahaneh Yehuda market in Jerusalem.[37] They approached the neighbourhood in a red Fiat and drove onto the sidewalk near the entrance into the market. They had planned on taking two suitcases packed with explosives into the market, which was then full of shoppers. However, before they could get out of

the car, evidently because of a technical problem, the suitcases exploded prematurely, killing them both and injuring
twenty-one citizens.[38]

It was not only prison experience that formed a catalyst for
commitment among members of Palestinian organizations.
Yossef Suiat and Nidal Jibali, who were also activists in
Palestinian Islamic Jihad and belonged to the Jenin group,
worked together as police officers. During the hours spent
together, their friendship grew closer. In their long talks,
they were very happy to find out that they shared joint commitment to the Palestinian cause and to the ideology of the
organization. Eventually, they offered themselves to a local
handler who dispatched them on a double suicide operation
which took place in the city of Hadera on 25 May 2001.[39]
They detonated the bomb inside the car they were driving
next to a bus laden with passengers, and thirty-six people
were injured.

Individuals may seek friends or community before they
become dedicated to a specific organization or cause. In some
cases, comradeship seems to be a force almost stronger than
anything. In his study of Al-Qaeda networks, Marc Sageman
emphasized the role of social networks in generating radical-
ism and terrorism.[40] He indicated the importance of pre-
existing social bonds with other people committed to the
same cause and to one another. A typical case is the home-
sick, drifting young man who is drawn to familiar settings,
especially mosques, to find friends who share common traits
and interests. Small clusters of friends that form in these
mosques often move in together and live in the same lodg-
ings. These groups go through a long process of intense social
interaction and peer socialization in these apartments and
develop a strong mutual confidence. As they become more
intimate, the moderate members of these groups adopt the
beliefs of the most extreme ones. They sever previous ties and
become increasingly involved in the group. At the end of this
process, they are ready to join the jihad. [41]

An example of such a network is the Istanbul cell that
carried out the November 2003 attacks. Mesut Cabuk, the

operative who blew himself up in the Beth Israel synagogue, was a member of this cell. Cabuk had lost his father at a very young age and this experience had a dramatic effect on his life. He began to look for comfort in religious books and was constantly looking for a community that would embrace him. In his teenage years, Cabuk finally found what he was looking for when a group of young religious militants offered him their friendship. A prominent figure in this group was the suicide bomber who was later to perpetrate the attack on the HSBC bank on 20 November in Istanbul. This was Azad Ekinci, the same person who recruited Gokhan Elaltuntas, whose case was described earlier. Cabuk and Ekinci became virtually joined at the hip. They travelled together to Pakistan, Iran and Afghanistan, where they were introduced to the *mujahidin*.[42] Even after their return, nothing could interfere with their close ties.[43] Despite the fact that he was married and had two children, Cabuk remained highly committed to his friend who served as a major source of encouragement for many years. Hence, when Ekinci approached him with the plan to attack the synagogues, Cabuk did not hesitate. He told his wife that he was leaving for a trip to Dubai and left the house with a few of his belongings.[44] Several days later, his young spouse read in the paper that Cabuk and his friends were the ones responsible for the attacks.[45]

Similar collaborations among friends are also evident on the Palestinian scene. These networks are usually formed outside the framework of any organization. In these small coteries of friends, the radicalization process occurs subsequent to intense social interaction and the aspiration of each member to prove to his friends how committed he is to the group and/or the cause they believe in.

One of the most significant examples of this process involved five childhood companions from the village of Assira al-Shamaliya (north of Nablus). Moawiya Jarara (23), Bashar Sawalha (24), Tawfiq Yassin (25), Youssef Shouli (22)[46] and Asadi Tul (24) grew up together and became close friends. At first, they all joined Fatah, but then they met Mahmoud Abu Hanude, a well-known Hamas activist, who recruited them to this Islamic organization. He was responsible for indoctrinating them with the belief that they should sacrifice their lives in the struggle against Israel. The special dynamic among the members of the group led them all to take part in suicide attacks. Two of them detonated themselves at the Mahaneh Yehuda market in July 1997, and the other three in September that same year in the *midrahov* (pedestrian mall) in Jerusalem, killing seven and injuring more than 200.[47]

Another powerful illustration of such a network is the incident involving members of the Hebron football club. Altogether, seven players from this team took part in several suicide attacks over a relatively short period of time. Fuad Al-Qawasme was one of them. On 18 May 2003, he carried out a suicide attack in his home town of Hebron, in which two Jewish settlers were killed.[48] In Al-Qawasme's case, the influence of social networking, whether it be kin or peer pressure, is even more prominent. Not only did his football team produce a considerable number of suicide bombers, his family did as well. In all, eight members of the Al-Qawasme *hamula* (extended family),[49] who in fact interacted on a regular basis, committed suicide attacks during the first few months of 2003. Some of them were also members of the football team.[50]

Networks based on families and friends became increasingly important during the years of the Al-Aqsa intifada. This was a result of the fact that some of the more established organizations underwent different degrees of dissolution due to the heavy military pressure imposed by Israel. Muhamad Hasnin and Ashraf Asmar from Jenin were close friends. Neither one of them belonged to any of the known terrorist organizations, yet they gradually became committed to the Palestinian struggle through their friendly interaction. When they felt ready to act, they made contact with Palestinian Islamic Jihad, and an activist supplied them with a truck laden with explosives and instructed them to crash it into a bus. They carried out their mission on 21 October 2002 by driving their vehicle laden with 70 kg of explosives into the vicinity of the IDF military camp 'Mahaneh 80', and exploding it near bus line 841, killing fourteen people and injuring forty-eight.[51]

A comparable example is the case of Muhammad Bastami, a twenty-one-year-old from Nablus, who appeared to have no ties to any known terrorist cell nor a specific motivation for volunteering for the suicide squads. Ultimately, he carried out an attack against citizens and soldiers at a petrol station located near the entrance to the settlement of Ariel. The only thing that seems to be relevant in explaining his decision to choose this path was his close relationship with his cousin, Hamed Sader, a well-known Hamas activist. It seems that Hamed introduced him to the ideology of Hamas and indoctrinated him with the virtues embedded in the act of martyrdom.[52]

Yet, one of the most significant examples of the powerful influence of a social network can be found in the case of Asif Muhammad Hanif and Omar Khan Sharif, both British citizens in their twenties. Hanif and Sharif, both of Pakistani origin,[53] grew up in Britain.[54] Hanif grew up in London and was an enthusiastic fan of football and cricket. After commencing studies in Cranford College, he began to get closer to Islam. He tried for a graduate degree in Kingston College, but after four months decided to go to Morocco and learn Islamic law. His travels also took him to Syria and Saudi Arabia. During this period, he became increasingly religious and, after returning to Britain, he began Islamic studies in Derby under Sheikh Omar Bakri Mohammed. In the course of those lessons he met Sharif and they become close friends. After six lessons[55] Hanif and Sharif offered their services to Hamas, unlike many other Europeans of Muslim or Arab origin who put their small radical cells at the disposal of Al-Qaeda. They travelled to Syria where they met Imad Al Alami, a Hamas leader in Syria who equipped and prepared them for their mission.[56] They entered Israel by way of Jordan as members of the Alternative Tourism Group (a peace-promoting solidarity movement), and in Gaza they met local Hamas activists who fitted them out with explosives. Hanif detonated his explosives belt at the entrance to a bar called *Mike's Place* in Tel Aviv. Sharif apparently drowned in unexplained circumstances, and his body was found a few weeks later, swept ashore on a Tel Aviv beach.[57]

To conclude, commitment is a strong motivating force for suicide missions. This should not come as a surprise. As observed in chapter 2, studies indicate that soldiers who storm enemy fire head on are neither crazy nor suicidal. They are simply committed to their country, often to an accompanying ideology and, above all, to their unit, commanders and comrades. This allegiance or 'kinship' factor significantly applies to many suicide terrorists who belong to an organization or even an independent cell. They do not exhibit mental pathologies or personal problems; they are simply strongly integrated into the social unit. A successful integration makes the unit and its members the most important factor in their lives, and they are willing to do anything for their friends and the common cause.

Personal Motivation for Suicide Attacks

However, not all suicide bombers are members of organizations or integrated into a social network. Many of them chose to become suicide bombers out of personal motivations, the majority of which are related to some type of crisis. Most of these latter perpetrators had never been members of an organization and were recruited, or in other cases specifically volunteered, for the purpose of carrying out the suicide mission.

Financial crisis as motivation

The first years in which suicide attacks became a prominent feature of the conflict in Lebanon may help to demonstrate the importance of a favourable social environment when recruiting individuals for such missions. Before Hezbollah and the other organizations understood the importance of a supportive environment and started planting the roots of the martyrdom idea in Shiite subculture, they had difficulties in mobilizing individuals for such actions.

Mohammed Mahmoud Berro is a good example of this kind of problem. He was captured by Israeli forces while trying to detonate a car bomb at the Israeli military headquarters in

Nabatiya on 23 February 1985. Berro was not religious, did not believe in heaven, nor did he show any signs of hatred towards Israelis.[58] He was inclined to set out on a suicide mission simply because his family needed the money and he was manipulated 'to volunteer' to become a live bomb.[59]

A few months earlier, Berro's father, who served as a police officer, was involved in a car accident. He ran over a young woman and was required to pay her medical expenses. Later, her family asked for further financial compensation and so the Berro family was under enormous pressure until the Shiite Amal movement entered the picture.[60] The organization's representatives offered the family assistance which should have taken care of their financial obligations. As members of the Shiite community, the Berro family was not surprised when they received this kind offer, as the organization had a very good reputation for helping Shiite families in crisis.[61] However, this time the Amal people had a different plan in mind. Shortly after transferring the money to the creditors, they approached Berro's father and asked him to pay back what he owed. Pushed into a corner, the father tried everything to avoid the people who were looking for him, so they decided to invite the young son to a meeting with an organization representative by the name of Abu-Hassan. In the course of the meeting, the younger Berro was asked to join the Amal military wing and fight the Israeli occupation in southern Lebanon.[62] In return, Abu-Hassan promised that the organization would take care of the family's financial problems. Berro was promised that he would not be put at any risk.[63]

Berro did not refuse the offer outright, as he was willing to hear more. Abu-Hassan then sent him to a religious cleric named Haj Ali. The cleric used a different rhetoric and talked to Berro about heaven and about the fact that people who die as *shahid*s did not actually expire but just moved on to a much better place. However, Berro was sceptical; the religious rhetoric did not appeal to him.[64] Abu-Hassan, for his part, was not ready to give up. When he saw that the religious inducement was not effective, he appealed to Berro's commitment to his family. Berro was told that his father was at a high risk of losing his job and that the whole family would be deprived of everything they had. However, if he chose to become a suicide bomber for Amal, the organization would offer the family a lifetime of financial stability. In his testimony, Berro said he felt trapped. He could not watch his father suffer any more and thus, quite unwillingly, he agreed to go out on the mission.[65] This was also the reason he was not eager to set off the explosives and ultimately he let the Israeli soldiers capture him.[66]

The stories of Zarema Muzhakhoeva and Mohammed Berro indicate that a financial crisis does not provide a very strong incentive to become a suicide bomber. In both cases, these individuals had no belief in the cause or felt no commitment to the organization. As a result, they were reluctant to fulfil their mission. This pattern repeated itself in the case of Mayilla Soufangi who also failed to detonate her explosive device. On 3 November 1985, the seventeen-year-old Sunnite woman was sent to blow up a mule she was leading towards a joint Israeli–SLA post.[67] Soufangi was a member of the Lebanese United Front, a small pro-Syrian faction which was actually operated by the Syrian intelligence services.[68] She had joined the organization shortly after she ran away from home following her mother's death.[69] She was desperate for money and the Syrian intelligence services were generous enough to offer her many of the things she needed.[70] In return, Soufangi was sent to basic military training in Rayak, a small town in the Lebanon valley and the site of a Lebanese Army and Air Force base.[71] After a short training period, she was told that it was her duty to carry out a suicide attack.[72] According to her testimony, she in fact wanted to kill Israelis; however she also stressed that she felt no hatred towards them. Thus, it seems that the main reason she set out on the mission was a sense of obligation to the people who helped her financially. As in the above-mentioned cases, Soufangi, too, was not eager to accomplish her mission and later regretted that she was persuaded to attempt it.[73] So, we may cautiously conclude that financial crisis on its own cannot be regarded as a strong motivating factor for carrying out suicide missions, especially in the absence of a supportive environment. This conclusion raises the question: are there other types of personal crises which are better or more reliable predictors of the engenderment of such a motivation?

Personal crisis as motivation

The answer to the question is positive. Individuals who have experienced a significant crisis in their personal life with strong emotional consequences, as well as individuals who have never found their place in the community and thus suffered from social sanctions and low self-esteem, have always been easy targets for the 'enlistment officers' of terrorist groups. These 'enlistment officers' knew exactly how to push the right buttons. In other words, they became experts in exploiting the pain and weaknesses of people for their own political objectives. Such recruitments were mostly successful in cases where the community supported the martyrdom idea and the individual was convinced that his act would be applauded.

Bilal Fahs, a member of the Lebanese Amal, was born to a poor family. His father left his mother soon after Bilal's birth, remarried and had a new family. Young Bilal grew up with his grandmother. However, this was not his sole predicament. His father's marriage with his mother was never properly registered and, under Lebanese law, Bilal was accordingly not recognized by the authorities and prevented from enjoying basic civilian rights such as education.[74] Consequently, he spent most of his days wandering the streets of Beirut until he was recruited by the Amal people. Finally, for the first time in his life, he had some sense of belonging.

When he turned seventeen, he met a young girl; they got engaged and the future seemed even brighter. However, Bilal's past, once again, came back to haunt him. Preparations for the wedding were frustrated by the fact that Bilal had no civil status and was not eligible to register for marriage. He was extremely discouraged by this indelible mark and bane on his life. Religious clerics who saw how devastated he was tried to talk to the authorities on his behalf, but nothing helped. Bilal underwent a dramatic change. His fiancée told reporters that he became obsessed with the fight against Israel in southern Lebanon and began to carry religious books and pictures of men who had perpetrated suicide acts against the Israeli forces. All his energy was transferred from his plans for marriage and starting a family to a full commitment to the jihad against the Israeli occupation. On 16 June 1984, he smashed a car full of explosives into an Israeli military convoy. Bilal was Amal's first suicide bomber.[75]

In many conservative societies, women who go through a personal crisis such as a divorce or an unintentional pregnancy suffer strong social condemnation and sanctions. In most cases, both these women and their families suffer from a dramatic decline in their social status. 'Enlistment officers' of the different Palestinian groups identified this category of women as an ideal target for recruitment to suicide missions.[76]

One of the most famous female suicide bombers to become elevated into the Palestinian pantheon of exalted champions was Wafa Idris. She was thirty-one years old when she detonated an explosive charge on Jaffa Street in the heart of Jerusalem on 27 January 2002. In the years prior to her suicide attack, Idris worked as a nurse in the Palestinian city of Ramallah. People who knew her reported that she had exhibited a strong empathy for the pain of Palestinians injured in clashes with Israeli forces and expressed much frustration with regard to the situation in the city. However, this cannot be regarded as the sole motivation for her to become a suicide bomber. Idris was very different from most Palestinian women of her age. She was born to a poor family and lost her father when she was very young. When she turned sixteen she married her cousin, Ahmad. Soon afterwards it became apparent that she could not have children and her husband asked for a divorce. Deeply shamed, Idris returned to her mother's house and put all her energy into voluntary activities. Her aunt, who was interviewed shortly after Idris's death, said that her former husband's insensitivity drove Idris to her death. From her bedroom window, Idris saw her ex-husband remarry and she even took part in the party he threw on the day he became a father. She was deeply humiliated but wanted to show the community that she still had her pride. Her friend, Raffa Abu Hamid, added that after the divorce, the conservative Palestinian society labelled her as a divorcee who could not have children. Feelings of emptiness and loss deprived her of all joy in life. The 'enlistment officers' of the Al-Aqsa Martyrs Brigades who heard about her situation took advantage of it and appealed to her strong identification with the suffering of the people whom she treated. Indeed, following her death, Idris, the former outcast, became a popular Palestinian hero.[77]

A careful scrutiny of the life stories of Palestinian women who became suicide bombers reveals that the story of Wafa Idris repeated itself, time and again, in different versions. Darine Abu Aisha, an English literature student from Al-Najah University in Nablus, who discharged an explosives belt at the Maccabim-Re'ut Junction on 27 February 2002,[78] was also a marginalized person.[79] She resented her parents' pressure to get married and rejected all the young men who asked for her hand. Her behaviour led the community to raise questions about her character and thus pile more pressure on the family.[80] The videotape that she left behind her was broadcast on the Arab satellite channel, ANN, but did not reveal the personal motivation for her act. She said she 'wanted to be the second woman – after Wafa Idris – to carry out a martyr operation and take revenge for the blood of the martyrs and the desecration of the sanctity of the Al-Aqsa Mosque'. Darine called attention to the crucial role of Palestinian women in the resistance: 'Let Sharon the coward know that every Palestinian woman will give birth to an army of martyrs, and her role will not only be confined to weeping over a son, brother or husband; instead, she will become a martyr herself.'[81]

The story of Shifa Adnan Al-Qudsi, a twenty-six-year-old from Tulkarm who was arrested before she was able to complete her mission, is rather similar.[82] Her status as a divorcee pushed her to the margins of the community.[83] At the same time, her sympathy for the pain which her people experienced

grew stronger.[84] The fact that her brother had planned to perpetrate a suicide mission and instead was shot and captured by
Israeli soldiers was the final trigger that prompted her to offer
herself to the representatives of the Al-Aqsa Martyr Brigades
for a suicide mission.

Ayat Al-Akhras was somewhat different. She was a brilliant
eighteen-year-old high-school student who on 29 March
2002, for no apparent reason, blew herself up at the entrance
to a supermarket in the Kiryat Yovel neighbourhood of
Jerusalem, killing two and injuring thirty.[85] Like her predecessors, Al-Akhras said in the videotape that she left that she
chose this path in order to protect the Palestinian people and
to show the Arab leaders who neglected the Palestinian cause
what one young woman was capable of doing.[86] Or in her
own words: 'I am going to fight instead of the sleeping Arab
armies who are watching Palestinian girls fighting alone . . .
It is an Intifada until victory.'[87] However, shortly after her
death, rumours started spreading that Al-Akhras had been
sexually active with her fiancé and had become pregnant.[88]
Afraid of the social sanctions she would be subjected to by
her family and community, she probably preferred to end her
life for a noble cause.

An almost identical incident is the case of the twenty-year-
old student, Andalib Takatka from Beit Fajar, who committed
a suicide act two weeks after Al-Akhras in the Mahaneh
Yehuda market in Jerusalem. In an interview prior to her
suicide mission, Andalib Takafka said, 'When you want to
carry out such an attack, whether you are a man or a woman,
you don't think about the explosive vest or about your body
being ripped into pieces. We are suffering. We are dying while
we are still alive.'[89] Following the attack, rumours started
spreading to the effect that she had been romantically
involved with a Fatah activist and had become pregnant by
him.[90] Although evidence with respect to the romantic relations in the last two accounts of the female suicide terrorists
is partial, it remains apparent that, in conservative societies,
setting out on a suicide mission can sometimes be a more
appealing alternative than living a life of condemnation on

the margins of society. A case clearly illustrating this point is that of Rim Salah Al-Riashi, the twenty-two-year-old mother of two from Gaza, who detonated an explosives belt at the Erez Crossing in the northern part of the Gaza Strip in January 2004. Al-Riashi, the first Hamas female suicide bomber, was known to have problems in her marriage and, according to some sources, was sent on the mission by both her husband and lover in order to help her avoid the social sanctions which are imposed on an unfaithful woman in a highly conservative society.[91]

Not only women choose to volunteer for suicide missions in order to avoid social sanctions. A reporter of the Qatar-based TV station, Al-Jazeera, presented the story of a sixteen-year-old boy from Nablus who detonated an explosives belt when he was approached by Israeli police officers on 16 June 2002. According to the story, the boy, whose name was not disclosed, was infected with the HIV virus when he received a blood transfusion during an operation a few months earlier. Unable to live with the stigma of being a person with AIDS, he preferred to die in a way that would bring back some of his dignity.[92]

Shadi Nassar from the village of Madama near Nablus suffered from a disability for many years. When he was four years old, he fell off a building and sustained a severe head trauma. Ever since that ill-fated day, he suffered from recurrent epileptic episodes and was rejected by his peers who thought he was insane. When he turned fifteen, Nassar could not take the mocking and humiliation any more and decided to quit school. He felt lonely and depressed and moved from one job to another. On 7 March 2002, he executed a suicide attack in the city of Ariel on behalf of the Popular Front for the Liberation of Palestine. Shortly after his death, posters with Nassar's image adorned every corner of his small village and, for the first time, he gained the respect he had so desperately yearned for when he was alive.[93]

His family members had no idea when and how he had been recruited for the mission and they did not approve of the act. His brother Rami said that a short time before the attack,

Shadi started expressing views against the occupation but there were no indications that he was planning to do something. According to Rami's assumption, organization recruiters took advantage of Shadi's physical and mental condition and manipulated him into this act. The fact that a few months prior to the attack he had been beaten by Israeli soldiers could also have been a trigger which made him more predisposed to engage in the mission.[94] This precipitating factor leads us to the motivation which seems to be the strongest indicator for the perpetration of a suicide act: revenge.

Revenge as motivation

The basic urge to inflict pain on those perceived as responsible for the anguish of the aggrieved party appears in many biographies of suicide bombers throughout the world. It should be noted, however, that revenge is not limited only to cases where an individual suffers a direct loss, such as an injury or losing a loved person in an action committed by the perceived aggressor. Revenge can also be in response to the continuous suffering of the community to which the perpetrator belongs. Many suicide bombers stated that they wanted to hurt the enemy in the same way that their people had been hurt by it, and they wanted to make this enemy feel and pay for what it had done to the community.

The story of Sana Mheidleh, who was the first female suicide bomber in Lebanon, may serve as a good example of this kind of revenge. Mheidleh was only sixteen years old when she drove a car bomb into an Israeli checkpoint on 9 April 1985.[95] Despite her Shiite origins, Mheidleh was not a member of Hezbollah but of the Syrian Social Nationalist Party.[96] Before embarking on her mission, she spoke to her comrades and left a letter.[97] When discussing her motives for perpetrating the attack, she clearly stated that religion had nothing to do with it. All she wanted was revenge. She stated that her act should be one of the consequences that the Israeli occupation of southern Lebanon would have to suffer for the way it had treated the Lebanese people.[98]

Almost sixteen years later, on 4 March 2001, Ahmad Alian, a twenty-two-year-old Palestinian from the Nur A-Shams refugee camp, detonated an explosives belt, killing three and injuring sixty in the Israeli city of Netanya.[99] Alian was a very religious person who worked in the local mosque as a muezzin. He was not a known member of any terrorist organization and it appears that he made the decision to become a *shahid* more or less on his own.[100] In a letter he left behind, Alian wrote: 'Israel is slaughtering the Palestinians and Jerusalem is still under occupation. Therefore, we Palestinians must sacrifice ourselves in any possible way for the Lord and for Jerusalem.'[101] Despite the strong religious rhetoric in Alian's statement, it seems that the main motivation for his act was the urge to protest against the Israeli occupation and to avenge the death of his fellow Palestinians.[102]

The desire to take revenge for the community's suffering became a recurrent motif among Palestinian suicide bombers during the years of the Al-Aqsa intifada. Jamal Nasser, a twenty-three-year-old electrical engineering student from Nablus, who detonated an explosive device near a school bus in Shavei Shomron on 29 April 2001, left a letter and a videotape. In the letter, he wrote that he made the decision to become a suicide bomber because he wanted 'to revenge the death of all the Palestinian *shahids*.'[103] In the videotape, he elaborated: 'I was driven to this act by my love for the Lord and the Al-Aqsa Mosque and by my desire to revenge the blood of the *shahids* . . . While Arab leaders and kings neglect their duty in protecting Palestine, I tell them: we do not want your money, your food or your medicine. We want your soldiers for the liberation of Palestine.'[104] Nasser was one of many Palestinian suicide bombers who made such statements prior to their deaths.

Less than a month later, on 18 May 2001, Mahmood Ahmad Marmash, a twenty-year-old carpenter from Tulkarm, activated his explosives belt at the entrance to the Sharon ('Hadarim') shopping mall in Netanya, killing six and injuring more than a hundred.[105] This time the only indication of a motive was found on a videotape distributed by Hamas.

In the tape, Marmash said, 'I will turn my body into a bomb which will explode the bodies of the Zionists who are ancestors of pigs and monkeys. I will revenge every drop of blood that was spilled on the soil of Jerusalem.' Later in the tape, he said that the death of a Palestinian baby, Iman Hiju, one week earlier in Gaza, had shocked his very being and triggered him to act at that point in time.[106] Following Marmash's death, his sister, Wahiba, made a comment that was not very different from the one made by Jamal Nasser. She said, 'My brother did what he had to do and it should be a good lesson to the [Palestinian] leaders who are doing nothing . . . I am very proud of him.'[107] Therefore, along with the urge to avenge the pain and humiliation of Palestinians by means of killing Israeli civilians, these suicide bombers also expressed their frustration at the incompetence of the Palestinian Authority, as they perceived it.

Over the following months, the idea of committing a suicide attack as an act of vengeance against the Israelis, while at the same time protesting the inadequacy of the Palestinian Authority, became a pattern. Ismail Al-Maswabi, a twenty-seven-year-old student at the University of Gaza, exploded himself and a group of Israeli soldiers near the Dugit settlement in the Gaza Strip on 22 June 2001. He left no explanation for his act, but his father, Bashir, who celebrated his son's death much in the manner of a wedding party, said, 'This is not an ordinary wedding, which anyone can have. This is a wedding that only very special people are entitled to – a wedding with heaven . . . My son resisted the occupation and the wrong way of some of our leaders . . . he did it out of our desire for freedom . . . he did not kill himself . . . he sacrificed himself for the Lord and for our homeland.'[108]

Similar statements were made by the family members of Mohammed Saeed Al-Hotary, a twenty-two-year-old Palestinian from Qalqilya, who had resided in Jordan for many years[109] and was responsible for the attack on the beachside club *Dolphi Disco* in Tel Aviv on 1 June 2001.[110] This attack claimed the lives of twenty-one people, most of them young immigrants from the former USSR who were waiting to enter the popular nightclub on a Friday night.[111] Hotary's family put the blame on Israel for his act. His father said, 'The Palestinian people believe in peace, but the Israelis left us with no other alternative but this one . . . I am very happy that my son did it; I wish that I had many more sons who could have committed such actions. I would have loved to do it myself.'[112]

This type of revenge seems to occur in communities that have experienced long periods of repression that impact, in one way or another, on almost every member of the community. Such acts of revenge are sparked off in cases where there is a collective sense that the situation must be changed but there is no one who is ready to do anything about it. Under such circumstances, individual members of the community feel it is their duty to make the oppressor pay, while at the same time they are also signalling to their leaders and allies that the community is frustrated and disappointed by their incompetence. In many cases, these perpetrators are regarded as heroes and their families garner a lot of support from the community.

Suicidal acts of revenge provoked by personal reasons are a different matter. These generally take place a short while after the perpetrator has suffered a significant loss and the action is a relatively individual one. This kind of attack was prevalent both among Chechen suicide bombers – mostly the women – and the Palestinian community during the course of the Al-Aqsa intifada.

Kaira was a twenty-two-year-old student when she took part in the tragic siege of the Moscow theatre. Despite the fact that she grew up in a religious Muslim family, she had always felt an affiliation with the West. She particularly loved European and American history, literature and music.[113] During the long years of the war in Chechnya, Kaira fell in love and got married. Shortly after the wedding, her husband joined the ranks of the rebels and six months later he was killed in action. For Kaira, this was just the beginning. The Russian army found out that she had been married to a rebel. A patrol stormed her family's house and took away her sixteen-year-old brother. Not long afterwards, the family recovered his mutilated body. It was clear to them that the boy had been severely tortured before he was executed. Over the next few months, Kaira also lost her cousin and, to make matters even worse, the family's house was destroyed in a Russian artillery attack.[114] Kaira was crushed. She felt guilty for marrying a rebel and bringing so many calamities on her family,[115] as well as anger against the Russians who were pitiless towards young children, women and older people.[116] According to an American friend of hers, these circumstances led her to join the group which attacked the theatre.[117]

Many more Chechen women turned to suicide bombing, spurred on by the urge to avenge the death of a loved one. The following are just a few illustrations. On 14 May 2003, Larisa Musalayeva detonated an explosives belt during a religious festival in Ilishkhan-Yurt. Her story begins six months earlier, when her brother, Imran, a well-known Chechen rebel, committed suicide[118] when the bodyguards of Akhmad Kadyrov (a Chechen leader loyal to President Putin) tried to catch and arrest him.[119] Subsequently, Larisa accused Kadyrov and his bodyguards of the death of her brother and resolved to take revenge. When she heard Kadyrov was going to be present at the festival, she tried to assassinate him in a suicide attack.[120] She perished in the blast and so did Kadyrov's bodyguards and many others, but Kadyrov himself was unharmed. Shahida Baymuradova, a forty-six-year-old woman, who also took part in the May 2003 attack in Ilishkhan-Yurt,[121] lost her husband during the 1999 fighting.[122] Luiza Gazuyeva, whose husband and two brothers were brutally killed by Russian troops, blew herself up near a group of soldiers.

One of the most illuminating cases in regard to this phenomenon is the account of a woman known as Kawa. She agreed to give a media interview before departing on her ultimate mission.[123] Kawa's husband was tortured to death by Russian soldiers and, as a result, she became a member of the 'Black Widows' of Chechnya, determined to avenge his death. The first thing she did was to join a group of rebels sent to locate her husband's killers. When they identified one of them, they tortured him to death in front of Kawa.[124] Then Kawa decided it was time to leave on her own mission. Despite her strong ties to the Wahhabist current of Islam, when asked about her motivation to become a suicide bomber, she never mentioned a religious cause. She said, 'Now I am left with one dream, to blow myself up in Russia and take with me as many Russians as possible. I want to be sent on such a mission. I want revenge. This is the only way to stop the Russians from killing Chechens. Maybe now they will understand the message and leave us alone.'[125] Later in the interview, Kawa discussed the roots of her hatred towards Russians in more detail. In 1995, when she was only fourteen years old, her father was killed during a raid by a Russian force on the family house. Later, she fell in love with Salman, who was two years older than her. He joined a small group of radical Muslim Chechens who aspired to free Chechnya and turn it into a Muslim theocracy. Shortly before he was killed, the Russians identified Salman as a prominent figure among the rebels and planned to ambush him. He was caught by surprise, tortured and then shot dead. The immediate trigger for Kawa's decision to leave her young daughter with Salman's mother and join the rebels was the fact that after his death, Salman's face was brutally mutilated in order to prevent identification. This act of cruelty horrified Kawa. When she heard the details, she made a commitment to take revenge.[126]

This type of individual retaliation is also present among men and women in other parts of the world, most prominently among Palestinians. A review of the records and accounts of over 180 Palestinian suicide bombers confirmed that close to half of them – and a larger number during the years of the Al-Aqsa intifada – embarked on their suicide missions shortly after they had lost a person very close to them. This person could have been a friend, family member or lover.

On 16 July 2001, Mustafa Abu-Shaduf,[127] a twenty-year-old from the city of Jenin, detonated an explosive device at the Binyamina train station. Two Israelis were killed and ten others injured.[128] Despite the fact that the organization which sent Mustafa, Palestinian Islamic Jihad, announced that this was in response to the continuation of crimes committed by Israel against the Palestinians,[129] other sources indicate that Abu-Shaduf was driven to the act by the loss of his brother seven months earlier in a clash with Israeli soldiers. Later, a friend of his who was a member of the local chapter of Palestinian Islamic Jihad was assassinated by a missile launched from an Israeli helicopter. To add to this, a few weeks prior to his departure on the suicide attack, Abu-Shaduf's best friend, Mahmud Juma Hamdan, disappeared.[130]

On 12 August 2001, three weeks after Abu-Shaduf's attack in Binyamina, Muhammad Nasser, a twenty-eight-year-old bachelor who was also a member of the northern group of Palestinian Islamic Jihad, detonated his suicide bomb at the *Wall Street Café* in Kiryat Mozkin (a suburb of Haifa), injuring twenty people.[131] His father, Mahmud, told reporters that Nasser had served in the police intelligence unit in Jenin but had decided to quit his job following the IDF assassination of his friend, Iyad Hardan, one of the prominent Palestinian Islamic Jihad leaders in Samaria. Nasser became obsessed with the wish to avenge Hardan's death. Prior to his departure on the suicide mission, he told his friends that all that was left for him was the desire to meet Iyad in heaven.[132]

Jihad Titi was motivated by a very similar reason. This eighteen-year-old from the refugee camp of Balata near Nablus activated his explosives belt on 27 May 2002, in Petah Tikva a week after three Fatah activists from Nablus were killed by Israeli soldiers. Among them was Mahmud Titi, Jihad's cousin.[133] This event drove the young man straight into the arms of the Al-Aqsa Martyrs Brigades, who were looking for a candidate to carry out a suicide mission in response to an attack on their people.[134]

A well-known and illustrative case of this phenomenon is the story of Hanadi Jaradat, which has already been discussed in chapter 1. Jaradat, who perpetrated one of the most deadly attacks against Israeli civilians, at the *Maxim* restaurant in Haifa, was a twenty-nine-year-old lawyer from Jenin.

Both Salah, her cousin and fiancé, and her brother, Fadi, were killed by Israeli soldiers. Fadi was shot near the house of her family[135] and the soldiers did not let her approach her dying brother and offer him help. Fadi was a role model for Jaradat. He supported her during her student years in Jordan and took care of their father who suffered from cancer. After Fadi's death, Jaradat assumed all his duties in the household, including taking care of her ailing father. This was another frustrating experience. Her father was being treated at the Rambam hospital in the city of Haifa and, on many occasions, as result of closures in Jenin, he missed his treatments and his health deteriorated. Family members described Jaradat as a volcano waiting to erupt. All she could think of was avenging the death of her loved ones and to make the Israelis pay for the pain they had inflicted on her family.[136] According to family members, four months before the attack she went to visit her brother's grave and swore to take vengeance. She said, 'Your blood will not have been shed in vain. The murderer will pay the price and we will not be the only ones crying.'[137]

Iyad Al-Masri was much younger than Jaradat when he activated his explosives belt; he was only seventeen years old. However, the circumstances which led him to carry out the attack were very similar. On 11 January 2004, Iyad left his parents' home and never came back. Later that afternoon, his mother was watching the broadcasts of the Hezbollah TV station, Al-Manar, and, at first, she did not make the connection between the story of a young Palestinian who detonated an explosive charge next to a group of Israeli soldiers and the disappearance of her son. Only later that night, she received the news. What drove the quiet adolescent into the arms of the 'enlistment officers' of Palestinian Islamic Jihad? This saga began a week earlier on 3 January. Amjad, Iyad's younger brother, who was only fifteen years of age, woke up one morning and went to school as usual to take a civic studies exam. When he arrived at the school gate, he saw that it was surrounded by soldiers. They refused to let him in and sent him back home. Frustrated, he left and waited with his friends on the roof of a neighbour's house. Up there, they kept track of the school premises, waiting for the soldiers to leave when, suddenly, Amjad fell down. He had been shot. According to his mother, all he did was observe the schoolyard. According to military sources, Amjad was throwing blocks at the soldiers. Amjad's mother, Abir, and his brother, Iyad, rushed to him and found him unconscious. They called an ambulance but on the way to the hospital, they were stopped several times at military checkpoints. By the time they reached the emergency room, there was nothing to be done.

Amjad was buried that same day, but that was not the end of the story. During the funeral, a group of youngsters started protesting against the presence of soldiers in the area. Military sources reported that Molotov cocktails and blocks were thrown at the soldiers. Muhammad, Amjad's cousin who, in the family's version, was carrying his body and, according to the military, took part in the riots, was shot dead. A day later, he was buried next to Amjad. In the following weeks, there were no prominent changes in Iyad's behaviour. He did not even mention revenge. However, there were a few, almost insignificant, signs. For example, he never left the house and he began to smoke, something he had never done before. Most importantly, he asked his mother to extend the mourning period a little longer. A few days later, Iyad himself was dead in the suicide attack he carried out against the Israeli army.[138]

Among the different crisis situations which may lead a person to commit a suicide attack, personal crises (except for financial ones) would be at the top of the list. It seems that a personal experience, whether it is the loss of a loved person and the urge to take revenge or an event which has a strong impact on the person's life, such as an unplanned pregnancy in a conservative society, would be the best predictor. Having said that, it should be stressed that the community has to view suicide terrorism as a positive phenomenon, and the person who perpetrates the act must be rewarded. In most cases, this reward will be the 'resurrection' of the person following his or her death and an elevation of the social status of this person's family. Without support from the community, the prospects of perpetrating a suicide attack, even for purposes of revenge, will diminish. As for a community crisis, embarking on a suicide mission solely on the basis of the community's distress is far less common. This type of behaviour will mostly characterize members of the community who are strongly integrated into it and are highly influenced by the collective feeling of hopelessness. Conditions reinforcing such behaviour will develop after a long period of repression and when the situation seems more hopeless than ever.

An Analysis of the Motivations of Palestinian Suicide Bombers

As mentioned at the beginning of this chapter, the attempt to construct a profile of suicide bombers based on psychological and socio-economic characteristics has for many years absorbed scholars and those engaged in military intelligence. While academics believe that a solid profile would enable them to figure out what kind of people sacrifice themselves in suicide missions, and what motivates them, intelligence officers are highly interested in such profiles for the purpose of identifying and stopping suicide terrorists before they are dispatched.

The first wave of suicide attackers launched by Hamas and Palestinian Islamic Jihad against Israeli targets consisted of thirty-three suicide bombers over a period of seven years until the outbreak of the Al-Aqsa intifada (April 1993–September 2000). In many aspects, this group fitted the profile of the Islamic *mujahidin*.[139] They were single (89.35 per cent) males (100 per cent) and their average age was 23.21 years. Most had a religious background (53.6 per cent)[140] and they were also highly educated. Only a small minority of this group had no more than an elementary education (10.75 per cent), while 39.3 per cent had a high-school education and 50 per cent were either in academies or university students. Most of these suicide bombers (69.6 per cent) were full- or part-time employed. Another common and important denominator was organizational affiliation. Over 71.4 per cent were long-time members of one of the organizations and had a record of involvement in terrorist activities. Many of them also spent time in Israeli prisons.

The group of Al-Aqsa intifada suicide perpetrators numbered 150 in only four years (October 2000–September 2004) and its composition was already quite a different matter. Men still constituted the vast majority of this group but women became increasingly involved in suicide terrorism over the years of this intifada (5.4 per cent). The number of unmarried perpetrators also increased during the course of the intifada and stood at 92.3 per cent (of whom 0.7 per cent were divorced). The increase in the number of single individuals could be attributed, at least partially, to the fact that the average age dropped to 21.71 years.

Yet, the most important differences between the two groups lie in other distinctions. Among Al-Aqsa intifada perpetrators, only a minority of 46.9 per cent had a religious background. Moreover, the level of education in this group was dramatically lower than that of their predecessors. Twelve per cent of Al-Aqsa intifada perpetrators had an elementary education, 55.6 per cent had a high-school diploma and only 32.4 per cent were either in academies or students in academic institutions. The levels of unemployed terrorists also increased and stood at 41.9 per cent. More strikingly, only 24.2 per cent of this group were members of a terrorist organization or had spent time in an Israeli prison.

Making solid inferences about the personal motivations of suicide terrorists on the basis of their changing characteristics as a group can be problematic. Yet, some ideas can be cautiously proffered. Since the outbreak of the Al-Aqsa intifada, suicide terrorism was no longer a unique trait of fundamentalist organizations which dispatched veteran activists who were mostly religious and educated men. Suicide terrorism became widespread among young Palestinians from very different backgrounds. Many of them were not highly ideological or religious and, furthermore, most of them were never active members of a terrorist organization.

The differences between the two groups lend some support to the commitment versus crisis dichotomy. The first generation of Palestinian suicide bombers was composed of a relatively small and homogenous group of members from Hamas and Palestinian Islamic Jihad, two religious fundamentalist organizations which objected to the peace process, once led by Arafat. The main motivation of these suicide bombers was to fulfil their duty as devout members of their organizations. During this period, both the role of socialization as well as ideological indoctrination – to be discussed in the next chapter – in becoming a member of the organization were of great import. Most suicide bombers from the much larger second group had no organizational affiliation. Many of them offered themselves for suicide missions and did not really care under which organizational designation they would be carried out. The fact that the second group was much bigger and more heterogeneous may indicate that this later wave of suicide terrorism was caused by the intensification of both personal and community crisis situations. In the months prior to the Al-Aqsa intifada, and especially after its outbreak, the entire Palestinian community plummeted from a state of high hopes for a better future into a bitter and painful war. Many members of the community suffered directly from this change in circumstances. The next chapter will illustrate how the different Palestinian organizations transformed the idea of martyrdom into a virtue and essentially planted the culture of death within Palestinian society. By doing so, they offered members of the community undergoing a crisis a channel for articulating their frustration, deprivation and, above all, their urge for revenge.

Summary

At the beginning of this chapter, two key questions were posed: who are suicide bombers and what motivates them? At this point, some conclusions can be offered. A suicide bomber can be almost anyone. Resorting to suicide terrorism, however, requires supporting preconditions as well as a triggering factor. Preconditions in most cases are related to the underlying values of the community and a situation of protracted conflict from which it has suffered. The combination of a culture which regards death as less threatening than the perception of death held by more Western cultures and a violent conflict which takes a high toll on the community can serve as a breeding ground for suicide terrorism. Yet, in order for this potential to materialize, there is a need for a strong organizational endorsement of the phenomenon, a subject which will be discussed in the next chapter, and a reserve of motivated candidates who will carry out suicide missions. The first precipitating motivational factor for such a mission would be a total commitment of the individual to an organization which endorses suicide terrorism or to a social network which regards the act of martyrdom as virtuous. The second triggering factor would be a crisis situation. This mostly applies to individuals who are members of the community but have no organizational affiliation. Under conditions of personal crisis, such as the loss of a loved person in a conflict, a divorce or an unplanned pregnancy in a conservative society and, in fewer cases, even a financial problem, a person may volunteer or become more susceptible to recruitment to a suicide assignment. Such a mission may be perceived by this individual as an ultimate vehicle for revenge, a way to gain personal rehabilitation and even a channel for securing the financial future of his or her family. A second type of crisis is related to cases where the individual's integration into the community is so profound that, overwhelmed by the pain inflicted on the community, this person regards the suicide attack as a reasonable action to help the group he or she identifies with.

7

The Recruitment and Socialization of the Suicide Terrorist

Murad Tawalbe was no different from most of his friends. He was born in the Palestinian city of Jenin in 1983. A boy with considerable political awareness, he was very much absorbed in the Palestinian struggle for independence. However, except for throwing stones and Molotov cocktails at Israeli soldiers like many of his peers, he had never been involved in more serious terrorist activities. In fact, when he turned eighteen, he even joined the Palestinian police force. Yet, Murad was different in one crucial aspect. His elder brother Mohammad was the charismatic leader of the military wing of Palestinian Islamic Jihad in Jenin.[1]

Following a routine confrontation with IDF soldiers, in which one of Murad's best friends, Amjad Hasnia, was shot dead, Mohammad noticed that his brother had changed. He was constantly upset and kept repeating that he wanted to avenge the death of his friend. Mohammad's response was not long in coming. He asked one of his comrades, Tabet Mardawi, to approach his younger brother and recruit him to Palestinian Islamic Jihad. Murad responded enthusiastically to the offer. At first, he was told that he would be sent on a mission to Haifa, which is only a thirty-minute drive from Jenin, and that he would be expected to open fire on passers-by in a crowded street. He had even undergone a short training period for this mission with another young member of the organization. However, in the end, the plan did not materialize.[2]

In May 2002, a few months later, Murad was approached directly by his elder brother. This time the offer was more concrete. The target again was downtown Haifa and this time Murad understood that he was expected to stab civilians with a knife in a final act of sacrifice. In other words, much like the eleventh-century Assassins, he was supposed to run down the street and stab people until he was either killed or stopped. Two months later, the plan was slightly modified. Mohammad and Mardawi invited Murad to Mohammad's apartment in the Jenin refugee camp where they described to him the virtues of becoming a *shahid*. They specifically emphasized the *shahid*'s role as the advocate for his parents and other family members in heaven on Judgement Day. He was also reminded of the fact that once he reached the gates of heaven as a *shahid*, he would be welcomed by seventy-two beautiful virgins. Murad was very impressed.

In the following days, he went through a brief training procedure. Besides hearing stories about the importance of the act of *istishad*, stories which were meant to strengthen his spirit, Murad also went through some tactical training. Only then, the true nature of the planned attack was revealed to him. Instead of stabbing Israelis, he was instructed to detonate an explosives belt in a crowded street. At this point, he showed no objection.[3]

The final stage in the training process took place in the house of Haj Ali Sphoori, one of the prominent leaders of Palestinian Islamic Jihad in Jenin. When Murad entered the room, he saw his brother waiting for him. He was instructed to write a will and then read it in front of a video camera. In his will, Murad asked his mother and brothers to be strong and patient until they would all be reunited one day in heaven. When the short ritual ended, he was sent back home with instructions to return to the same place the next day at 4 a.m.

The following day, he arrived at the house before dawn and was welcomed by his brother and Sphoori. The slim boy was wrapped in a 6 kg explosives belt and then covered with three shirts to make him look a little overweight. Before he was sent to pray for the last time, Murad was informed that he had two options regarding the destination of the attack. He could go either to the city of Afula or the original target, downtown Haifa. Murad chose Haifa. Following another short ritual, he boarded a taxi waiting for him outside Sphoori's house. The taxi dropped him off at the village of Anin, very close to Israeli territory. Another Jihad activist smuggled him into Um-al-Fahem, an Arab city inside Israel.

For the first time since his recruitment Murad was alone. He decided to join a group of Arab workers and boarded a taxi to Haifa. Thirty minutes later, he left the taxi near a mosque in the Arab quarter of the city. Not far from the mosque, he noticed a group of about 150 people who were shop owners and customers at the local flea market. Murad knew that this was an ideal opportunity. He approached the crowd and had moved his hand to the activation button of the explosives belt when, suddenly, he froze. In a statement which he later gave, he said that he suddenly was overcome with fear. 'I was afraid. I was flooded with thoughts of my mother and brothers. I decided not to blow myself up with all these people. I felt sorry for them. They did nothing wrong.' Later, he added that he saw some Arab faces in the crowd and was afraid that he would harm them as well. Scared and confused, Murad fled the scene.

A few minutes later, he tried to summon up his courage, and returned to the market. However, once again, he just could not do it. Finally, he ran to a deserted building where he took off the belt. Then he called his brother from a payphone and told him that he had failed to accomplish the mission due to an electrical failure which prevented the detonation. Later on, when he tried to flee the scene, he was detained by a police patrol and revealed the whole story. Ultimately, he was prosecuted and is now serving a seven-year sentence in an Israeli prison.[4]

Despite his failed mission, the story of Murad's recruitment, training and dispatching sheds light on the process of how a young person, who is sometimes bitter, upset and eager for revenge, is transformed into a live bomb. In the following sections of this chapter, I will investigate the training process of suicide bombers and dispute the contention that suicide terrorism is a trait of a certain culture or religion. On the contrary, I will argue that this phenomenon is to a large extent a result of favourable environmental conditions and a well-orchestrated organizational process. However, prior to this, I will discuss the role of the environment in supporting the recruitment processes of potential suicide terrorists in different parts of the world. Then, I will conduct a comparative analysis of the organizational process, that is, the recruitment, training and dispatching of suicide bombers by different groups, and finally, I will highlight similarities and differences.

The Environmental Setting of Suicide Terrorism

As mentioned in previous chapters, many academic voices have recently been heard linking Muslim religion and Arab culture to suicide terrorism.[5] Yet, as I have shown, suicide terrorism generally runs its course in short-term campaigns, mostly lasting up to three years. This indicates that there is a person or organization who decides when to start and end it. Moreover, suicide terrorism rarely appears in a non-organized form. Therefore, it should not be treated as a spontaneous phenomenon but more as well designed and planned. People do not just take to the streets and begin to set off explosive devices. They are trained for this mission by an organization which has a set of goals.

Thus I believe that the arguments which stress that suicide terrorism is a product of a certain culture or religion should be carefully examined. I do, however, consider that culture and religion are utilized for the purpose of training the suicide bomber and that some societies are more vulnerable to this phenomenon than others.

The chances of finding suicide terrorists in affluent and prosperous societies are not very high. The same is true for societies in which life is a dominant value and the aspiration to preserve life is superior to all other goals and dreams. Yet, suicide terrorism is also not present in most poor societies or societies where life is considered as no more than a path that must be taken before the individual reaches his/her eternal destination.

So what are the conditions which allow some societies to show understanding and support for this phenomenon? As presented in chapter 2, a survey of areas in the world where suicide terrorism has emerged and is perceived as a virtue by large parts of the population underscores the factor of a long-lasting conflict with a powerful enemy that has inflicted much pain on that society. This predicament generates frustration and results in the dehumanization of the other side.[6]

As strange as it may sound, in certain societies that perceive themselves as weak and who feel hopeless and oppressed by a powerful enemy, suicide terrorism, with its potential to cause considerable pain, damage and confusion to the aggressor, can empower that society. It may even offer hope that things will eventually change; it may at least ensure that the aggressor suffers. In some cases, perception of the enemy as evil and dehumanized makes it easier for people to support acts in which not only soldiers and politicians but also innocent civilians and children are killed. One interesting fact should be emphasized. Social support for suicide terrorism, or the 'culture of death', as it is described in other places,[7] is very rarely a grass-roots phenomenon. In fact, it is a highly calculated, top-down phenomenon.

The organization that adopts this strategy is greatly concerned with its public image and the level of support it receives from its potential constituency. Hence, the organization's leadership is engaged in trying to mobilize support, and one of the prominent ways of doing this among societies which are oppressed and feel weak and hopeless is by supplying heroes and hope.

Hezbollah was the first organization to launch waves of suicide attacks. Early suicide campaigns carried out by this organization were marked by high levels of secrecy.

Organization leaders wanted to leave no traces of their involvement in order to prevent counter-attacks against the organization. Moreover, as Sheikh Subhi al-Tufeili explained, the organization was reluctant to take responsibility for the attacks so that no specific person or organization, but Islam in general, would be glorified. However, a few years later this picture began to change as Hezbollah leaders realized the political power of martyrdom.[8]

The first sign of an attempt to create a supportive culture with respect to suicide bombers was the case of Ahmad Qasir, which was discussed at the beginning of the previous chapter.[9] It took Hezbollah over two years to reveal the identity and picture of the fifteen-year-old suicide bomber,[10] but soon after the release of his photo, Qasir became a mega-celebrity both in Lebanon and Iran. This was a result of a concentrated effort by Iran and Hezbollah to market him as a hero. Huge posters of Qasir's image rising from the ruins of the Israeli barracks were positioned along roadsides and inside the Shiite villages of southern Lebanon. The Iranian leadership erected a memorial site in the name of Qasir, the Islamic hero, in Tehran. The anniversary of his lethal act has been commemorated by Hezbollah every year since then. Dozens of potential *shahids* declaring they are ready to walk in Qasir's footsteps march along the streets, and the number of supporters attending these annual events continues to grow every year.[11]

This approach has proved to be highly effective. Almost ten years after Hezbollah stopped sending its members on suicide missions, Sheikh Naim Kassem, one of its leaders, claimed that the organization's reserve of potential suicide bombers had expanded. Swayed by the 'culture of death' created and nurtured by the organization, many people responded to the huge recruitment posters in the streets of southern Lebanon, offering themselves for suicide missions. The organization has been so persuasive that it did not have to deploy special operatives for the recruitment of new members for suicide missions. All its leaders had to do was pick out the best people for the job from the many applicants.[12]

The question is, what has made Hezbollah's efforts to establish this 'culture of death' so successful? There are arguments that Islamic religion looks favourably upon acts of martyrdom, yet the case is not so simple; Islam in fact has many faces. Hezbollah started launching suicide attacks under fairly auspicious conditions. Lebanon was torn apart by a long-drawn-out civil war, during which the Shiite population, and Hezbollah's constituency, suffered greatly. The organization's leadership, backed by Iran, learned quickly how to turn a deaf ear to those authoritative voices in the Muslim world which objected to the idea of suicide (*intihar*, in Arabic). Hezbollah eventually adopted the Iranian stance on the issue which was developed by Ayatollah Khomeini, according to which such attacks are not considered suicide acts.

During the war with Iraq in the 1980s, the Iranian army, suffering from military inferiority, recruited young boys whose function was to walk into Iraqi minefields. Sometimes they even carried explosive devices on their bodies and were required to run towards Iraqi tanks. These children proved to be an effective tactical tool and Khomeini did not want to lose this advantage. However, he needed popular support for sending young children to die on the battlefield and so he used his religious authority to make the distinction between a condemnable suicide act and a praiseworthy act of self-sacrifice (*istishad*, in Arabic). This religious justification was important for the children's families and for Iranian society, yet it was not appealing enough for the children themselves. In order to attract them, Khomeini cultivated an ethos of self-sacrifice.[13] The army officers who recruited these children promised them the keys to the gates of heaven and fitted them out with headbands flaunting the slogan 'Long Live Khomeini'. Steadily, the idea of joining the army and becoming a hero or even a martyr spread among boys in Iran. This cultural phenomenon, created by the top-down approach of the regime, was translated into peer pressure and even became a trend among Iranian youths. A great number of these children succumbed to the pressure of their friends and, bearing in mind the social rewards they would receive once they became heroes, went off and enlisted in the army, often without the approval of their parents, many of whom remained sceptical about the idea of *istishad* or 'martyrdom'.[14]

Hezbollah was not the only organization to adopt this approach successfully. Years after it stopped dispatching suicide bombers, this strategy was passed over to Palestinian organizations, using the same 'marketing' approach. As mentioned in previous chapters, Palestinian organizations did not need much encouragement to turn to suicide terrorism. They were fighting the same Israeli enemy as Hezbollah, and were inspired by the fact that suicide bombing had proved to be effective in Hezbollah's struggle against Israeli forces. They also realized it was not enough to prove to the Palestinian people the strategic advantages of this phenomenon; it would have to become something prestigious and desirable. Therefore, both Hamas and Palestinian Islamic Jihad adopted Hezbollah's approach of glorying self-sacrifice and creating a 'culture of death'.

However, during the 1990s, when both organizations started sending suicide terrorists off to Israeli cities, Palestinian society was not really eager to embrace this type of culture. Many Palestinians saw the Oslo Accords as the prospect of a better future. However, before long, the hope for a bright future was once more replaced by despair. Disappointment with the Israeli lack of will to implement the Accords coupled with anger towards the Palestinian National Authority – which did not show any real commitment to improving the living standards of the average Palestinian – served the efforts of terrorist organizations in disseminating a 'culture of death' in Palestinian society.

At first, this consisted of turning out posters of *shahids* with the Al-Aqsa Mosque in the background which were circulated and posted in the streets. Later, and especially following the outbreak of the Al-Aqsa intifada, the streets were covered with graffiti in praise of the *shahids*. Songs in their honour were written and broadcast on the radio. Mass rallies were devoted to the presentation of dramatic pieces which depicted suicide attacks, and Internet sites were created in memory of perpetrators. This time, the organizations were highly successful in cultivating this mindset. The idea of *istishad* became a virtue and was associated with symbolic capital. Young children started playing the '*shahid* game' in which they imitated suicide attacks. Public support for suicide terrorism increased and the number of volunteers for such operations reached new peaks.[15] The Palestinian *shahid* became a cultural icon and society regarded this model as a powerful manifestation of hope rather than one of despair.[16] There is evidence of the creation of death or martyrdom cultures in other places as well. For example, in the case of the PKK, women who volunteered for, or were even forced into suicide missions, received the support of parts of the Kurdish community in southeast Turkey for these activities and enjoyed an elevation in their social status.[17] Even Tamil communities in Sri Lanka felt empowered by the LTTE's decisive struggle and in some cases supported the martyrdom acts of their children for the greater cause of national liberation.[18] Another interesting example of the emergence of a 'culture of death' can be found in Chechnya. Since the advent of suicide terrorism in this part of the world in the early years of the twenty-first century, mostly perpetrated by the unit of 'Black Widows', their social environment has shown growing support for these women and their acts. They have become the heroes of the rebels. Admirers have glorified their acts, written songs of praise and used the Internet to encourage wider support for the phenomenon.[19]

In cultural terms, suicide terrorism can thus be described as a result of a spiralling feedback process between an organization and its constituency. In order to sustain a suicide campaign, every terrorist organization needs the support of the community. Raising such support depends upon the organization's success in instilling ideas among members of the society about the importance of martyrdom and glorifying these notions by religious, nationalistic or other means. Under certain conditions, such as ongoing repression, desperation and hopelessness, certain societies will be willing to embrace these cultural elements and to close the circle by providing the organization with support for instigating suicide acts.

This chain of events can be broken under two conditions. If the organization's leadership decides that suicide terrorism is no longer effective, it will stop fostering this type of culture. Alternatively, if there is a change in external circumstances and the community becomes hopeful and sees prospects of a better future, the appeal of martyrdom will diminish.

This analysis helps break the myth of the connection between Islam and suicide terrorism. First, as mentioned earlier, a 'culture of death' can be created by non-religious organizations which justify martyrdom with nationalistic or ethnic rhetoric. Second, all cases of Islamic suicide terrorism have been initiated by organizations that have also cultivated the surrounding culture. Hence, culture or religion is not the source of the phenomenon as suicide terrorism did not just spring unaided from this type of society. As described in previous chapters, the first phase of a suicide campaign begins with a decision made by the organizational elite. In order to maintain campaign momentum, the organization needs support from its constituency; religious rhetoric or any other strong rhetoric can be useful for this purpose. These means are also highly important in the recruitment and training segments of prospective suicide bombers.

At this stage, I will proceed to analyse the organizational process which starts out with the identification of a potential suicide bomber, continues with his or her training and is completed when the individual is sent on his or her last mission. As was the case with collecting data on the perpetrators, obtaining comparative data on the organizational process was not a simple task; many organizations maintain high levels of secrecy and prevent any disclosure of information. The following analysis is based on data which have been collected over a long period of time from publications and studies on organizations as well as from the testimonies of members and ex-members.

Recruitment

In cases where organizations have succeeded in fostering strong communal support for suicide terrorism, the recruitment stage is far easier than when such support is absent. Nonetheless, finding the right person for the particular mission, recruiting him or her to the organization and coaxing this person into sacrificing his or her life for the organization is not an easy task.

The recruitment mechanism of potential suicide bombers varies among the different organizations. However, recruitment methods can generally be classified into three main types. The first is when a person approaches the organization and offers him- or herself for a suicide mission. The second is the grass-roots mobilization of a group of people who are committed to a certain cause and who are willing to die for it. These people sometimes approach the organization for specific guidelines regarding the suicide mission. The third method, which is the most common, is active recruitment. This is when the organization's 'enlistment officers' are sent to recruit new members. In the majority of cases, new members are first given the offer of becoming fighters, and only after the training process are some singled out for suicide acts.

Individuals seeking to become suicide bombers and who approach organizational operatives on their own accord are most common in societies which adhere to a 'culture of death'. Once the idea of martyrdom becomes deeply rooted in society and receives strong popular support, members of this society will alter their views on the act of sacrifice. Culture shapes the way we perceive reality. A culture which perceives martyrdom as a virtue has the potential to incite people in certain situations to do almost anything in order to attain this goal.

It would not be true, however, to claim that anyone can be persuaded to perform such a deed. Otherwise, we would see thousands of candidates waiting in line to become suicide bombers. A more accurate description would be that when the suicide method is endowed with a positive image, people who are highly committed to a cause or in certain crisis situations, as described in the previous chapter, may be more likely to volunteer for this sort of mission.

The second method of recruitment for suicide missions should be approached from a network perspective. This recruitment method is particularly relevant in the case of Al-Qaeda but lately became highly visible in other instances as well, most prominently the Palestinian. For many years, Al-Qaeda was markedly interested in recruiting Muslim and Arab youngsters residing in Arab and Western countries, with the aim of conscripting these youths to fight under the flag of Islam.[20] The liaison operative sent by the organization for the recruitment mission was usually a former member of the organization who had gone through military and primarily ideological training in one of the *mujahidin* camps. Many of these liaison officers, after a period of training, were sent back to their countries of origin and, if they were posted to Western countries, they received very specific instructions on how to assimilate, primarily by marrying local women. Many of them found positions in mosques which allowed them to get to know the local Muslim community, identify potential candidates for recruitment and initiate their training process.[21] Following a period of preliminary training and evaluation, novices were invited to become members of Al-Qaeda.[22]

As remarked earlier, the American invasion of Afghanistan has hurt the core of Al-Qaeda in a dramatic way. The organization in effect has lost its stronghold in Afghanistan, a fact highly visible in the reduction of the extent of its terrorist operations as well as in its reduced geographical dispersion. Following this invasion, the importance of its overseas social clusters has increased, and they have become the major source of terrorism under the umbrella of the global jihad. Since 2002, it has become evident that many of the cells operating under the name of Al-Qaeda were actually local cells with very loose ties to the organizational core.[23]

However, the most common recruitment method is still by means of 'enlistment officers'. One of the most explicit manifestations of this recruitment method is evident in the case of the LTTE. For many years, representatives of the organization were sent to Tamil communities, especially in Jaffna, for the purpose of recruiting children aged twelve to sixteen who dropped out of school, mainly due to family economic difficulties. These recruiters were instructed to go from one house to another in pursuit of potential candidates. However, not only school drop-outs were conscripted. In some Tamil areas, the LTTE gained control over many aspects of civilian life, including the education system. This privileged status allowed organization operatives access to schools. In the first stage, teachers were instructed to indoctrinate their students about the importance of the Tamil struggle and the leading role of the LTTE in this struggle. Then, during school hours, members of the organization would enter classrooms and talk to the children about the LTTE and its goals. One specific way to attract the young children was by showing them movies featuring earlier successful operations. Many of the children who became highly enthusiastic were immediately signed up; in other cases, children who were not eager to join the organization were forced to enlist.[24]

The recruitment process to the PKK was rather similar. Many PKK fighters who were recruited from the Kurdish diaspora in Europe were approached by organization 'enlistment officers' in Kurdish cultural centres where many youths spent their time. There is evidence that, at these centres, young men went through a process of indoctrination, the aim of which was to build up their Kurdish identity and introduce them to the PKK.[25] A similar process took place in Kurdish summer camps. Children were approached in their schools by representatives of the PKK and were invited to cultural camps all over Europe where they learned about the Kurdish struggle. Some of these children never returned home but rather were sent directly to the battle zone in southeast Turkey.[26]

The PKK's method of recruiting specifically for suicide missions was slightly different. Most suicide attacks mounted by the organization were carried out by women, and organization activists usually approached younger, under-educated potentials from large, poor families residing in Turkey.[27] Some of these women were reported to have lost their close family in combat with the Turkish forces. It is hard to find evidence indicating that financial incentives were offered to the women during the recruitment phase and religious rhetoric was also not visible. The most prominent incentives evidently were the urge for vengeance, commitment to the Kurdish cause and devotion to the leader of the PKK, Abdullah Ocalan.[28]

A similar recruitment technique was also employed by leaders of the Chechen rebels. Some Arab and Muslim fighters perceived the Chechen fight against the Russians as another chapter in the *mujahidin* struggle which began in Afghanistan and voluntarily joined the Chechen forces, but the rebels also relied on local manpower. Once again, unemployed young persons were the most vulnerable group for recruitment. One of the main incentives for joining the rebel forces was the salary offered by recruiters. Other reasons, as discussed in the previous chapter, were hatred of the Russian forces and the desire to avenge the death of a friend or relative killed by the Russians.[29] It appears that, as with the PKK, Islamic rhetoric, often regarded as having a crucial effect, was not as relevant as one might expect in the recruitment stage.[30]

Recruitment of male suicide bombers for the Chechen campaign of terrorism was equivalent to the mobilization for other units. Here, again, potential members joined the unit mostly as a result of personal incentives. Prospective female bombers were recruited in a slightly different manner. The 'Black Widows' unit identified women who were at a vulnerable phase in their lives. Like the Kurds, some of them had lost a husband or a loved one during the fighting. Others may have suffered from financial difficulties or some other personal crisis. These women were then approached by a woman called Black Fatima, whose real name was Lyuba.[31] Fatima was a legendary figure in the 'Black Widows' unit; according to one of the failed perpetrators, each time she recruited a woman for a mission, she used a different approach to suit the specific candidate. In some cases she offered revenge; in many other cases she offered money and, even more important, financial support for family members to be left behind by the suicide bomber.[32]

At first, the recruitment procedure to Palestinian groups was quite similar to the above-mentioned organizations. Hamas would find potential suicide bombers among members of its university chapters as well as in schools, mosques, social clubs formed by the organization and in Israeli jails. The 'enlistment officers' sent by the organization looked for youngsters who showed interest in religious studies and were drawn to the organization's doctrine.[33] Prior to the Al-Aqsa intifada, the organization was very cautious. It generally refrained from accepting unfamiliar volunteers for suicide missions and carefully examined the background of each potential candidate or group of candidates. One thing which was of particular importance to the organization was to ensure that the recruit's motivation for the mission was rooted in ideological reasons and not in the individual's desire to improve his or her family's financial status. It was also important to make sure that the potential recruit did not suffer from mental problems. The organization did not want to be portrayed as taking advantage of sick people or individuals who were not responsible for their actions.[34] The recruitment process for Palestinian Islamic Jihad was almost identical although, due to the smaller size of this organization, it was hard to find cases of mass mobilization for suicide missions. For the most part, 'enlistment officers' operated in the well-known Jihad strongholds in the cities of Jenin, Beit-Lehem, Nablus and Hebron.[35]

The Al-Aqsa intifada altered the whole recruitment process. As mentioned earlier, Palestinian organizations employed suicide terrorism as a leading strategy and hence began to need a growing number of bombers. Competition among organizations also intensified the use of such perpetrators, and the relatively long and selective process of recruitment became irrelevant.

Fatah, which joined the scene of suicide terrorism only in late 2001, like its predecessors, sent 'enlistment officers' to

universities, schools and mosques. They were looking mostly
for young people who had a history of confrontation with the
Israelis or who had lost family or friends in incidents with the
Israeli army.[36] However, unlike Hamas, Fatah was less hesitant about recruiting volunteers who were not previously
known to the organization.[37]

In fact, with the dramatic increase in the number of suicide
attacks in the year 2002, the recruitment methods of all the
organizations began to collapse.[38] The leaderships of these
organizations had suffered targeted attacks by the Israeli
army and this had loosened their control over recruitment
and training processes. As a result, many of the attacks that
were launched against Israeli targets after the beginning of
2002 were local initiatives rather than top-down organizational decisions. Hence, it came as no surprise that many
attacks were credited to more than one organization. Local
activists from different groups were cooperating in order to
launch the attacks, and, in many cases, the whole process of
recruitment and training took no more than a few hours.

Unlike other organizations which adhered to one recruitment method, Palestinian organizations adopted all three.
Changing patterns of recruitment and especially the transition from a careful culling of candidates by trained recruiters
to a mass mobilization of volunteers emphasizes the success
of the organization in planting the roots of a 'culture of death'
in a society which in return provided endless numbers of
prospective bombers in times of need.

Training

A comparative appraisal of the training processes among the
different organizations reveals an interesting picture. As noted
above, the majority of terrorist organizations do not recruit
candidates specifically for suicide missions, and consequently
preliminary training processes involve a combination of an
introduction to basic military techniques and ideological – in
many cases, religious – indoctrination. Preparation courses for

suicide attacks take place at a later stage and are delegated to only a select group of people. At this point, the most important instruction course is the mental one. The organizations' main concern now is to make sure that the potential bombers do not back down, a move that would not only jeopardize the specific mission but could also disclose organization members and tactics.

In tactical terms, the course of preparation is rather short. Suicide bombers often have some kind of background in guerrilla and terrorist tactics, yet this is not always necessary. Organizations handle the perpetrator as if he or she were a weapon, and this weapon is not responsible for the selection of a target, gathering intelligence or tactical preparations. Moreover, in most cases, the suicide potential is escorted by organization operatives until the target is nearly reached and he or she receives instructions up to the very last stage. This reinforces the importance of mental preparation. In order to complete the mission, the suicide bomber must reach the target calm, confident and focused.

Hezbollah, the organization which launched the first suicide bomber, was also the first to develop a two-stage training programme for such missions. At first, knowledge on how to prepare for and execute a suicide attack was acquired from representatives of the Iranian Revolutionary Guards, who were closely involved in the activities of Hezbollah in its early days. These connections were so close that not only were Hezbollah suicide bombers trained by Iranians in the early 1980s, but the actual training procedure also took place in camps in Iran.[39] Later, with the help of Iranian officers, Hezbollah established its own training camps in the Beqaa valley in Lebanon. The selection of this location was not random. The Beqaa valley population is mostly Shiite and the Syrian army has a strong influence there. Hence, these camps were relatively secure from Israeli attack.

One of the camps, Ein Kawkab, resembled the type of basic training camp that could be found in any army. New recruits lived in tents while their trainers resided in separate quarters. On the camp's premises, there was a mosque and an auditorium. The first phase of the training process included the introduction of guerrilla tactics, which consisted of, among other assignments, laying landmines, infiltration of enemy camps, how to use automatic weapons and rockets, and learning techniques of self-defence. Yet, religion and political courses were of no less importance in grooming the Hezbollah militant for action.

Only the trainees who exhibited the strongest commitment to the cause and a willingness to die for Islam were selected for the more advanced training stages. This phase, during which religious indoctrination was intensified, also included preparation for highly sophisticated guerrilla attacks as well as suicide missions.[40] Once Hezbollah abandoned the suicide strategy in the mid-1980s, traditional guerrilla tactics were given a much bigger role in the training process. This reached a point where, by the mid-1990s, Hezbollah no longer had a specific programme for suicide bombers.[41]

The LTTE, known to have connections with Hezbollah, imitated and improved Hezbollah suicide techniques and also adopted their training methods. Every new recruit to the LTTE, most of whom were children, had to go through a basic training period of four months. Basic training included an introduction to military tactics and of course indoctrination in the organization's ideology. Much emphasis was given to glorifying and idolizing the organization's leader, Prabhakaran.

A typical daily routine at LTTE camps began with an early wake-up call at 5 a.m. The children then underwent two hours of physical training in the jungle, followed by lessons in the martial arts. In the afternoon, they attended classes, where they were introduced to the history of the organization and the Tamil people. In order to toughen them up and take the edge off their doubts about killing, instructors showed them war movies and later sent them to attack designated targets, applying the knowledge acquired from the movies. Evenings were mostly devoted to classes in intelligence gathering and the handling of explosive devices.

Throughout the training period, children were isolated from their families and subject to the draconian rules of the camp. For example, there are testimonies about trainees who were caught drinking alcohol being punished by death. At the same time, in order to keep families happy while their children were going through the training period, the organization provided them with financial support.[42]

Only after the basic training period did the selection process for the suicide squad, the Black Tigers, begin. Prospective suicide bombers were selected according to their achievements in the initial training period.[43] Specific training for suicide missions lasted for a few more weeks during which trainees learned the suicide tactic in great detail. However, in the vein of Hezbollah, mental preparation was even more important. The instructors' objective was to get the recruit to commit fully to the mission and make sure he or she would not have second thoughts.[44]

One of the mechanisms used by the organization to ensure the commitment of the Black Tigers to their mission was by dubbing them the most important warriors of the organization. As a result of this classification, all other LTTE members looked up to them and this helped the organization accomplish two important goals. First, the potential suicide bomber felt uplifted, 'a chosen one', for this elite status was very appealing.[45] Second, he was at the same time hard-pressed; this admiration created very strong social pressure which made it virtually impossible for the potential suicide bomber to leave the unit. However, in cases where the social pressure was not effective enough and a person decided to back down at the last moment, the LTTE could apply formal sanctions in order to make the novice reconsider.

Not surprisingly, the training process of the PKK was not much different. One striking resemblance to the LTTE was the nature of the programme which the suicide bomber underwent during the training process. Again, the organization did everything possible to prevent the person from having second thoughts. Much like the LTTE, both social and formal sanctions were applied in cases where a prospective suicide bomber showed hesitation. In some cases, unsure candidates were even threatened with execution if they refused to fulfil their mission.[46] However, there are also other similarities in the training processes of these two organizations.

Most PKK training camps were located in Syria, Lebanon and the northern Kurdish part of Iraq. Training went on for a period of three months and included instruction in an assortment of guerrilla tactics, primarily, the operation of light weapons and explosives, collecting intelligence and, of course, mental education – again, similar to the LTTE's methods. However, rather than committing to a religious or ideological doctrine, allegiance to the charismatic leader of the organization, Abdullah Ocalan, and the Kurdish national cause stood at the centre of this indoctrination. Another parallel to the LTTE, and even Hezbollah, is the fact that the basic training of all these organizations resembled standard army training. Once they arrived at 'boot camp', trainees were required to turn over their identity cards and were prohibited from leaving camp or making contact with their families.[47]

A far less structured training process is evident in the case of the Chechen groups. During the first stages of the Chechen struggle against the Russians, the rebels relied mostly on traditional tactics and training processes. However, the growing number of Al-Qaeda-affiliated Arab militants who joined them in the 1990s made them change their tactics and affected the training process. Yet, while it is quite apparent that the method of suicide terrorism is a part of the Arab influence on Chechen rebels, the training process for suicide missions remained separate from standard guerrilla training.

According to Russian intelligence sources, many Chechen rebels made use of the infrastructure of *mujahidin* training camps in Pakistan and sometimes in Georgia. Chechen as well as Arab trainees, all of them men, arrived at camps and went through a three-month training programme, which included guerrilla and terrorist tactics, such as mountain combat techniques, convoy attacks and kidnapping. This was accompanied by Islamic religious indoctrination.[48] Following this initial training period, just a select few were chosen for suicide missions. These prospective suicide bombers were subject to further training in intelligence methods. The purpose of this specific training was to assist them in getting through Russian roadblocks and penetrating Russian territory without being discovered.[49]

However, many of the Chechen suicide bombers were women who went through a different training process. The period of grooming female potentials for suicide missions was in fact minimal and lasted around two weeks during which they became acquainted with basic terrorist tactics.[50] Descriptions of the training of female suicide bombers in Chechnya are rare and often biased. However, there are several testimonies of women who claimed that they had been drugged during the mental preparation process. Others maintain that they had been whipped up into an ecstatic frenzy. They describe how they were taken into large rooms where they were ordered to repeat a sentence over and over again and move their bodies in monotonous motions until they lost control.[51] It seems that the introduction of drugs in the training process of Chechen women has made an impression on other organizations. There are indications that since the American invasion of Iraq, the use of drugs as part of the preparation of suicide bombers has increased. Suicide bombers under the patronage of Abu Musab al-Zarqawi were reported to have taken antipsychotic pills during the training process and before setting out on their mission.[52]

Brief inculcation programmes for suicide operations have also been highly significant for Palestinian organizations in which neither women nor men underwent an official training period. There are two basic explanations for the absence of a more comprehensive training programme. First, the Palestinian territories are closely monitored by the Israeli army. Hence, it is almost impossible to operate a semi-military camp without giving away its location. Second, as mentioned earlier, in the late 1990s, and especially during the years of the Al-Aqsa intifada, the surrounding culture became highly supportive for suicide missions and helped provide potential perpetrators with strong incentives to go out on missions. Thus, the need for long psychological preparation – usually meant to reduce the objections of potential perpetrators – was eliminated and all that remained was to provide the person with instructions on activating the explosive device and infiltrating Israeli territories.

Nonetheless, during the pre-intifada period, some similarities to other terrorist organizations employing the suicide technique were evident. For example, many suicide bombers sent out by Hamas and Palestinian Islamic Jihad had been long-time members of these organizations and were active in other forms of terrorism in the past.[53] Moreover, the training process in Hamas included psychological elements and religious indoctrination. The prospective perpetrator went through long sessions with the recruiters, who talked about the religious importance of the act and also tried to remove the fear of dying. This would include taking the recruit to a cemetery and placing him or her inside a grave.[54]

After the outbreak of the intifada, even this short training process was discarded. Since the leaders of the organizations became targets for the Israeli army, much of the responsibility for suicide missions fell on the shoulders of the lower-ranking local activists. The selection process became irrelevant and almost anyone who volunteered for a suicide mission was immediately accepted and put through a short training course. Sometimes this lasted no longer than a few hours in which the candidate was praised for choosing this path and given basic technical instructions regarding the activation of the device.[55] In order to compensate for the lack of real preparation, the suicide bomber was accompanied by his or her operators from the start of recruitment until he or she entered Israeli territory. In some cases, perpetrators were allowed to spend the last night before their mission with their families. Since this act became so prestigious in Palestinian society, there was almost no concern that the family of the prospective suicide bomber would try to prevent him or her from going out on the mission even if he or she were to tell them about the plans.[56]

Al-Qaeda features the most interesting example in the training process of suicide terrorists. The fact that this is a multinational organization requires high levels of coordination. Prior to 11 September 2001, recruitment for the most part took place in Muslim and Western countries while training camps were based in Afghanistan. Hence, following the recruitment of a candidate or a group of candidates, it was necessary to send them off to these camps. Candidates approved by the Al-Qaeda leadership received flight tickets, money and the necessary documents for the journey. Most of the new recruits were trained and indoctrinated at these camps and then sent back to their countries of origin in order to help establish new cells. The more capable candidates went through intensive military training and remained in Afghanistan; only a select few were singled out for suicide missions.[57]

As indicated in chapter 5, the number of suicide attacks initiated by Al-Qaeda and its affiliates prior to 9/11 was relatively small. Hence, suicide terrorists were trained in similar fashion to other members of the organization. The most important part of their training was the psychological phase. The organization put most of the emphasis on bringing the recruits to a mental state in which they were fully committed to the organization and its goals and were willing to sacrifice everything, including their own lives, for its sake. The key procedure was a constant indoctrination of the organization's perception of Islam and the importance of maintaining the superiority of Islam against challenges posed by infidels. In some cases, psychological training led all the way up to the very attack itself. On a few occasions, such as the Hamburg group which participated in the 9/11 episode, suicide terrorists were instructed to live together and help each other prepare for the mission. In general, it seems that the actual tactical preparation for the mission was relatively brief.[58] A comparative review of the occurrences in which Al-Qaeda initiated suicide attacks indicates that the organization leadership felt that the success of the operation mostly depended on the mental resilience of the perpetrators rather than their tactical skills.[59]

In the post-9/11 era, this mindset changed. The fact that training camps in Afghanistan were destroyed in the wake of the American invasion forced Al-Qaeda to adapt. Hence, the core of the training process shifted from sites in Afghanistan to countries where candidates were recruited.[60] This increased the organization's reliance on modern technology and, most prominently, the Internet. This tool has served many organizational objectives, including the dissemination of ideological propaganda, mobilization of support, transference of strategic and tactical manuals to active cells and providing intelligence information and operational commands prior to an attack.[61]

Dispatching

The most critical time in the process of executing a suicide mission is the minutes and sometimes hours from the moment the suicide bomber leaves his or her operators until the perpetration of the attack. This could be a very risky point in time for the dispatchers, as well as for the success of the operation, since the prospective perpetrator is already on his or her way to the target destination and the chances that he or she might be caught are much higher.

There is also another risk for the organization at this stage. As the time of the attack draws closer, the greater are the chances that the prospective terrorist might start having second thoughts or even become paralysed with fear. His or her colleagues are no longer on hand to raise the spirits or take away doubts. It is therefore crucial to get the suicide candidate to commit deeply beforehand to the mission and to bolster their confidence before finally setting out.

Hezbollah found an effective mechanism to solve this problem which was later adopted by almost every organization that deployed suicide bombers. Since the mid-1980s, the organization has prepared and released a short video of the suicide candidate prior to departure on his or her mission. This tactic has two objectives. The more important and psychological purpose of this ritual is to get the individual to commit totally to the operation. After shooting a video in which the prospective bomber justifies his or her act, prays and says last goodbyes to his or her loved ones, there is almost no way back. In some organizations, such as Hamas and Palestinian Islamic Jihad, from the minute the tape is shot until the actual bombing, the perpetrator is referred to by his or her comrades as *al-shahid al-hai* (the living martyr). The psychological pressure at this point is so great that even if the person still has doubts – a situation which occurs from time to time – it is impossible for him or her to back out without suffering considerable injury to their social status. This means being condemned by his or her close circle of comrades inside as well as outside the organization, which may even include his or her own family members.[62]

These tapes have another, secondary, purpose. They enhance the celebrity status of suicide bombers and further reinforce the 'culture of death'. In most cases, these tapes are brief, yet very powerful. Suicide aspirants wear military uniforms and headbands and may proudly brandish their weapons. Often, there are flags of the organization and religious symbols in the background. The Islamic religious organizations also make sure that the 'living *shahid*' is holding the Koran. The fact that most suicide bombers appear calm and resolute and ask their parents not to cry for them helps their families cope with the act and increases the community's admiration.

Despite the fact that the ritual of videotaping has become an integral part of the training process of suicide bombers in most organizations, there are different versions of these 'last rites'. Chechen women, for example, are videotaped wearing the black clothes of a widow and, unlike their Palestinian and Lebanese counterparts, their tapes are characterized by less emphasis on Islamic rhetoric.[63] The LTTE has also adopted a slightly different version of the videotape ritual. In the night prior to his or her departure for the suicide mission, the prospective perpetrator is invited to sup at the table of Prabhakaran, the charismatic leader of the organization.

During the course of dinner, the prospective bomber receives the highest honours and his or her picture is taken standing next to the leader. Soon afterwards, and before the dinner ends, the picture is developed and hung on the wall next to the pictures of all former suicide bombers of the organization. This has a very similar effect to the videotape procedure; the prospective bomber sees his or her picture on the wall next to a long succession of the association's past heroes. As in the videotaped ritual of other organizations, at this point the person becomes a living martyr and after this 'last dinner', the chances of turning back decline dramatically.[64]

Following the completion of the videotape, suicide bombers in religious organizations such as Al-Qaeda, Hamas and Palestinian Islamic Jihad undergo a ritual of religious purification which prepares them for entering the gates of heaven.

Recent testimonies collected mainly from Israelis who survived a suicide attack and witnessed the last moments of the suicide bomber before the explosion, underscore the power of this psychological training process. Most bombers were reported to be calm, quiet, even smiling.[65] It is very uncommon to find an occasion where the suicide bomber was detected due to his or her nervous behaviour and apprehended before detonating the explosive device.

Summary

In this chapter I described the preparation process of suicide bombers for their mission based on evidence from various testimonies and narratives from different organizations. I argued that a specific culture or religion cannot be held as solely responsible for suicide terrorism. As demonstrated, it seems that the evolution of a 'culture of death' depends on the combination of a long period of experiencing hopelessness in a certain community together with the presence of an organization which offers a way out of this predicament through the ultimate sacrifice.

A supportive culture is very important for an organization which chooses the suicide strategy. It offers a considerable reserve of potential perpetrators and makes the recruitment phase much easier. Furthermore, as mentioned in previous chapters, terrorist organizations are like political parties, both of which are highly interested in endorsement by their constituencies. If a 'culture of death' is deeply rooted in society, the organization will gain approval and be acclaimed rather than condemned for employing the suicide strategy.

An understanding of the training and dispatching processes of suicide terrorists also helps detract from the argument that this phenomenon is linked to a certain culture or religion. All organizations put a strong emphasis on psychological preparation. Indoctrination can be religious, nationalistic or any other type as long as it hits a sensitive point in the prospective perpetrator. The fact that most organizations train their people in closed-off and remote camps increases this effect even more. Isolation, a strong, dominant organizational culture and peer pressure are highly important in the process of getting the prospective suicide bomber to commit fully to the mission. In other cases, most prominently the Palestinian ones, the training process takes place inside the community, which is highly supportive of the act and provides cultural support to the training process.

8
The Consequences of Suicide Terrorism

In the last seven chapters, I have portrayed the phenomenon of suicide terrorism and offered explanations for its emergence and expansion. In this concluding chapter, I will look into the various effects of suicide terrorism on the victimized societies and offer a response model, which is aimed both at its symptoms and root causes.

The Effects of Suicide Terrorism

The idea that the main goals of any terrorist organization in causing harm to a civilian population is actually to draw attention to the group's demands, create an atmosphere of fear in the victimized society and, as a result, bring about policy changes, has been known in the literature for many years.[1] The devastating nature of suicide terrorism has multiplied the effect of terrorism on individuals, societies and political systems, and thus created a grave, new and immediate challenge for many societies.[2]

Due to the magnitude of the 9/11 attacks, the ramifications of these particular events have gained a lot of scholarly attention.[3] However, similar effects are present also among other societies that are victims of suicide attacks. The first three sentiments reported by individuals in many of these societies are anxiety, confusion and especially the fear of recurrence of such an attack, which could harm them and their loved ones.[4] In many cases, these feelings are transformed into a form of attenuated behaviour.[5] In the period following the 9/11 attacks, the citizens of New York and other metropolitan areas were extremely unwilling to leave their homes to visit places of entertainment, shopping malls, public or civic centres, or even to go to their workplaces. Clearly, this behaviour had a direct effect on the slowdown of the economy.[6]

A similar pattern has taken place in Israel. Following the first few waves of suicide attacks on shopping centres and buses, the number of individuals prepared to go out to restaurants and shopping malls decreased and many small businesses had to close down.[7] I remember driving the streets of Tel Aviv on the day after the Purim suicide attack on 4 March 1996. Typically, on the Purim holiday, the streets of all major Israeli cities, and especially Tel Aviv, are crowded with children in costumes who gather to watch or join the city's carnival parade. This time, the streets were deserted, the buses were almost empty and even the Gan Ha'ir shopping mall in the heart of Tel Aviv was almost completely abandoned.

Indeed, when suicide attacks happen on a recurrent basis and assume the pattern of a campaign, a process of 'habituation' takes place in many societies. People seem to get used to the situation; sometimes they repress it and try to maintain a facade that everything is normal.[8] However, this can be misleading. Terrorism has profound psychological effects which are not always immediately visible. The most prominent among them is post-traumatic stress disorder (PTSD), which manifests itself in various forms, most notably in repeated, disturbing memories, thoughts or images of the terror attacks and the aftermath of these events. One of the indications of PTSD often is avoiding activities or situations that remind the individual of traumatic events and feelings, while thoughts about the attacks may interfere with routine functioning at home or elsewhere.[9]

PTSD symptoms were found to be prevalent among many United States citizens after 9/11 and also among Israelis following waves of Palestinian suicide attacks,[10] as well as among Russians who were exposed to ongoing suicide campaigns of Chechen factions[11] and Sri Lankan citizens. The results of a Sri Lankan study which explored the effects of terrorism on refugees who fled conflict-ridden areas are of particular interest. This study revealed that the effects of terrorism were not limited merely to the psychological realm. Individuals who took part in this survey reported severe medical conditions, many of which were found to be closely connected to the constant exposure to terrorism and ongoing emotional stress.[12]

One of the major problems associated with high levels of fear due to exposure to suicide terrorism is that this fear has a substantial influence on sentiments and behaviours in the social realm as well. An immediate response of almost any society that becomes a victim of a mass-casualty attack is the 'rally around the flag' syndrome.[13] American society in the wake of the 9/11 events is a good example of this pattern. In the days following the attacks, people expressed strong patriotic sentiments. American flags were hanging from almost every window, firemen and police officers were treated like heroes, and even the media coincided with positions held by the administration.[14] Furthermore, over 60 per cent of Americans attended memorial services in order to express their identification with community and country. More than 30 per cent donated money or blood for victims of the attacks.[15]

However, this is only one side of the coin. Alongside patriotic sentiments and community-oriented activities, which seem to be harmless and even constructive, other sentiments take root in societies exposed to suicide attacks as well as other forms of mass casualty terrorism. These include mistrust of other people, disillusionment with the government's ability to protect them, sceptical attitudes towards prospects of reconciliation and peace and, above all, militant and hostile attitudes towards the terrorists and communities they claim to represent.[16]

Pursuant to the 9/11 attacks, American politicians expressed concern over a probable wave of Islamophobia and the appearance of exclusionary sentiments towards minority groups from the Middle East and Asia. Indeed, many Americans supported the restriction of civil liberties and displayed anti-Arab sentiments. They also exhibited hawkish positions with regard to the war on terror.[17] In two other countries, Russia and Israel, which suffer from suicide terrorism on a continuous basis, fear of terrorism was found to be correlated both with higher levels of animosity towards minority communities and with a desire for harsh governmental reprisal aimed at terrorists and their 'constituencies'. Moreover, exposure to terrorism predisposed all of these societies to be more willing to give up some democratic freedoms in order to enable their governments to protect them effectively from terrorism.[18] A survey conducted in Russia after Chechen terrorism attacks showed that 25 per cent were willing to establish an emergency regime in order to fight terrorism, while another 21 per cent approved giving the security forces more power in the war against terrorism and 10 per cent advocated tougher anti-terrorism legislation.[19] In a survey conducted in Israel in April 2002, 72 per cent of the Israeli population declared that any military operation against terrorism was justified.[20]

In democracies and semi-democracies, such public sentiment incites elites who are eager to satisfy their constituencies – and who sometimes experience the same sentiments themselves – to take fierce action. The fact that the terrorized public is impatient to see a quick solution to the threat, and thus exhibits militant positions, can help or even convince the leadership to reach a decision to declare a state of war (as is the case with the United States, Russia and, Israel) or to launch wide-ranging military operations (as in Sri Lanka and Turkey). In most of these countries, elites also relied on the public's willingness to impose limitations on civil rights during the course of the war on terrorism. Such limitations were manifested in the American Patriot Act as well as in a long string of counter-terrorism laws adopted after the events of 9/11.[21] They were also manifested in

Israeli and Sri Lankan policies of closures and pre-emptive detentions. In Sri Lanka, for example, the 1979 law against acts of terrorism authorized the government to hold a person under arrest for eighteen months without trial.[22] In Israel, the law for the detention of illegal combatants granted the Israeli government the mandate to hold a suspect for up to six months and possibly more without trial.[23] However, above all, there are President Putin's reforms in Russia. The federal law for the protection of constitutional rights, civil liberties and the security of the Russian Federation, which was adopted on 30 June 2002, was one important step in the major political reform that took place in Russia. In essence, it limited many democratic freedoms in the country, reduced the level of autonomy given to the different components of the federation, and accorded the ruling elite in Moscow much more power.[24]

In other cases, the urgency in trying to solve the problem may lead democratic governments in completely opposite directions. The Spanish change of government which took place shortly after the terrorist attacks in Madrid on 11 March 2004, and the decision of the new government to pull out Spanish forces from Iraq reflected, to some degree, the Spanish public's desire not to be exposed to similar attacks in the future. These events were perceived as an important triumph among terrorists all over the world. The message from Spain, as they saw it, was that terrorism is a low-cost winning strategy.

Hence, mass-casualty terrorism can have problematic consequences for democratic administrations in two opposing ways. On one hand, it can sway such governments to wage war on terrorism. In most cases, this will not put an end to the phenomenon but, at the same time, it can easily undermine the moral democratic foundations of the ruling administration and may deepen political cleavages. On the other hand, it can encourage governments to acquiesce to terrorists' demands and consequently send an encouraging message to terrorists all over the world. The question of how to respond to mass-casualty terrorism, given the possibility that each of the above-mentioned modes of response may end up with an unfavourable outcome, is a major dilemma facing democracies under attack. Unfortunately, this is not the only dilemma that may arise in the efforts to formulate an effective response to this challenge.

The Response to Suicide Terrorism

Suicide attacks manifest themselves in various forms. Many (36.9 per cent)[25] of these attacks take place on the battlefield or are aimed at inflicting damage on military compounds. Here, the question of how to respond seems to be less complicated than in other cases. As demonstrated in the case of Hezbollah, when Israel restructured and reinforced its military compounds and shortened the routes of its military convoys, suicide attacks became less effective and subsequently less appealing to the organization. Therefore, when suicide attacks are used as part of guerrilla warfare on the battlefield, the challenge of responding to them remains confined to tactical and strategic considerations and they should not be treated differently from any other kind of guerrilla tactic.

However, in many (39.6 per cent) instances, organizations dispatch their perpetrators to highly populated urban areas.[26] As discussed earlier, the implications of this tactic go far beyond its immediate damage and eventually put a lot of pressure on political elites.

Contrary to other types of terrorism, even a short-term, effective response to suicide terrorism is hard to accomplish. Suicide terrorism requires very few means and little preparation. All the organization needs in order to carry out a successful attack is a perpetrator and an explosives belt. In democratic societies which keep their borders relatively open and do not place military checkpoints on their highways, such a perpetrator can quite easily cruise through the country and reach the heart of its urban centres. Therefore, measures must be taken to prevent suicide bombers from arriving at their designated target, and ways must be found to minimize the damage if, in spite of the many precautions the explosion does take place.

Furthermore, as mentioned earlier, responding to terrorism always takes a high toll on democratic societies. A lot has been written on the methods of response to terrorism, and most scholars are in agreement that using military rather than police enforcement in response to a terrorist threat in a democratic state is unacceptable.[27]

However, can police officers, whose actions generally are more in conformity with democratic values than those of the military, respond effectively to the challenge of suicide terrorism? This form of terrorism requires first-rate counter-intelligence capabilities that would enable agencies to monitor the organization and prevent the recruitment and launching of a potential suicide bomber. In circumstances where the per-petrators have already been dispatched on a suicide mission, substantial tactical capabilities are necessary in order to stop them from reaching their destination. Finally, if the attack was not thwarted, there is a need for a highly organized force to coordinate rescue efforts.

In most Western countries, expecting the police to assume responsibility for all these tasks seems almost unreasonable. Thus, many countries choose to put much of the burden of responding to suicide terrorism on the shoulders of military or semi-military forces, even while knowing the democratic price of such decisions. This type of policy is based on the policymakers' belief that the overall risks are justified in order to protect the civilian population from this deadly type of terrorism. Such belief can be a result of the high level of influence that the armed forces enjoy over policy-making processes in democratic regimes undergoing a crisis situa-tion. In many cases, army generals and heads of security services will advocate forceful military responses, either because they are trained to believe that these are the best solutions for countering terrorism effectively or because such a response will serve the interests of the organizations they lead.

Yet, over the years it has become evident that this belief is somewhat unfounded. Despite the military's capacity to reduce the number of suicide attacks in the very short run, such a response exacts a high price in the long run. Military operations inflict a great deal of suffering on the wider society rather than just on the terrorist organizations themselves. Hence the anger, and with it the incentive to perpetrate more attacks, will only increase, even among people who until that time had no intention of becoming terrorists. Thus, the cycle of terrorism and counter-terrorism will only escalate, and the military option becomes highly counter-productive in the long run.[28]

So what can be done to protect civilians from suicide bombers in the short run and deal with the causes of this phenomenon in the long run? In the following paragraphs, I will offer an integrative approach for responding to suicide terrorism. This approach shifts much of the weight from short-term offensive measures aimed at the symptoms of the problem to longer-term and defensive measures, which have the potential to offer a better answer to both the roots of the problem and its manifestations. Having said that, there is a need to be very cautious before dismissing more aggressive modes of response altogether; the use of these approaches

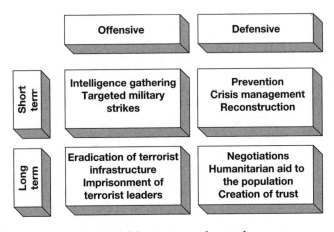

Figure 8.1 *Model for coping with suicide terrorism*

may become inevitable under certain circumstances. However, any resort to them should be made only under extreme circumstances and only for a short while.

As seen in the figure, the model is divided between short-term responses whose aim is to protect the population from suicide attacks in the midst of a campaign, and long-term responses, which are meant to address the root causes of the problem. Another distinction is between offensive and defensive measures. While the first is relevant to the response to terrorist organizations and the perpetrators themselves, the second is relevant to the victims of suicide terrorism as well as the constituencies that support these organizations.

Short-term offensive responses

Short-term offensive measures in this model are confined to small-scale operations aimed directly at the leaders and members of the organization who are responsible for planning attacks and launching perpetrators. The objective of this kind of policy is to prevent an attack which is already under way. Such counter-operations should not necessarily end in the death of the perpetrator or his or her dispatchers; if possible, they should be disarmed and arrested. It should be re-emphasized that such operations will not solve the problem of terrorism but only offer 'first aid' for its symptoms. It is also important to avoid using mass military force when resorting to this kind of response and to try to keep the operation as limited as possible. Large-scale strikes will miss the very purpose of this type of response, since they may inflict extensive damage on civilians who have nothing to do with terrorism; in this way, they just generate more hatred, hopelessness and urge for revenge.[29] Thus, whenever a government carries out an offensive strike aimed at preventing a suicide attack, all possible consequences should be brought into consideration and, in some cases, if the price of such a strike is too high, it should be avoided entirely, even at the cost of tolerating the suicide attack.

Short-term defensive responses

This leads me to the second and, in my view, more important short-term response: the defensive one. I would like to take up Robert Pape's analysis, which puts an emphasis on the importance of defensive mechanisms in coping with suicide terrorism, and to elaborate on this mode of response.[30] As mentioned earlier, even in cases when military strikes against terrorists are highly effective, the probability that a certain number of suicide attacks will be carried out regardless is relatively high due to the nature of this type of terrorism. Moreover, one suicide attack can cause vast damage. It will most likely kill and injure many people and terrify many more.

Based on the understanding that such attacks cannot be completely prevented, we should think of ways to minimize their consequences. Three important stages are involved in this process: prevention, crisis management and reconstruction.[31] The first stage is aimed at preventing the terrorist from detonating the device in an environment possibly abounding with targets. One possible way to do this is by building physical barriers between the terrorists and their potential targets. If such a barrier is impossible to build due to the geopolitical nature of a given territory, or if a perpetrator succeeds in crossing the barrier, there is need for a second line of defence.

Soft targets, which include infrastructure facilities, shopping centres, hospitals, schools and public transport, as well as many other sites which may be appealing in the eyes of the terrorists, should be heavily guarded by police or other agencies that are designated for such missions. True, being checked at the entrance to a government building, shopping mall and even restaurant is unpleasant. However, ever since the wave of terrorist hijackings in the 1970s, we have all become accustomed to airport security. If we calculate the effects of security checks in the prevention of suicide terrorism in comparison with the brief unpleasantness, I believe that the price is worthwhile. At any rate, governments should reassess the prospects for potential suicide terrorist attacks every few months. If the chances for such attacks drop dramatically, there is no need to continue to disturb the everyday lives of civilians or to allocate considerable funds for such security inspections.

The second stage is crisis management. This becomes highly important in cases where the suicide bomber has succeeded in overcoming all barriers and was able to detonate the explosive device. Examples from different parts of the world show that, time and again, rescue agencies have failed to respond effectively to such incidents. There are numerous problems that should be dealt with in the minutes after the occurrence of a suicide attack. The vicinity must be secured in order to make sure that a second suicide bomber is not waiting for rescue services to arrive to then detonate his or her bomb and possibly an external explosive device in order to inflict more damage. Victims should receive first aid and then be rushed to medical centres. This means that roads should be clear so that ambulances will be able to arrive on and leave the scene with maximum speed. It is also necessary to administer first aid to indirect victims of the attack. These include individuals who were exposed to the event and developed symptoms of anxiety.

The key words in such a situation are coordination and planning. There should be one agency responsible for the management of such a crisis situation and all other agencies involved must follow its directions.[32] In order to assure the effectiveness of the response, the agency in charge should develop guidelines for coping with suicide attacks. Moreover, all agencies involved must train together on a regular basis and thus improve their coordinated response to different scenarios of suicide attacks as well as other types of mass-casualty terrorism.

The last stage, reconstruction, is aimed at bringing life back to normal as soon as possible and thus to minimize the long-term effects of the attack. This stage involves continuous medical, psychological, social and even economic support for all direct victims of the attack and their family members as well as psychological treatment of indirect victims. This stage also includes the physical reconstruction of the stricken area and allocation of budgets for compensating business owners and other individuals who sustained financial damage in the attack.

Another important aspect is the reconstruction of inter-personal trust as well as trust in the government following an attack.[33] An effective response should include programmes for both children and adults whose aim is to reduce the psychological and social outcomes of the exposure to terrorism. Such programmes can be communicated through schools and the media.

To sum up, defensive measures have an added value beyond the enhanced coping capabilities of urban centres. An effective defensive response will limit the number of fatalities and casualties of suicide terrorism. It will also minimize secondary psychological, social and economic damage. If we believe that most terrorist organizations act in a rational fashion, we may assume that once suicide attacks lose a certain degree of their effect, this tactic will lose some of its appeal for terrorists. This does not mean, however, that terrorist organizations will necessarily revert to more traditional tactics. If defensive measures are not comprehensive enough nor accompanied by policies addressing the causes of the phenomenon, it is highly likely that organizations will look for soft spots which would allow them to initiate other types of mass-casualty attacks.

Long-term offensive responses

As mentioned earlier, short-term responses are aimed at the symptoms of suicide terrorism. However, they will not have an effect on its causes. One of the clearest conclusions of this study, as well as of other inquiries, is that suicide terrorism is a product of an organizational process.[34] Therefore one method of coping with the phenomenon would be to reduce the organization's interest in initiating such attacks. Many countries affected by suicide terrorism, including the United States, Russia, Israel, Sri Lanka and Turkey, have opted for the military response. Their decision was based on the supposition that they were capable of overpowering these organizations. Yet, many contemporary terrorist groups do not correspond with the old hierarchical structures but rather with a network-based one.[35]

This being the case, a clampdown on one of the organization's branches will have very little impact on the operational capabilities of other chapters of the same group (both internationally, e.g., Al-Qaeda, and domestically, e.g., Hamas). Thus, on the organizational level, it is necessary to make a concerted effort where the goal is to identify the main figures and cells of the organization, put them under constant surveillance and undermine their activities in almost any possible way, starting with ongoing arrests and ending with freezing assets and bank accounts. This will not diminish the organization's capabilities in carrying out suicide missions but it will shift the focus of the elite's energy from initiating attacks to saving its own skin.

The same logic applies for leaders of organizations and cells. The continuous killing of these leaders without trial cannot become an acceptable policy. Democratic countries cannot afford to lapse into this kind of response. Morally, it will undermine the very foundations of the governing system and, tactically, such actions have the potential of turning dead leaders into martyrs in the eyes of their constituencies and increasing the motivation for revenge. These leaders should be captured and brought to trial as the Turks did with Abdullah Ocalan. In this case, not only did Turkey maintain some level of democratic standards, it was also highly successful in dissolving the organization.[36]

Yet, targeting the organization and its leadership are not enough. As noted above, it is imperative to take one step further and tackle the deepest roots of the phenomenon. This essentially means addressing the key grievances of the constituencies which support the organizations.

Long-term defensive responses

Suicide terrorism does not appear out of thin air. In most cases, it surfaces after long periods of conflict and following the exhaustion of many other warfare tactics. Furthermore, in most cases, organizations considering the option of suicide terrorism will seek the support of their constituency when adopting this tactic. It follows that, in order to confront the roots of suicide terrorism, there is no alternative but to explore the needs of these constituencies and to undertake to meet some of their demands in order to reduce their support for such actions. In the majority of the cases (Lebanon, Palestine, Sri Lanka, Turkey, Chechnya), the basic demand of these populations was to be free in their homelands.[37] To be sure, in many instants, this demand was shrouded in clerical rhetoric but religious motivation should be considered only secondary to the main grievances. Hence, it could be assumed that once some of the aggrieved population's demands are met or, at least, a point is reached where the injured party believes its adversaries are upfront and ready to compromise, its incentive to support the organization dispatching suicide terrorists will diminish.

The case of Al-Qaeda and its affiliates is a little more complicated in this respect. Osama Bin Laden and his allies have placed the religious conflict rhetoric at the forefront of their agenda. However, I am not convinced that both Bin Laden and his adherents are interested in waging war on the Western world and, most prominently, the United States. They are far more realistic. Many Muslim and Arab communities in the world who support Bin Laden are not anti-American. Actually, in some respects, America is perceived in a mixed way by the Middle East and Asia. On one hand, these communities admire the power of the American economy and even find some cultural elements very appealing. On the other hand, they fear the power of the United States and are suspicious of the American leadership's real intentions. They do not really understand why the United States has a military presence in the Middle East, or why it has always favoured Israel and especially why it supports Arab regimes often considered corrupt and far from being democratic. Beefing up American military forces in the region following the invasion of Iraq has only increased the perception of threat among many people in the region who are now sure that the United States is trying to establish a permanent presence in the Middle East.[38]

Having said that, I am not implying that the United States or other countries should completely alter their foreign policies or accept the demands of terrorist organizations. On the contrary, there is a need to sidestep these organizations and eliminate their role as brokers. The countries under attack by suicide bombers should approach both moderate leaders and people on the other side in an honest way and leave out the militant rhetoric (which sometimes equally applies to its domestic politics).

The key factor in addressing these populations is trust. In order to undercut support for terrorist organizations, there is a need to reduce the levels of perceived threat among these communities and create basic levels of trust in the intentions of the other side. This is not a simple task, but if intentions to confront the root causes of suicide terrorism are sincere and elites are ready to pay a price for this resolution, it is not unworkable.

There are various methods of implementation. In terms of leadership, it is necessary to engage in serious negotiations with moderate leaders who have the respect and legitimacy of their people. If negotiations are honest and fruitful, the constituency will most probably shift its support from the radical to the more moderate organizations. However, if talks fail and no trust is created between the two parties, prospects for further radicalization will only increase.

In terms of the community, it is necessary to let members know that their opponents do not perceive them as the evil enemy and, by the same token, they respect their needs and aspirations. Military strikes are not helpful in this respect, nor is propaganda and psychological warfare. The community needs to know that the other side is trustworthy. The ways to start the process is by making life easier for the population and imposing as few restrictions as possible. In cases where there is a need for humanitarian aid, it should be provided, but not in a paternalistic way. Rather, food and medication can be transferred to the population through the moderate leadership or international humanitarian organizations.

Above all, it is highly important to leave the population out of the cycle of violence. Even if a military strike is inevitable, civilian populations should not be involved. In cases where such an operation would harm innocent civilians, it should be reconsidered even at the price of letting terrorists off the hook. Inflicting pain on a civilian population will eliminate trust and simply drive more people into the unremitting cycle of violence and revenge.

8
Afterword

The London Bombings: Challenges for the Future

During the summer of 2005 suicide bombings became an integral part of almost every news broadcast. Alongside the continuous wave of attacks in Iraq, which was unprecedented in its magnitude compared to such waves in the past, suicide bombers were launched again at targets in countries such as Turkey, Israel and Egypt.

The most lethal attack took place in the tranquil resort of Sharm El-Sheikh, Egypt, on Saturday 23 July 2005. Two cars driven by suicide bombers exploded shortly after 1.15 a.m. in front of the Ghazala Gardens Hotel and at the Movenpick Hotel in the Naama Bay area. A third vehicle, a minibus, exploded in a parking lot next to the city's Old Market. Eighty-eight people, most of them Egyptian citizens, but also several tourists from Europe, were killed instantly.

Most of the television stations that received the first news about the events in Egypt were busy at the time covering the failed attacks in London, which had taken place two days earlier on Thursday 21 July, exactly two weeks after the horror of the actual bomb attacks in London. For a few days it seemed that suicide terrorism was the single most important issue with which the world had to deal. This pattern of terrorism is now reaching every corner of the world and threatens the everyday life of European, American, Asian and Middle Eastern citizens alike.

The attacks in London on 7 July were particularly noteworthy for three major reasons. First, it was the single most brutal terrorist attack against the British capital in contemporary history. Fifty-six people were killed in the attacks and more than 700 were injured. Second, the attacks were carefully planned. Three of them took place in the tunnels of the London underground system during the morning rush hour, a fact which maximized the damage; the fourth attack was carried out on a bus in Tavistock Square. Third, all the perpetrators – Hasib Hussain, Jamal (Germaine) Lindsay, Mohammad Sidique Khan and Shehzad Tanweer – were British citizens.

None of the perpetrators, who arrived in London from West Yorkshire in the early hours of the morning of 7 July, had a police record, and none was known to the intelligence forces prior to the attacks. They were all picked up for the first time on a security camera at Kings Cross Station, minutes before the attacks. Later that day an organization called Al-Qaeda in Europe claimed credit for the events.

What can we learn from these events? The unfortunate conclusion is that coping with suicide bombing is becoming a bigger challenge as days go by. The attacks are becoming more sophisticated and rapidly spread to different corners of the world with the explicit aim of hurting Western citizens. The response should be on both defensive and offensive levels.

The best defensive mechanism for this type of challenge is the enhancement of security in transportation systems, shopping malls, schools, hospitals, churches and synagogues, as well as in sensitive strategic locations such as ports, nuclear power stations and factories which produce and use dangerous chemicals and biological materials. This may be uncomfortable for residents of countries in the West who are used to complete freedom, and such measures will, of course, be criticized by some. However, as mentioned in my concluding chapter, it is a relatively small price to pay for saving hundreds of lives.

The bigger challenge relates to the offensive level. There seems to be a gradual change in the nature of the groups that launch suicide bombers. Until the late 1990s, and even the first years of the current decade, these were well structured and hierarchical organizations, such as Hezbollah, the LTTE, the PKK, Hamas and even Al-Qaeda, prior to the American invasion of Afghanistan. Today, these organizations are being replaced by far more elusive terrorist networks. The fact that these networks claim to represent Al-Qaeda serves as no indication that they truly operate under the guidance of the core leadership of this group.[1]

The overall assessment is that the networks that operate under the name of Al-Qaeda in different parts of the world represent more local and idiosyncratic interests. The questions are: what is it that motivates networks such as the one that was responsible for the attacks in Madrid in March 2004 or those in London in July 2005? How do they form? How are they structured and operated?

I believe that neither scholars nor intelligence officers have any real answers to these questions at this point, and addressing these issues should be given the highest priority in our new research agenda. I also believe that the models developed for the understanding of suicide terrorism, including the one presented in this book, can be useful for the next stage of research. In the following paragraphs I will offer some initial thoughts with regard to the analysis of this phenomenon.

Concerning the perpetrators, I accept Marc Sageman's approach, according to which young Muslim immigrants or sons of immigrants – especially in European countries – feel either alienated from the surrounding culture or unable to fit into the local labour market. They find comfort in each other's company and in religious activities.[2] These youngsters go through a process of radicalization, which is inflamed by preachers who direct their animosity towards the society which they believe has rejected them. The fact that they spend most of their time together reinforces the peer social-ization process and contributes to its radicalization.

The bigger enigma concerns the elite level. Who is it that mobilizes these radicalized young people, gives them instruc-tions and explosives and dispatches them to the designated target? And why do they do it? As mentioned earlier, we no longer look at organizational frameworks with clear strata of leadership. The new networks have no uniform, cadres, history or even a name. In most cases, they form for a specific attack, then dismantle, then form again in a different structure – and so on. The major actors in these groups – the elites – are the individuals who initiate the attacks. In social network lan-guage, these individuals are referred to as the 'hubs'. They are located at the centre of the net and all the links lead to them.

In order to figure out the motivations of these hubs, the same rationale that is used to analyse decisions of elites in structured organizations should be applied. We should avoid falling into 'cultural' traps such as seeing religion as a moti-vating factor. The challenge is to identify the network and its main hubs, to understand their goals and to cope effectively with the social conditions that breed the next wave of per-petrators. This is a new and more elusive challenge than ones we have encountered in the past, which requires a lot of effort and resources. Only by facing up to it will we be able to understand and cope with this newest infrastructure of suicide bombings.

Notes

CHAPTER 1   WHAT IS SUICIDE TERRORISM?

1   Ariel Merari 'The Readiness to Kill and Die: Suicidal Terrorism in the Middle East' in Walter Reich (ed.) *Origins of Terrorism: Psychologies, Ideologies, Theologies, State of Mind*, New York: Woodrow Wilson International Center for Scholars and Cambridge University Press, 1990, pp. 193–4.

2   For Durkheim's typology of the different types of suicide, see Emile Durkheim, *Suicide*, London: Routledge & Kegan Paul, 1952.

3   Under the broad category of altruistic suicide, Durkheim distinguished three sub-categories: obligatory, optional and acute altruistic suicide. While Ariel Merari maintains that the type most applicable to the suicide terror phenomenon is in fact optional altruistic suicide, my view is that the acute altruistic suicide sub-category is the most relevant to the description of the phenomenon. For a discussion of this matter, see Ariel Merari 'Social, Organisational and Psychological Factors in Suicide Terrorism' in Tore Bjorgo (ed.) *The Root Causes of Terrorism*, Proceedings of an Expert Meeting on the Root Causes of Terrorism (9–11 June 2003), Oslo: The Norwegian Institute of International Affairs, 2003; also, Durkheim *Suicide*, pp. 217–40; Young Lung-Chang 'Altruistic Suicide: A Subjective Approach', *Sociological Bulletin* (1972), 21(2): 103–21.

4 Kathryn Johnson 'Durkheim Revisited: Why Do Women Kill Themselves?', *Suicide and Life-Threatening Behaviour* (1979), 9: 145–53; Steven Stack 'Durkheim's Theory of Fatalistic Suicide: A Cross-National Approach', *The Journal of Social Psychology* (1979), 107: 161–8; Steven Taylor *Durkheim and the Study of Suicide*, London: Hutchinson, 1982.

5 See: Rex Brynen 'The Dynamic of Palestinian Elite Formation', *Journal of Palestinian Studies* (1995), 24(3): 31–43; Hussein Sirriyeh 'Democratisation and the Palestinian National Authority: From State in the Making to Statehood', *Israel Affairs* (2000), 7(1): 49–62.

6 Lung-Chang 'Altruistic Suicide' 106.

7 Ami Pedahzur, Arie Perliger and Leonard Weinberg 'Altruism and Fatalism: The Characteristics of Palestinian Suicide Terrorists', *Deviant Behaviour* (2003), 24(4): 405–23.

8 For a discussion of the two approaches on the definition of suicide terrorists, see: Robert A. Pape 'The Strategic Logic of Suicide Terrorism', *American Political Science Review* (2003), 97(3): 345 n. 1.

9 For a discussion of the features of martyr terror, see Merari 'The Readiness to Kill and Die' 194.

10 For a more in-depth analysis of martyr terror, see Shaul Shay *The Shahids: Islam and Suicide Attacks*, Herzliya: Interdisciplinary Centre Press, 2003, pp. 26–7 [Hebrew].

11 Mia M. Bloom *Dying to Kill: The Global Phenomenon of Suicide Terror*, 2004, ch. 4 (website), New York: Columbia University Press, 2005.

12 Ehud Sprinzak 'Rational Fanatics', *Foreign Policy* (2000) 120: 69.

13 Karin Andriolo 'Murder by Suicide: Episodes from Muslim History', *American Anthropologist* (2002), 104 (3): 738–9.

14 Ibid. 739.

15 Shay *The Shahids*, pp. 51–5.

16 Pape 'The Strategic Logic of Suicide Terrorism' 345; Boaz Ganor 'Suicide Terrorism: An Overview', *Countering Suicide Terrorism*, Herzliya: International Policy Institute for Counter-Terrorism [hereafter ICT], 2001, pp. 134–45.

17 Mia M. Bloom 'Palestinian Suicide Bombing: Public Support, Market Share and Outbidding', *Political Science Quarterly* (2004), 119(1): 61–88.

18 Bloom *Dying to Kill*, ch. 4.

19   Scott Atran 'Genesis of Suicide Terrorism', *Science* (2003),
     299(5619): 1534.
20   Shay *The Shahids*, pp. 24–5.
21   Pape 'The Strategic Logic of Suicide Terrorism' 346–7.
22   For further elaboration on the advantages which terrorist
     organizations gain from using suicide terrorists, refer to Bruce
     Hoffman and Gordon H. McCormick 'Terrorism, Signaling,
     and Suicide Attack', *Studies in Conflict and Terrorism* (2004),
     27(4): 243–81.
23   This study relied on a database consisting of a list of terror inci-
     dents perpetrated by suicide terrorists worldwide. It covers a
     period of time beginning on 19 March 1977, the day of the
     assassination of Congo President Marien Ngouabi, and con-
     cludes on 22 February 2004 with the explosion of a suicide ter-
     rorist on a Jerusalem bus in Israel. In all, the catalogue includes
     418 suicide assaults which took place in twenty-nine different
     countries and were carried out by twenty-five different organ-
     izations. The database was compiled in several stages and is the
     property of the National Security Studies Centre in the
     University of Haifa. First, data was collected from various aca-
     demic sources (articles and books) in order to identify the
     countries, organizations and periods which have proved to be a
     part of the realm of suicide terror. In the second stage, each
     region and group of organizations was assigned to a researcher
     whose function was to search for information on suicide attacks
     that was relevant to their assigned domain. The sources of infor-
     mation on which the database was established are numerous
     and diverse: articles and academic texts (*Encyclopaedia of World
     Terrorism*, 1997; *Almanac of Modern Terrorism*, 1991; Pape 'The
     Strategic Logic of Suicide Terrorism'), databanks found on the
     Internet (Cdiss Terrorism Programme, ICT Database), Internet
     sites dealing in various terror organizations or terror in the
     world, as well as a broad use of Israeli and international media
     sources. In the final stage, the amassed information was encoded
     in an SPSS file according to the specific variables chosen. At the
     same time, a qualitative database was constructed which
     included descriptions of the incidents and their features, as well
     as indication of the organizations which perpetrated them.
     Variables included in the quantitative database on which the
     analysis was based are: (1) date of incident; (2) place of incident
     (country); (3) features of the incident; (4) the organization

responsible; (5) ideology of the perpetrating organization; (6) suicide tactic; (7) the assaulted target [e.g., restaurant, military force); (8) a profile of the target of attack [e.g., citizens, soldiers); (9) number of fatalities and wounded; (10) number of terrorists participating in attack; (11) gender of terrorists participating in attack; (12) religious affiliation of terrorists.

24 Pape 'The Strategic Logic of Suicide Terrorism' 347.

25 Ibid.

26 Except for the Palestinian incidents related to the Al-Aqsa intifada as well as incidents in Chechnya and Iraq.

27 Pape 'The Strategic Logic of Suicide Terrorism' 346–50.

28 Shimon Shapira *Hezbollah: Between Iran and Lebanon*, Tel Aviv: Hakibbutz Hameuchad, 2000, pp. 164–9 [Hebrew].

29 Rohan Gunaratna *Inside Al-Qaeda: Global Network of Terror*, New York: Columbia University Press, 2002, p. 74.

30 Shaul Mishal and Avraham Sela *The Hamas Wind: Violence and Coexistence*, Tel Aviv: Miskal Yedioth Ahronoth Books and Chemed Books, 1999, p. 126 [Hebrew].

31 Pape 'The Strategic Logic of Suicide Terrorism' 345.

32 Atran 'Genesis of Suicide Terrorism' 1535.

33 Bloom *Dying to Kill*, ch. 4; Martha Crenshaw 'The Logic of Terrorism: Terrorist Behaviour as a Product of Strategic Choice' in Walter Reich (ed.) *Origins of Terrorism: Psychologies, Ideologies, Theologies, State of Mind*, New York: Woodrow Wilson International Center for Scholars and Cambridge University Press, 1990, pp. 7–24.

34 Bloom *Dying to Kill*, ch. 4.

CHAPTER 2   HOW CAN SUICIDE TERRORISM BE EXPLAINED?

1 See, for example, Harvey W. Kushner 'Suicide Bombers: Business as Usual', *Studies in Conflict and Terrorism* (1996), 19(4): 349–67.

2 See, for example, Emad Salib 'Suicide Terrorism: A Case of Folie à Plusieurs?', *British Journal of Psychiatry* (2003), 182(6): 475–6; John Rosenberger 'Discerning the Behaviour of the Suicide Bomber: The Role of Vengeance', *Journal of Religion and Health* (2003), 42(1): 13–20; Harvey Gordon 'The "Suicide" Bomber: Is it a Psychiatric Phenomenon?', *Psychiatric Bulletin* (2002), 26(8): 285–7.

3 Kim Taewoo 'Islamic Terrorism and the Clash of Civilisations', *Korean Journal of Defence Analysis* (2002), 14(1): 97–117. Raphael Israeli focuses specifically on Islamic culture and calls the phenomenon 'Islamikaze'; Raphael Israeli 'Islamikaze and their Significance', *Terrorism and Political Violence* (1997), 9(3): 96–121. For more information, see Scott Atran 'Mishandling Suicide Terrorism', *Washington Quarterly* (2004), 27(3): 75.

4 Atran 'Mishandling Suicide Terrorism' 67–90.

5 Mia M. Bloom 'Palestinian Suicide Bombing: Public Support, Market Share and Outbidding', *Political Science Quarterly* (2004), 119(1): 61–88.

6 Radio interview with Iyad Saraj and Ariel Merari 'Today's Suicide Bombers are the Children of the Previous Intifada', *Studio* (2002), 134: 27 [Hebrew]; Bruce Hoffman 'The Logic of Suicide Terrorism', *The Atlantic Monthly* (2003), 291(5): 40–7.

7 Scott Atran 'Genesis of Suicide Terrorism', *Science* (2003), 299(5619): 1534.

8 Martha Crenshaw 'The Logic of Terrorism: Terrorist Behaviour as a Product of Strategic Choice' in Walter Reich (ed.) *Origins of Terrorism: Psychologies, Ideologies, Theologies, State of Mind*, New York: Woodrow Wilson International Center for Scholars and Cambridge University Press, 1990, p. 8. For a discussion of the different modes of decision-making process among elites of terrorist organizations, refer to Gordon H. McCormick 'Terrorist Decision Making', *Annual Review of Political Science* (2003), 6: 473–507.

9 Robert A. Pape 'The Strategic Logic of Suicide Terrorism', *American Political Science Review* (2003), 97(3): 343–61. Pape's assumption that suicide terrorism targets democratic countries has been the object of much criticism. Apart from certain countries where this type of terrorism has surfaced, such as Saudi Arabia and Tunisia, which don't even fill the minimum requirements of a democratic polity, there is considerable doubt also in regard to the types of rule in terror-stricken Sri Lanka, Turkey and Israel and whether they possess the features of a democratic polity. For a discussion of this issue, see Bloom 'Palestinian Suicide Bombing'; Mia M. Bloom *Dying to Kill: The Global Phenomenon of Suicide Terror*, 2004, ch. 4 (website), New York: Columbia University Press, 2005.

10 Pape 'The Strategic Logic of Suicide Terrorism' 346.
11 In Pape's study, he in fact presents an assumption according to which more than half of the organized campaigns of suicide terrorism in different places in the world between 1980 and 2001 wound up with various degrees of success for the organization that led the campaign; Pape 'The Strategic Logic of Suicide Terrorism' 351.
12 Bruce Hoffman and Gordon H. McCormick 'Terrorism, Signaling, and Suicide Attack', *Studies in Conflict and Terrorism* (2004), 27(4): 243–81; Ehud Sprinzak 'Rational Fanatics', *Foreign Policy* (2000), 120: 68.
13 Bloom 'Palestinian Suicide Bombing'; Bloom *Dying to Kill*, ch. 4.
14 Leonard Weinberg 'Turning to Terror: The Conditions Under which Political Parties Turn to Terrorist Activities', *Comparative Politics* (1991), 23(4): 423–38; Leonard Weinberg and Ami Pedahzur *Political Parties and Terrorist Groups*, London: Routledge, 2003.
15 Bloom *Dying to Kill*, ch. 4.
16 Pape 'The Strategic Logic of Suicide Terrorism' 346–7.
17 Samuel Huntington 'The Clash of Civilisations?', *Foreign Affairs* (1993), 72(3): 22–49. For discussion of Huntington's contentions in this context, refer to: John R. Oneal and Bruce M. Russett 'A Response to Huntington', *Journal of Peace Research* (2000), 37(5): 611–12; Dieter Senghaas 'A Clash of Civilizations – An Idée Fixe?', *Journal of Peace Research* (1998), 35(1): 127–32; Jonathan Fox 'Two Civilizations and Ethnic Conflict: Islam and the West', *Journal of Peace Research* (2001), 38(4): 459–72; Errol A. Henderson 'Culture or Contiguity: Ethnic Conflict, the Similarity of States, and the Onset of War, 1820–1989', *Journal of Conflict Resolution* (1997), 41(5): 649–68; Giacomo Chiozza 'Is There a Clash of Civilizations? Evidence from Patterns of International Conflict Involvement, 1946–97', *Journal of Peace Research* (2002), 39(6): 711–34; Bruce M. Russett, John R. Oneal and Michaelene Cox 'Clash of Civilizations, or Realism and Liberalism Déjà Vu? Some Evidence', *Journal of Peace Research* (2000), 37(5): 583–608; Jonathan Fox 'Religion and State Failure: An Examination of the Extent and Magnitude of Religious Conflict from 1950 to 1996', *International Political Science Review* (2004), 25(1): 55–76.

18   Pape 'The Strategic Logic of Suicide Terrorism' 349.
19   Mamoru Iga 'Suicide of Japanese Youth', *Suicide and Life-Threatening Behaviour* (1981), 11(1): 17–30; Mamoru Iga *The Thorn in the Chrysanthemum: Suicide and Economic Success in Modern Japan*, Berkeley: University of California Press, 1986; Charles R. Chandler and Yung-Mei Tsai 'Suicide in Japan and the West: Evidence for Durkheim's Theory', *International Journal of Comparative Sociology* (1993), 34(3–4): 244–59.
20   Dennis Warner and Peggy Warner with Sadao Seno *The Sacred Warriors: Japan's Suicide Legions*, New York: Van Nostrand Reinhold, 1982.
21   Stephan F. Dale 'Religious Suicide in Islamic Asia: Anti-Colonial Terrorism in India, Indonesia and the Philippines', *Journal of Conflict Resolution* (1988), 32(1): 52–3.
22   Ibid.
23   Ariel Merari 'Social, Organisational and Psychological Factors in Suicide Terrorism' in Tore Bjorgo (ed.) *The Root Causes of Terrorism*, Proceedings of an Expert Meeting on the Root Causes of Terrorism (9–11 June 2003), Oslo: The Norwegian Institute of International Affairs, 2003.
24   For further discussion of the relative deprivation theory and suicide terrorism, see Atran 'Mishandling Suicide Terrorism' 77–9.
25   Bloom *Dying to Kill*, ch. 4.
26   Ghassan Hage 'Comes a Time We Are All Enthusiasm: Understanding Palestinian Suicide Bombers in Times of Exighophobia', *Public Culture* (2003), 15(1): 79–80.
27   Atran 'Genesis of Suicide Terrorism' 1535.
28   They had in mind terrorists who operated on their own and without the backing of an organization and who, many times, were in fact found to be suffering from mental pathologies.
29   Ariel Merari 'The Readiness to Kill and Die: Suicidal Terrorism in the Middle East' in Walter Reich (ed.) *Origins of Terrorism: Psychologies, Ideologies, Theologies, State of Mind*, New York: Woodrow Wilson International Center for Scholars and Cambridge University Press, 1990, p. 203; Atran 'Genesis of Suicide Terrorism' 1537; Ariel Merari 'Suicide Terrorism' in R. Yufit and D. Lester (eds) *Assessment, Treatment and Prevention of Suicide*, New York: John Wiley, 2004.
30   Edwin S. Shneidman *Definition of Suicide*, New York: Wiley, 1985.

31 John Lackhar 'The Psychological Make-Up of the Suicide Bomber', *Journal of Psychohistory* (2002), 20: 349–67; Lloyd DeMause 'The Childhood Origins of Terrorism', *Journal of Psychohistory* (2002), 29(4): 340–8.

32 Lackhar 'The Psychological Make-Up of the Suicide Bomber'; DeMause 'The Childhood Origins of Terrorism'.

33 Merari 'Social, Organisational and Psychological Factors in Suicide Terrorism' in Bjorgo (ed.) *Root Causes of Terrorism*.

34 David Lester, Bijou Yang and Mark Lindsay 'Suicide Bombers: Are Psychological Profiles Possible?', *Studies in Conflict and Terrorism* (2004), 27(4): 283–95.

35 Assaf Moghadam 'Palestinian Suicide Terrorism in the Second Intifada: Motivations and Organisational Aspects', *Studies in Conflict and Terrorism* (2003), 26(2): 72.

36 Karin Andriolo 'Murder by Suicide: Episodes from Muslim History', *American Anthropologist* (2002), 104(3): 736–8; Dale 'Religious Suicide in Islamic Asia'.

37 Moghadam 'Palestinian Suicide Terrorism in the Second Intifada' 72.

38 Ibid.; Hage 'Comes a Time We Are All Enthusiasm' 76.

39 Moghadam 'Palestinian Suicide Terrorism in the Second Intifada' 72.

40 Atran 'Genesis of Suicide Terrorism' 1536.

41 Moghadam 'Palestinian Suicide Terrorism in the Second Intifada' 72–3; Bloom *Dying to Kill*, ch. 4.

42 Moghadam 'Palestinian Suicide Terrorism in the Second Intifada' 76.

43 Jessica Stern *Terror in the Name of God: Why Religious Militants Kill*, New York: HarperCollins, 2003, pp. 48–50; Anat Berko *The Moral Infrastructure of Chief Perpetrators of Suicidal Terrorism: Cognitive and Functionalist Perspectives*, Ph.D. thesis (2001), Ramat Gan, Israel: Bar-Ilan University, p. 5 [Hebrew].

44 Bloom *Dying to Kill*, ch. 4.

45 Moghadam 'Palestinian Suicide Terrorism in the Second Intifada' 68.

46 Edgar H. Shein 'The Chinese Indoctrination Program for Prisoners of War: A Study of Attempted "Brainwashing"', *Psychiatry* (1956), 19(2): 149–72; Robert J. Lifton *Thought Reform and Psychology of Totalism*, New York: W. W. Norton, 1961.

210   *Notes to pages to pages 40–45*

47 Merari 'The Readiness to Kill and Die' in Reich (ed.) *Origins of Terrorism*, pp. 199–200.
48 From an interview with Ariel Merari conducted by CBS network, 'Mind of the Suicide Bomber', CBS News, 26 May 2003. The interview can be found at: http://www.cbsnews.com/stories/2003/05/23/60minutes/main555344.shtml
49 Ibid.
50 Atran 'Genesis of Suicide Terrorism' 1537.
51 For further discussion of the role of commitment in terrorist groups, refer to Marc Sageman *Understanding Terror Networks*, Philadelphia: University of Pennsylvania Press, 2004.
52 Joseph A. Blake 'Death by Hand Grenade: Altruistic Suicide in Combat', *Suicide and Life-Threatening Behaviour* (1978), 8(1): 46–59; Jeffrey W. Riemer 'Durkheim's "Heroic Suicide" in Military Combat', *Armed Forces and Society* (1998) 25(1): 103–20; Merari 'The Readiness to Kill and Die' in Reich (ed.) *Origins of Terrorism*, pp. 201–2.
53 Merari 'The Readiness to Kill and Die' in Reich (ed.) *Origins of Terrorism*, pp. 201–2.
54 Ibid., pp. 198–9.
55 Merari 'Social, Organisational and Psychological Factors in Suicide Terrorism' in Bjorgo (ed.) *Root Causes of Terrorism*.

CHAPTER 3   TURNING TO SUICIDE TERRORISM: HEZBOLLAH
AND THE PALESTINIAN ORGANIZATIONS

1 Robert A. Pape 'The Strategic Logic of Suicide Terrorism', *American Political Science Review* (2003), 97(3): 343–61; Bruce Hoffman and Gordon H. McCormick 'Terrorism, Signaling, and Suicide Attack', *Studies in Conflict and Terrorism* (2004) 27(4): 243–81.
2 Mia M. Bloom 'Palestinian Suicide Bombing: Public Support, Market Share and Outbidding', *Political Science Quarterly* (2004), 119(1): 61–88.
3 Mia M. Bloom *Dying to Kill: The Global Phenomenon of Suicide Terror*, 2004, ch. 4 (website), New York: Columbia University Press, 2005.
4 Leonard Weinberg and Ami Pedahzur *Political Parties and Terrorist Groups*, London: Routledge, 2003, pp. 1–35.

5   Cristoph Reuter *My Life is a Weapon: A Modern History of Suicide Bombing*, Princeton, N.J.: Princeton University Press, 2004.

6   Ibid., p. 62.

7   Shimon Shapira *Hezbollah: Between Iran and Lebanon*, Tel Aviv: Hakibbutz Hameuchad, 2000, pp. 164–9 [Hebrew].

8   Reuter *My Life is a Weapon*, p. 57.

9   Shapira *Hezbollah*, p. 123.

10 Yoram Schweitzer, 'Suicide Terrorism: Developments and Characteristics', ICT, 21 April 2000. http://www.ict.org.il

11 About a year and a half after the strike on the American embassy in Beirut, it was again bombed at its new location. A booby-trapped truck carrying dynamite driven by a suicide bomber was detonated close to the embassy building, causing the deaths of eleven people and injury to fifty-eight; Shaul Shay *The Shahids: Islam and Suicide Attacks*, Herzliya: ICT, 2003, pp. 65–6 [Hebrew].

12 Shay *The Shahids*, pp. 64–6.

13 Pape 'The Strategic Logic of Suicide Terrorism' 348.

14 The organizations responsible for this increase were: the Syrian National Party, the PAS, the Lebanese Communist Party and the Socialist Nasserist Party; Shaul Shay 'Suicide Terrorism in Lebanon', *Countering Suicide Terrorism*, Herzliya: ICT, 2001, p. 131.

15 All the suicide attacks, fifteen in total, that took place in Lebanon between July 1985 and November 1986 targeted soldiers of the SLA.

16 Three suicide attacks occurred between the time of the retreat of the Israeli army to the security zone and the complete withdrawal from Lebanon. The first incident took place on 19 October 1988, when a truck bomb carrying 200 kg of dynamite driven by a suicide operative blew up next to an IDF convoy in the vicinity of the Fatma Gate on the Israel–Lebanon border. In this episode, eight Israeli troops were killed and seven more were injured. In the second attack, in which a Hezbollah suicide militant detonated an explosive device amidst an IDF convoy on 20 March 1996, an Israeli officer was killed. In the third incident, on 29 December 1999, one soldier was killed and twelve others were wounded when a suicide operative driving a car bomb crashed into a convoy of military vehicles.

17 Shay 'Suicide Terrorism in Lebanon' 133.
18 Gal Luft 'Israel's Security Zone in Lebanon – A "Tragedy"?',
    Middle East Quarterly (2000) 7(3). http://www.meforum.org/
    artice/70
19 Reuter *My Life is a* Weapon, p. 67.
20 For further details, see Martin Kramer 'The Moral Logic of
    Hezbollah' in Walter Reich (ed.) *Origins of Terrorism:
    Psychologies, Ideologies, Theologies, State of Mind*, Washington,
    DC: Woodrow Wilson Center Press, 1990, p. 142.
21 For elaboration on the notion of sacrifice in the Shiite tradition,
    refer to Augustus Richard Norton 'The Shi'i Muslims of
    the Arab World', *American for Middle East Understanding*
    (1988), 21(5). http://www.ameu.org/printer.asp?iid=154&aid
    =198# content
22 Kramer 'The Moral Logic of Hezbollah' in Reich (ed.) *Origins
    of Terrorism*, p. 142.
23 Magnus Ranstorp 'The Strategy and Tactics of Hezbollah's
    Current "Lebanonization Process"', *Mediterranean Politics*
    (1998), 3(1): 95–126.
24 During the elections that took place in 2000, the list allying
    Hezbollah, Amal and other Shiite organizations won all
    twenty-three of the seats apportioned to southern Lebanon.
    This was Hezbollah's greatest achievement since setting foot
    in the political arena of Lebanon. Ten out of twenty-three par-
    liamentary seats were reserved for Hezbollah representatives.
    All told, Hezbollah chalked up twelve parliamentary seats and
    Amal secured nine.
25 For elaboration of Hezbollah's shift to party politics, refer to
    Augustus Richard Norton 'Walking Between Raindrops:
    Hizballah in Lebanon', *Mediterranean Politics* (1998), 3(1):
    81–102; Clive Jones 'Israeli Counter-Insurgency Strategy and
    the War in South Lebanon', *Small Wars and Insurgencies*
    (1997), 8(3): 82–108.
26 Shay *The Shahids*, p. 78.
27 Augustus Richard Norton 'Lebanon's Malaise', *Survival*
    (2000–1), 42(4): 38.
28 Yoram Schweitzer 'Hezbollah: A Transnational Terrorist
    Organisation', ICT, 1 September 2002. http://www.ict.org.il
29 Anat Kurz, Maskit Burgin and David Tal *Islamic Terrorism and
    Israel: Hezbollah, Palestinian Islamic Jihad and Hamas*, Tel
    Aviv: Papyrus, Tel Aviv University, 1993, p. 174 [Hebrew].

30 Shaul Mishal and Avraham Sela *The Hamas Wind: Violence and Coexistence*, Tel Aviv: Miskal Yedioth Ahronoth Books and Chemed Books, 1999, pp. 101–5 [Hebrew].

31 Ibid., pp. 109–18.

32 Pape 'The Strategic Logic of Suicide Terrorism' 353.

33 Ibid. 354.

34 Ibid. 353.

35 Mishal and Sela *The Hamas Wind*, pp. 78–80.

36 Ibid.

37 Israel Ministry of Foreign Affairs 'HAMAS – The Islamic Resistance Movement – Jan 93', *MFA Library*, 1 January 1993. http://www.mfa.gov.il/mfa/mfaarchive/1990_1999/1993/1/hamas++the+islamic+resistance+movement+-+jan-93.htm.

38 Bloom 'Palestinian Suicide Bombing'.

39 Andrew Kydd and Barbara F. Walter 'Sabotaging the Peace: The Politics of Extremist Violence', *International Organization* (2002), 56(2): 263–4.

40 The three campaigns that failed to cause significant disruptions took place in October–November 1993, April 1994 and October 1994. For details, see Kydd and Walter 'Sabotaging the Peace' 279–84.

41 See, for example, 'The Peace Index 1996', The Tami Steinmetz Center for Peace Research (TSC) [Hebrew]. http://spirit.tau.ac.il/socant/peace/peaceindex/1996/files/Jan96.pdf

42 'Armed Attacks, Negotiations, "Separation", Elections, Unemployment, and Palestinian-Jordanian Relations', *CPRS Polls*, Public Opinion Poll #15, 2–4 February 1995. http://www.pcpsr.org/survey/cprspolls/95/poll15a.html

43 'The American Initiative, Armed Attacks, Palestinian State, Cabinet Reshuffle, Corruption, Democracy, Election of the President and Vice President, Ownership of Satellite Dishes and Computers, and Subscription to the Internet Service', *CPRS Polls*, Public Opinion Poll #34, 25–27 June 1998. http://www.pcpsr.org/survey/cprspolls/98/poll34a.html

44 Pape 'The Strategic Logic of Suicide Terrorism' 355.

45 Bloom 'Palestinian Suicide Bombing'.

46 'Camp David Summit, Chances for Reconciliation and Lasting Peace, Violence and Confrontations, Hierarchies of Priorities, and Domestic Politics', *CPRS Polls*, Public Opinion Poll #1, 27–29 July 2000. http://www.pcpsr.org/survey/polls/2000/p1a.html#violence

47 In between the two campaigns that succeeded, there was an additional suicide campaign in the period July–October 1998, at the time of the signing of the Wye Agreements between Netanyahu and Arafat; however, Hamas did not achieve its goals by means of this campaign. Kydd and Walter 'Sabotaging the Peace' 286–7.

48 Results were not long in coming. In a survey conducted a short while after the commencement of suicide attacks by the PFLP, rates of support for the organization had returned to their original levels. Bloom *Dying to Kill*, ch. 4.

49 Bloom 'Palestinian Suicide Bombing'.

50 While Arafat's popularity dropped from 46 to 33 per cent and that of Fatah from 37 to 29 per cent, support for Islamic organizations increased from 17 to 27 per cent. These figures are taken from 'The Mitchell Report, Cease Fire, and Return to Negotiations; Intifada and Armed Confrontations; Chances for Reconciliation; and, Internal Palestinian Conditions', *CPRS Polls*, Public Opinion Poll #2, 5–9 July 2001. http://www.pcpsr.org/survey/polls/2001/p2a.html

51 Ronen Bergman *Authority Given*, Tel Aviv: Miskal-Yedioth Ahronoth Books and Chemed Books, 2002, pp. 25–8 [Hebrew].

52 IDF spokesperson 'Documents: The Palestinian Authority Employs Fatah Activists Involved in Terrorism and Suicide Attacks', *Kokhaviv Publications*, 23 April 2002. http://www.kokhavivpublications.com/2002/israel/04/0204231229.html

53 Bergman *Authority Given*; Bloom 'Palestinian Suicide Bombing'.

54 Pape 'The Strategic Logic of Suicide Terrorism' 348.

CHAPTER 4   TURNING TO SUICIDE TERRORISM: THE LTTE AND THE PKK

1 'Liberation Tigers of Tamil Eelam (LTTE)', organization profile in the Terrorist Organizations Database, ICT. http://www.ict.org.il

2 Bruce Hoffman and Gordon H. McCormick 'Terrorism, Signalling and Suicide Attack', *Studies in Conflict and Terrorism* (2004), 27(4): 243–81.

3 Mia M. Bloom 'Tamil Attitudes Toward Terrorism', *Tamil Eelam*, 5 November 2004. http://www.tamilcanadian.com/pageview.php?ID=1687&SID=52; Mia M. Bloom 'Sri Lanka:

In the Tigers' Belly', *World Press Review*, 22 April 2003.
http://www.worldpress.org/Asia/1015.cfm.
4   Hoffman and McCormick 'Terrorism, Signaling, and Suicide
Attack' 259.
5   Ibid. 260.
6   Oren Yiftachel and As'ad Ghanem 'Understanding
"Ethnocratic" Regimes: The Politics of Seizing Contested
Territories', *Political Geography* (2004), 23(6): 647–76.
7   Christoph Reuter *My Life is a Weapon: A Modern History of
Suicide Bombing*, Princeton, N. J.: Princeton University Press,
2004, p. 158.
8   Ibid.
9   Mia M. Bloom 'Ethnic Conflict, State Terror and Suicide
Bombing in Sri Lanka', *Civil Wars* (2003), 6(1): 64.
10 Pauletta Otis and Christopher D. Carr 'Sri Lanka and the
Ethnic Conflict', *Conflict* (1988), 8: 212–13.
11 Ralph R. Premdas and S. W. R. de A. Samarasinghe 'Sri Lanka's
Ethnic Conflict: The Indo-Lanka Peace Accord', *Asian Survey*
(1988), 28(6): 676–90.
12 Manoj Joshi 'On the Razor's Edge: The Liberation Tigers of
Tamil Eelam', *Studies in Conflict and Terrorism* (1996), 19(1):
21–2.
13 Ibid. 23.
14 Tom Cooper 'Sri Lanka Since 1971', *ACIG Journal*,
29 October 2003. http://www.acig.org/artman/publish/
article_337.shtml
15 Bloom 'Ethnic Conflict, State Terror and Suicide Bombing in
Sri Lanka' 61.
16 Ibid. 64.
17 Joshi 'On the Razor's Edge' 24.
18 Kingsley M. De Silva (ed.) *Conflict and Violence in South
Asia: Bangladesh, India, Pakistan and Sri Lanka*, Kandy:
International Centre for Ethnic Studies, 2000, pp. 407–8.
19 Bloom 'Ethnic Conflict, State Terror and Suicide Bombing in
Sri Lanka' 72.
20 Ibid. 64.
21 Sarah Wayland 'Ethnonationalist Networks and Transnational
Opportunities: The Sri Lankan Tamil Diaspora', *Review of
International Studies* (2004), 30(3): 405–26.
22 Bloom 'Ethnic Conflict, State Terror and Suicide Bombing in
Sri Lanka' 69.

23 Bloom 'Tamil Attitudes Toward Terrorism'.
24 Richard Gorman 'Tracking the World's Suicide Bombers', *Rutgers Focus*, 18 November 2003. http://ur.rutgers.edu/focus/index.phtml?Article_ID=1214.
25 Reuter *My Life is a Weapon*, p. 162.
26 Bloom 'Tamil Attitudes Toward Terrorism'.
27 Bloom 'Ethnic Conflict, State Terror and Suicide Bombing in Sri Lanka' 54–5.
28 'Kurdistan Worker's Party (PKK)' organization profile in the Terrorist Organizations Database, ICT. http://www.ict.org.il.
29 For a discussion of the PKK's primary goals, refer to Nur Bilge Criss 'The Nature of PKK Terrorism in Turkey', *Studies in Conflict and Terrorism* (1995), 18(1): 17–37; and Michael Radu 'The Rise and Fall of the PKK', *Orbis: A Journal of World Affairs* (2001), 45(1): 47–63.
30 ERNK = Eniya Rizgariya Netewa Kurdistan (National Liberation Front of Kurdistan).
31 According to Ergil, the PKK tried to create a myth of Turkish colonialism and convince the Kurdish population that it should fight against the Turks who took their land; Doğu Ergil 'Suicide Terrorism in Turkey', *Civil Wars* (2000), 3(1): 40–1.
32 ARGK = Arteshen Rizgariya Gelli Kurdistan (People's Liberation Army of Kurdistan).
33 Criss 'The Nature of PKK Terrorism in Turkey' 20.
34 'Enter the PKK' 25. http://wwics.si.edu/subsites/ccpdc/pubs/kur/chap02.pdf
35 Radu 'The Rise and Fall of the PKK' 52.
36 Ergil 'Suicide Terrorism in Turkey' 46; Yoram Schweitzer 'Suicide Terrorism: Development & Characteristics', ICT, 21 April 2000. http://www.ict.org.il/articles/articledet.cfm?articleid=112
37 Ely Karmon 'The Showdown Between the PKK and Turkey: Syria's Setback', ICT, 22 November 1998. http://www.ict.org.il/articles/articledet.cfm?articleid=55
38 Salah Aziz 'Turkey's Hard Choice'. http://www.kakarigi.net/salah-aziz/turkey.htm
39 Ibid.
40 'Authorities Put on Brave Face after Fatal Suicide Attack', *Turkish Daily News*, 27 October 1996. http://www.turkishdailynews.com/oldeditions/10_27_96/dom.htm;Schweitzer

'Suicide Terrorism'. http://www.ict.org.il/articles/articledet. cfm?articleid=112

41 'Turkey Defies Pleas to End Kurdish War', CNN, 20 May 1997. http://www.cnn.com/WORLD/9705/20/turkey.iraq/index.html

42 Karmon, 'The Showdown Between the PKK and Turkey'.

43 Ibid.

44 Ergil 'Suicide Terrorism in Turkey' 45–7.

45 'Turkish Government Policies in the Southeast' 133. http://wwics.si.edu/subsites/ccpdc/pubs/kur/chap05.pdf

46 Criss 'The Nature of PKK Terrorism in Turkey' 20.

47 Radu 'The Rise and Fall of the PKK' 57–8; 'Enter the PKK' 22. http://wwics.si.edu/subsites/ccpdc/pubs/kur/chap02.pdf

48 For a more detailed comparison, refer to Mia M. Bloom, 'Devising a Theory of Suicide Terror', paper submitted to the ISER Seminar of Contentious Politics. http://www.iserp.columbia.edu/downloads/bloom.pdf

49 Three last suicide attacks were carried out just after the sentencing, but this small wave was ended by August 1999.

50 'World: Europe Revenge Bombings Halted', BBC News, 13 July 1999. http://news.bbc.co.uk/1/hi/world/europe/393611.stm.

51 In fact, Turkey's decision not to carry out the death penalty on Ocalan was more influenced by the EU than by Ocalan's statements.

52 Radu 'The Rise and Fall of the PKK' 50.

CHAPTER 5   THE TRANSITION TO SUICIDE TERRORISM: AL-QAEDA AND THE NETWORK OF ISLAMIC FUNDAMENTALIST GROUPS

1 For more information, see *Patterns of Global Terrorism*, Appendix B, US Department of State. www.state.gov/documents/organization/31946.pdf

2 See Daniel L. Byman 'Al-Qaeda as an Adversary: Do We Understand Our Enemy?', *World Politics* (2003), 56: 139–63.

3 Magnus Ranstorp 'Interpreting the Broader Context and Meaning of Bin Laden's "Fatwa"', *Studies in Conflict and Terrorism* (1998), 21: 321–30; 'Jihad Against Jews and Crusaders', *fas.org*, 23 February 1998. http://www.fas.org/irp/world/para/docs/980223-fatwa.htm; 'Bin Laden's Fatwa',

Online News Hour. http://www.pbs.org/newshour/terrorism/
international/fatwa_1996.html

4   It should be mentioned, though, that there is still an ongoing
    debate regarding the question of Al-Qaeda's connection to
    Wahhabism. Some scholars see a direct link to this tradition:
    see, for example, Mike Millard *Jihad in Paradise: Islam and
    Politics in Southeast Asia*, New York: M. E. Sharpe, 2004, p. 35;
    Stephen Schwartz *The Two Faces of Islam: The House of Sa'ud
    from Tradition to Terror*, New York: Doubleday, 2002, p. 180.
    Other scholars do not find such a link: see, for example, Azzam
    Maha 'Al-Qaeda: The Misunderstood Wahhabi Connection
    and the Ideology of Violence', The Royal Institute of
    International Affairs, Briefing Paper 1 (2003).

5   The person most associated with the idea of Salafi jihad is the
    Egyptian Sayyid Qutb (1906–66), a member of the Muslim
    Brothers. His book, *Milestones*, which was published in 1964,
    became the movement's manifesto. For further information, see
    www.nmhschool.org/tthornton/sayyid_qutb.htm. For analysis
    of the Salafi school and the writings of Qutb, see Marc Sageman
    Understanding Terror Networks, Philadelphia: University of
    Pennsylvania Press, 2004, pp. 7–17.

6   Yoram Schweitzer and Shaul Shay *An Expected Surprise: The
    September 11th Attack and its Ramifications*, Herzliya: ICT,
    2002, p. 17 [Hebrew].

7   Ted Thornton 'The Wahhabi Movement, Eighteenth
    Century Arabia', History of the Middle East Database, 20
    April 2004. http://www.nmhschool.org/tthornton/wahhabi_
    movement.htm

8   Jonathan Fighel 'Sheikh Abdullah Azzam: Bin Laden's spiritual
    mentor', ICT, 27 September 2001. www.ict.org.il; H. A. R.
    Gibb and J. H. Kramers *Concise Encyclopaedia of Islam*, fourth
    impression, Boston, Mass.: Brill Academic Publishers, 2001,
    p. 618.

9   Schweitzer and Shay *An Expected Surprise*, p. 36.

10 Rohan Gunaratna *Inside Al-Qaeda: Global Network of Terror*,
    New York: Columbia University Press, 2002, p. 74.

11 Schweitzer and Shay *An Expected Surprise*, p. 126.

12 See Byman 'Al-Qaeda as an Adversary' 145.

13 The question about the true goals of Al-Qaeda is still debated
    by many scholars. For elaboration, see Byman, 'Al-Qaeda as an
    Adversary'; also, Anon. *Through Our Enemies' Eyes: Osama Bin*

Laden, Radical Islam, and the Future of America, Washington, DC: Brassey's, 2002.

14 Shaul Shay *The Shahids: Islam and Suicide Attacks*, Herzliya: ICT, 2003, pp. 153–4 [Hebrew].

15 Ibid., p. 154.

16 Alan Cullison 'Inside Al-Qaeda's Hard Drive', *The Atlantic Monthly*, September 2004. http://www.theatlantic.com/doc/prem/200409/cullison

17 Bruce Hoffman 'Al-Qaeda, Trends in Terrorism, and Future Potentialities: An Assessment' *Studies in Conflict and Terrorism* (2003), 26(6): 434.

18 Shay *The Shahids*, pp. 120–1.

19 'Armed Islamic Group: Algeria, Islamists', Council on Foreign Relations, in http://cfrterrorism.org/groups/gia.html; 'In the Spotlight: Armed Islamic Group', *CDI*. 29 July 2002, in http://www.cdi.org/terrorism/gia.cfm

20 Based on data from MIPT Terrorism Knowledge Base: http://db.mipt.org/Faqs.jsp.

21 Joe Bob Briggs, 'The Q-Man', *National Interest* (2003–4), 74: 115–20; Stephen D. Collins 'Dissuading State Support of Terrorism: Strikes or Sanctions? (An Analysis of Dissuasion Measures Employed Against Libya)', *Studies in Conflict and Terrorism* (2004), 27: 1–18; Zachary Abuza 'Tentacles of Terror: Al Qaeda's Southeast Asian Network', *Contemporary Southeast Asia* (Dec. 2002), 24(3): 427.

22 Zachary Abuza 'Tentacles of Terror' 427–66.

23 Sageman *Understanding Terror Networks*.

24 Amy Chew 'The Roots of Jemaah Islamiyah', CNN, 26 February 2004. http://www.cnn.com/2003/WORLD/asiapcf/southeast/07/24/indo.JI.roots/

25 Ibid.

26 'Abu Sayyaf Group (ASG)', organization profile in the Terrorist Organizations Database, ICT. http://www.ict.org.il

27 Zachary Abuza 'Tentacles of Terror: Al-Qaeda's Southeast Asian Network'.

28 'Suspect Mastermind Behind Saudi Bombing in Custody', *Chinadaily.com*. 27 June 2003. http://www.chinadaily.com.cn/en/doc/2003-06/27/content_241343.htm

29 'Morocco Spells Death to 4 for Casablanca Bombing', *The Daily Star*, 20 August 2003. http://www.thedailystar.net/2003/08/20/d30820130184.htm

30 Yossi Melman 'Al-Qaeda is in Crisis, but the Spirit of the Global Jihad is More Alive than Ever', *Haaretz*, 4 December 2003. For examples of Bin Laden's direct connections with large-scale attacks, see Internet Desk 'Hand of Al-Qaeda at Casablanca', Radio Netherlands, 19 May 2003. http://www.rnw.nl/hotspots/html/mor030519.html; 'Al-Qaeda Accused of Involvement in Riyadh Attacks', CNN Student News, 13 May 2003. http://www.cnn.com/2003/fyi/news/05/13/saudi.bombings/index.html.

31 'Call for Suicide Attacks against Westerners', *The Star*, 22 May 2003. http://www.thestar.co.za/index.php?fSectionId=132&fArticleId=150004; 'The Wills of the Perpetrators of the Suicide Attacks in Riyadh', Memri: The Middle East Media Research Institute [Hebrew]. http:// www.memri.org.il/Memri/LoadArticlePage.asp?entID=1339&entType=4&language=Hebrew

32 On 15 November 2003, two suicide bombers exploded two trucks full of dynamite at the entrances to the Beit Yisrael and Neve Shalom synagogues in Istanbul, and on 20 November, two suicide bombers detonated two car bombs at the entrances to the British consulate and the British Bank in Istanbul. Altogether, fifty-seven people were killed in the two attacks and hundreds were wounded.

33 Karl Vick 'Turkish Suspects Tied to Guerrillas', *Washingtonpost.com*, 24 November 2003.

34 The ABC News Investigative Unit, 'New Findings in Turkish Bomb Investigation', *ABCNEWS.com*, 24 November 2003.

35 Mike Boettcher 'Tracing the Trail of Radical Turks', *CNN.com*, 26 December 2003. http://edition.cnn.com/2003/WORLD/europe/ 11/25/turkey.alqaeda/index.html; '"The Cars of Death Will Not Stop. . ."', *Guardian Unlimited*, 21 November 2003. http://www.guardian.co.uk/turkey/story/0,12700,1090545,00.html; Ian Mather '"The Cars of Death Will Not Stop. . ."', *Scotland on Sunday*, 23 November 2003. http://static. highbeam.com/s/scotlandonsundayedinburghscotland/november232003/thecarsofdeathwillnotstop/

36 Damien McElroy and Philip Sherwell 'Bomb Attacks Were Planned in Internet Café', *Telegraph*, 23 November 2003.

37 Shay *The Shahids*, pp. 139–41.

38 Ibid., p. 142.

39 Andrei Skrobot and Dmitry Simakyn 'Black Holiday in Tushino', *Nezavisimaya Gazeta*, 7 July 2003.

40 'Vzriv v Metro Sovershila Jenchina Samoubiiza', *Izvestia*, 6 February 2004; 'FSB Rassmatryvaet dve Versii Terakta', *Izvestia*, 8 February 2004.

41 Rod Nordland 'Is Zarqawi Really the Culprit?', *Newsweek*, 6 March 2004.

42 Deborah Orin 'Bush Pledges US Staying Power in Iraq', *New York Post*, 29 October 2003; Michael Howard. 'Baghdad Bombings: Foreign Fighters Blamed for Day of Carnage: Investigation Arrest of Would-Be Bomber with Syrian Passport Strengthens US Belief that Outside Insurgents are Behind Wave of Violence', *Guardian*, 28 October 2003.

43 Nordland 'Is Zarqawi Really the Culprit?'

44 For more information, see Renuen Paz 'Arab Volunteers Killed in Iraq', *Prism Series of Global Jihad* (2005), 1(3), 1–7.

45 Rod Nordland, Tom Masland and Christopher Dickey 'Unmasking the Insurgents', *Newsweek*, 7 February 2005.

CHAPTER 6   WHO BECOMES A SUICIDE TERRORIST?

1 Martin Kramer 'Sacrifice and "Self-Martyrdom" in Shi'ite Lebanon', *Terrorism and Political Violence* (1991), 3(3): 30–47. http://www.geocities.com/martinkramerorg/Sacrifice.htm

2 Ibid.

3 Ibid.

4 'Eastern Turkish Town of Bingol in Shock After Suicide Attacks', *News-Star.com*, 28 November 2003. www.news-star.com/stories/112803/new_20.shtml.

5 Nicolas Bourcier 'Turkish City that is a Cradle of Unrest', *Manchester Guardian Weekly*, 17 December 2003

6 Soraya Sarhaddi Nelson 'Turkey's Latest Terrorism Act Hatched in Internet Café', *Knight Ridder – Washington Bureau*. 21 November 2003. http://www.realcities.com/mld/krwash ington/7321680.htm

7 'Naive Bomber and the Avenger Who Lit his Fuse', *Times* (London), 29 November 2003.

8 Nicholas Birch, 'Friends Seduced by Islamic Terror Suicide Bombings in Istanbul Have Put the Focus on a Sinister Terror Group, the Kurdish Hizbullah', *Irish Times*, 22 November 2003.

9 Nelson 'Turkey's Latest Terrorism Act Hatched in Internet Café'.

10 'Naive Bomber and the Avenger Who Lit his Fuse'.

11 Ibid.

12 '"Parallels" to Al-Qaeda Cited in Istanbul Synagogue Blasts: Investigators Identify Two Bombers from Same Eastern Province', *Washington Post*, 20 November 2003.

13 'Turkey's Town of Terrorists', *The Times* (London), 8 December 2003.

14 Birch 'Friends Seduced by Islamic Terror Suicide Bombings . . .'.

15 'Turkey's Town of Terrorists'.

16 Soraya Sarhaddi Nelson, 'Remote Kurdish City Produced Terrorist Plot: Long Struggles among Factions May be to Blame', *San Jose Mercury News* (California), 23 November 2003. http://www.sanluisobispo.com/mld/mercurynews/news/world/7331721.htm

17 'Naive Bomber and the Avenger Who Lit his Fuse'.

18 Lawrence Uzzell 'Profile of Female Suicide Bomber', *Chechnya Weekly* (11 Feb. 2004), 5(6): 3–6. http://www.jamestown.org/images/pdf/chw_005_006.pdf

19 Ibid.

20 Ibid.

21 Ariel Merari 'The Readiness to Kill and Die: Suicidal Terrorism in the Middle East' in Walter Reich (ed.) *Origins of Terrorism: Psychologies, Ideologies, Theologies, State of Mind*, New York: Woodrow Wilson International Center for Scholars and Cambridge University Press, 1990, p. 203; Scott Atran 'Genesis of Suicide Terrorism', *Science* (2003), 299 (5619): 1537; Ariel Merari 'Suicide Terrorism' in R. Yufit and D. Lester (eds.) *Assessment, Treatment and Prevention of Suicide*, New York: John Wiley, 2004.

22 In very few cases evidence was found for some kind of mental condition or other illness; however, because this is such a small minority of the cases, it doesn't say much about the larger phenomenon. There is evidence that some of the Sri Lankan, Kurdish and Chechen perpetrators, mostly women, were coerced to engage in suicide attacks, but, again, this occurred in only a small minority of the cases.

23 For a detailed description of the problems involved in the study of suicide terrorists, see Merari 'The Readiness to Kill and Die' in Reich (ed.) *Origins of Terrorism*.

24 Doğu Ergil *Suicide Terrorism in Turkey: The Workers' Party of Kurdistan*, Countering Suicide Terrorism: An International Conference, Herzliya: ICT, 2000.
25 Ayla H. Schbley 'Torn Between God, Family, and Money: The Changing Profile of Lebanon's Religious Terrorists', *Studies in Conflict and Terrorism* (2000), 23: 175–96.
26 Merari 'The Readiness to Kill and Die' in Reich (ed.) *Origins of Terrorism*; Anat Berko *The Path to the Garden of Eden*, Tel Aviv: Miskal Yedioth Ahronoth Books and Chemed Books, 2004 [Hebrew].
27 We constructed a database specifically for this purpose. The database was created in two stages. First, we detected all terrorist events (suicide attacks) which had taken place in Israel over the last decade. This was done by conducting a careful scrutiny of the Israeli daily *Haaretz*, with the help of a group of specially trained students. Each retrieved terrorist event was encoded according to a detailed codebook. Regarding incidents where it was difficult to obtain information, we made use of other resources, notably, Internet sites of the terrorist's organization or other daily newspapers. In the second stage, we established a quantitative database which included characteristics relevant to terrorist profiles. The whole process of retrieving and encoding data was cross-checked in order to prevent any possibility of bias or loss of data. This methodology, which has become relevant over the years in the study of social protest as well as political violence, is termed 'events data'. It allowed us to obtain longitudinal and reliable information with regard to the studied phenomenon as well as in terms of its characteristics and causes.
28 The commitment/crisis dichotomy has a lot of similarities to the altruistic and fatalistic types of suicide as proposed by Durkheim. For further elaboration on the relevance of Durkheim's typology on the study of suicide terror, refer to Ami Pedahzur, Arie Perliger and Leonard Weinberg 'Altruism and Fatalism: The Characteristics of Palestinian Suicide Terrorists', *Deviant Behaviour* (2003), 24(4): 405–23.
29 Bernard N. Grofman and Edward N. Muller 'The Strange Case of Relative Gratification and Potential for Political Violence: The V-Curve Hypothesis', *American Political Science Review* (1973), 67(2): 514–39; Ted R. Gurr *Why Men Rebel*, Princeton, N.J.: Princeton University Press, 1970; Randy Hodson, Dusko Sekulic and Garth Massey 'National Tolerance in the Former

Yugoslavia', *American Journal of Sociology* (1994), 99(6): 1534–58.

30   Dalal Saoud 'Feature: Bombings – Suicide or Martyrdom?', *United Press International*, 3 May 2001; Catherine Taylor 'Jihad Widows Keep the Faith – Middle East Mayhem', *The Australian*, 7 October 2003; Red Harrison 'Fundamental Rite', *The Weekend Australian*, 4 October 1997.

31   'Nations aren't Innocent', *Sangam.org*. http://www.tamil.net/list/2001–08/msg00211.html

32   'Suspected Killer Identified by Sri Lankan Police', *The Xinhua General Overseas News Service*, 4 May 1993; Rohan Gunaratna, 'The Employment of Suicide in Terrorism and Guerrilla Warfare: The Threat and Likely Trends', *atimes.com*, in *Vers une privatisation des conflits?*, Recherches et Documents no. 22, April 2001: 43–60.

33   'Time's Wasting Hours: Trends in the Tamil Struggle', Report 13, ch. 6. http://www.uthr.org/Reports/Report13/chapter6.htm

34   In general, Israel allows Palestinian prisoners some degree of autonomy while they are serving their sentences. They elect their leadership, run their everyday life and give each other lessons on different subjects. Often, prisoners gather in groups based on their ideological affiliations. The closeness that life in prison imposes on them creates and reinforces their camaraderie and commitment to their organization. Moreover, spending a length of time in an Israeli prison is often considered a commendable rite of passage when becoming a Palestinian fighter.

35   'Islamic Jihad Claims Responsibility for Bombing', *Morningsun.net*, 8 November 1998. http://www.morningsun.net/stories/110898/usw_1108980023.shtml;   'Palestinians Boost Anti-terrorism Efforts After Attack', *CNN.com*, 7 November 1998. http://edition.cnn.com/WORLD/meast/9811/07/israel.bomb.02/

36   Roni Shaked, Doron Meiri and Alex Fishman 'The Terrorists Came from a Territory Under Israeli Control', *Yedioth Aharonoth*, 8 November 1998: 15 [Hebrew].

37   Ibid.

38   'Islamic Jihad Blamed for Jerusalem Car Bombing', *CNN.com*, 6 November 1998; 'Palestinians Arrest Jihad Activists after Bombing', *CNN.com*, 7 November 1998.

39   'The Perpetrators of the Attack', *Maariv Online*, 26 May 2001 [Hebrew].

40 It is important to note that Sageman was not referring specifi-
    cally to suicide terrorism: Marc Sageman *Understanding Terror
    Networks*, Philadelphia: Pennsylvania University Press, 2004.

41 'The Global Salafi Jihad', statement by Marc Sageman to the
    National Commission on Terrorist Attacks upon the United
    States, 9 July 2003. http://www.globalsecurity.org/security/
    library/congress/9–11_commission/030709-sageman.htm.
    See also Sageman *Understanding Terror Networks*.

42 Birch 'Friends Seduced by Islamic Terror Suicide Bombings . . .'.

43 'Turkish Suspects Tied to Guerrillas; Government's Backing of
    Islamic Group Arouses Scrutiny after Blasts', *Washington Post*,
    24 November 2003.

44 Damien McElroy, Olga Craig, Philip Sherwell, Colin Brown
    and Yigal Schleifer 'How the Message Was Brought Home. The
    State Visit by George W. Bush Was Running Like Clockwork,
    Then, 1,500 Miles Away, Two Massive Bombs Exploded',
    Sunday Telegraph (London), 23 November 2003.

45 'Widow of Synagogue Bomber Says She Found Out He Died
    From Press', *Agence France-Presse*, 21 November 2003.
    http://quickstart.clari.net/qs_se/webnews/wed/bp/Qturkey-
    attacks-widow.Rq6O_DNL.html

46 http://edition.cnn.com/WORLD/9709/24/israel/four.shot.jpg;
    'Israel Demands Arrest of Militants Linked to Bombings',
    CNN.com, 24 September 1997. http://edition.cnn.com/
    WORLD/9709/24/israel/index.html; 'Israel Says 4 Suicide
    Bombers from West Bank', *CNN.com*, 23 September 1997.
    http://edition.cnn.com/WORLD/9709/23/israel.bombers/
    index.html

47 Sami Sokol, Eitan Rabin and Amira Hess 'The 4 Suicide Bombers
    Were Wanted by Israel Since September 96 When They Escaped
    the Palestinian Prison', *Haaretz*, 24 September 1997 [Hebrew];
    Eitan Rabin 'DNA Tests of the Family Members Confirmed the
    Suicide Bomber's Identity', *Haaretz*, 24 September 1997
    [Hebrew]; Simone Bitton *The Bombing* (1999), film by Simone
    Bitton. About the film, see http://www.frif.com/pdf/mid
    east2004.pdf p. 8; for a review of the film, see: Pamela Nice
    'Deconstruction of a Bombing', *Al Jadid Magazine* (2001),
    7(35). http://www.aljadid.com/film/ 0735nice.html

48 Itzik Saban and Eitan Glickman 'Bicycle of Death', *Yedioth
    Aharonoth*, 20 May 2003: 7 [Hebrew].

49 For more on the involvement of the Qawasme family in terror

incidents, see 'The Qawasme Family is Responsible for the Murder of about 100 Israelis and for the Injury of Hundreds', *The News Room*, 31 August 2004 [Hebrew]. http://newsroom. co.il/?id=30809

50 Arnon Regular 'The Six Suicides from Hebron: Friends in the Football Team', *Haaretz*, 29 May 2003 [Hebrew].

51 Itzik Saban, Roni Shaked, Eran Navon and Eitan Glickman 'Suspect: Israeli Arabs Were Involved in Attack', *Yedioth Aharonoth*, 23 October 2002: 9 [Hebrew].

52 Roni Shaked, Itzik Saban and Haim Broida 'Person Responsible for Attack in Ariel Eliminated', *Yedioth Aharonoth*, 5 November 2002: 9 [Hebrew].

53 Gal Berger 'One Year Later: Hamas Assumes Responsibility for the Attack on Mike's Place', *MSN.co.il*, 8 March 2004 [Hebrew]. http://nfc.msn.co.il/archive/001-D-41827–00. html?tag=15–33–27.

54 'Suicide Bomber "Had WTC Article"', *ic Newcastle*, 6 May 2004. http://icnewcastle.icnetwork.co.uk/0100news/0200national/ tm_objectid=14216982&method=full!&siteid=50081& headline=suicide-bomber–had-wtc-article–name_page.html.

55 'Cover Story: Passport to Terror – The Times, UK', *Islamic News Updates*, Message 3035, 8 May 2003. http://groups. yahoo.com/group/IslamicNewsUpdates/message/3035.

56 Nick Fielding 'Passport to Terror', *Sunday Times* (London), 4 May 2003; Daniel McGrory 'Israel Asks for Help to Trace "British Bombers"', *The Times* (London) 27 October 2003.

57 Israel Ministry of Foreign Affairs, 'Details of April 30th, 2003, Tel Aviv Suicide Bombing', Ministry of Foreign Affairs website: http://www.mfa.gov.il/MFA/Government/Communiques/ 2003/; Sharon Sadeh 'Britain: Indictments against Family of Terrorist on the Promenade', *Walla News*, 9 May 2003 [Hebrew]. http://news.walla.co.il/?w=//384918; Associated Press 'Suicide Bomber's Brother and Sister Face Retrial', *News.jpost.com*, 8 July 2004. http://www.jpost.com/servlet/ Satellite?pagename=JPost/JPArticle/ShowFull&cid=1089257 369089&p=1078397702269.

58 Edward Walsh 'Suicide Recruit to Captive of Israel: 16-Year-Old, Among Shiites Demanded by Hijackers, Describes Growing Up in Lebanon', *Washington Post*, 18 June 1985.

59 Thomas L. Friedman 'Boy Says Lebanese Recruited Him as Car Bomber', *New York Times*, 14 April 1985.

60 Walsh 'Suicide Recruit to Captive of Israel'.
61 Ibid.
62 Ibid.
63 Friedman 'Boy Says Lebanese Recruited Him as Car Bomber'.
64 Walsh 'Suicide Recruit to Captive of Israel'.
65 Friedman 'Boy Says Lebanese Recruited Him as Car Bomber'.
66 Walsh 'Suicide Recruit to Captive of Israel'.
67 'Captured Suicide Bomber Wanted to Ride Mule to Paradise', *Associated Press*, 20 November 1985.
68 'Syrians Paid "Suicide" Girl', *Herald*, 20 November 1985.
69 'Captured Suicide Bomber Wanted to Ride Mule to Paradise'.
70 'Syrians Paid "Suicide" Girl'.
71 'Captured Suicide Bomber Wanted to Ride Mule to Paradise'.
72 Ibid.
73 For more information, refer to http://www.iaf.org.il/Templates/Kills/FirstDown.IN.aspx?lang=HE&lobbyID=43&folderID=43&subfolderID=293&docfolderID=293&docID=1268&docType=ARTICLE.
74 Kramer 'Sacrifice and "Self-Martyrdom" in Shi'ite Lebanon'.
75 Ibid.
76 For the full stories of the Palestinian suicide bombers, refer to Barbara Victor *Army of Roses: Inside the World of Palestinian Women Suicide Bombers*, Emmaus, Pa: Rodale Books, 2003.
77 'Palestinian Women Martyrs against the Israeli Occupation – Wafa Idriss: January 27, 2002'. http://www.aztlan.net/women_martyrs.htm; Amit Cohen and Sa'id Baderan 'The [Female] Terrorist in Haifa: A Lawyer from Jenin', *Maariv Internet*, 5 October 2003 [Hebrew]; http://www.nrg.co.il/online/archive/ART/551/742.html
78 Chen Kotz-Bar 'I Dreamed of Killing More than a Hundred', *Maariv*, Weekend Supplement, 23 January 2004: 16 [Hebrew].
79 'Suicide Attacks Using Women', Intelligence and Terrorism Information Center at the Center for Special Studies, March 2004 [Hebrew]. http://www.intelligence.org.il/sp/4_04/women.htm
80 Victor *Army of Roses*, pp. 100–1.
81 'Palestinian Women Martyrs against the Israeli Occupation – Dareen Abu Aysheh: February 27, 2002'. http://www.aztlan.net/women_martyrs.htm
82 ' "She is Having a Fine Time with God" Said the Terrorist about her Friend', *Haaretz*, 14 April 2002 [Hebrew].

83 Itamar Eichner and Haim Broida 'This is How [Female] Suicide Terrorists are Recruited', *Yedioth Aharonoth*, 24 Hours, 12 January 2003: 13 [Hebrew].

84 '"She is Having a Fine Time with God"'.

85 'Suicide Attacks Using Women'.

86 Kotz-Bar 'I Dreamed of Killing More than a Hundred'.

87 Ibrahim Hazboun 'The Palestinian Authority's "Angels of Death"', *OPSICK*, 31 March 2002. http://www.operation sick.com/articles/20020331_paangelsofdeath.asp

88 'Suicide Attacks Using Women'.

89 'Palestinian Women Martyrs against the Israeli Occupation – Andaleeb Takafka: April 12, 2002'. http://www.aztlan.net/ women_martyrs.htm.

90 'Suicide Attacks Using Women'.

91 Ibid.

92 Harel Amos and Jonathan Lis 'Jerusalem Police on High Alert for Suicide Bomber', *Haaretz*, 18 June 2002 [Hebrew]. http://www.haaretzdaily.com/hasen/pages/ShArt.jhtml?item No=177250&contrassID=1&subContrassID=0&sbSubContr assID=0

93 Natasha Muzgobiah 'Our Son is a Terrorist', *Yedioth Aharonoth*, 24 Hours, 11 February 2003: 7 [Hebrew].

94 Ibid.

95 Rima Salameh 'Lebanon's Militia Women Fight and Become Suicide Bomb "Martyrs"', *Associated Press*, 7 April 1986.

96 Scheherezadd Faramarzi 'Girl Who Drove Car Bomb First Sent Mother Present', *Associated Press*, 12 April 1985.

97 Ibid.

98 Ibid.

99 'Israel Bomb Kills 4', *CNN.com*, 4 March 2001.

100 'The Executive of the Attack: We Must Sacrifice Ourselves', *Ynet*, 7 March 2001 [Hebrew]. http://www.cs.biu.ac.il/~ zultia/about%20me/shlomit/013.htm

101 Ibid.

102 Ibid.

103 In this case, the term *shahid* was not used to describe fellow suicide bombers but people who died as a result of Israeli military assaults.

104 *Ynet News* Archive, 29 April 2001. http://www.ynet.co.il/ home/0,7340,L-8,FF.html [Hebrew].

105 'Six Dead in Mideast Resort Bomb', *CNN.com*, 18 May 2001. http://edition.cnn.com/2001/WORLD/meast/05/18/bomb. netanya.02/index.html; 'Israel Launches Strikes after Suicide Bombing', *CNN.com*, 18 May 2001. http://edition.cnn.com/2001/WORLD/meast/05/18/bomb.netanya.03/index.html

106 *Ynet News* Archive, 19 May 2001. http://www.ynet.co.il/home/0,7340,L-8,FF.html; *Maariv Online* Archive, 19 May 2001. http://www.nrg.co.il/online/HP_0.html

107 Ibid.

108 *Ynet News* Archive, 23 June 2001. http://www.ynet.co.il/home/0,7340,L-8,FF.html

109 'Bomber Identified as 22-year-old Palestinian', *CNN.com*, 3 June 2001. http://edition.cnn.com/2001/WORLD/meast/06/03/tel.aviv.bomber/index.html.

110 'The Perpetrator of the Attack: A Qalqilya Resident who Served in the Jordanian Army', *Ynet News*, 3 June 2001 [Hebrew]. http://www.ynet.co.il/articles/1,7340, L-785548,00.html

111 'Special: A list of the twenty-one young persons who were killed in the attack', *Ynet News* [Hebrew]. http://www.ynet. co.il/home/0%2C7340%2CL-1258%2CFF.html

112 'The Perpetrator of the Attack: A Qalqilya Resident . . .'.

113 Chris Kline and Mark Franchetti 'The Woman Behind the Mask', *Sunday Times* (London), 3 November 2002.

114 Ibid.

115 Ibid.

116 Ed Bradley 'Terror in Moscow: New Documentary Features Hostage Drama in Moscow Theatre Last Year When Chechen Rebels Took 800 People Hostage', *60 Minutes* (7:00 PM ET) – CBS 26 October 2003.

117 Kline and Franchetti 'The Woman Behind the Mask'.

118 Sharon LaFraniere and Peter Baker 'Moscow's New Fear: Women with Bombs: Chechen Rebels Recruit War Widows', *Washington Post*, 11 July 2003.

119 Sergei Dyupin 'Ripped Off Head Started Talking', *What the Papers Say* (Russia) 2 July 2003.

120 LaFraniere and Baker 'Moscow's New Fear: Women with Bombs'; Viktor Paukov, Aleksandr Raskin and Vremya Novostei 'Suicide Bombings Kill 75, Injure 400 in Chechnya, Terrorist Holiday: Akhmad Kadyrov Was Shielded by Bodyguards', *Current Digest of the Post-Soviet Press*, 11 June 2003.

121 'Chechen Interior Ministry Blames Blast on Rebel Comman-der', *BBC Monitoring International Reports*, 14 May 2003.
122 Paukov, Raskin and Novostei 'Suicide Bombings Kill 75 . . .'.
123 Mark Franchetti '"Wish Me Luck", Said the Suicide Widow Waiting to Kill Russians', *Sunday Times* (London), 17 August 2003.
124 Ibid.
125 Ibid.
126 Ibid.
127 'Suicide Bomber Kills Two Israeli Soldiers', *CNN.com*, 16 July 2001.
128 'The Jihad Takes Responsibility on Hezbollah Television', *Maariv Internet*, 17 July 2001 [Hebrew].
129 Ibid.
130 Ibid.
131 'My Son Made His Family Proud', *Maariv Internet*, 13 Aug 2001 [Hebrew].
132 Ibid.
133 Amir Rapaport and Itamar Eichner 'The Target: Nablus', *Yedioth Aharonoth*, 28 May 2002: 6 [Hebrew].
134 Ibid.
135 Yitzhak Yoav and Yifat Gadot 'A Woman Suicide Terrorist Blew Herself Up at Maxim Restaurant in Haifa', *News First Class*. www.nfc.co.il [Hebrew]; Amit Cohen and Sa'id Baderan 'The [Female] Terrorist in Haifa: A Lawyer from Jenin', *Maariv Internet*, 5 October 2003 [Hebrew].
136 John Ward Anderson and Molly Moore 'For Two Families in Haifa, Three Generations of Victims', *Washington Post*, 6 October 2003; 'Face of Suicide Bomber; She Kills 16 Adults 3 Kids and Wounds this Tiny Child', *Sunday Mail*, 5 October 2003.
137 Vered Levi-Barzilai 'Ticking Bomb', *Haaretz*, 17 October 2003 [Hebrew].
138 Gideon Levy 'All the Sons are Dead', *Haaretz*, Supplement, 30 January 2004 [Hebrew].
139 Sageman *Understanding Terror Networks*. There are, however, some interesting differences. While the majority of the subjects in Sageman's analysis were married and had a back-ground of secular education, among Palestinian suicide bombers of the first wave the majority were single and had a background of religious education.

140 Religious background in this case has been determined
     according to the type of school that the perpetrator attended.

CHAPTER 7   THE RECRUITMENT AND SOCIALIZATION OF THE
                      SUICIDE TERRORIST

1   Arnon Regular 'With his Hand on the Switch, the Terrorist
    Decided not to Explode', *Haaretz*, 23 May 2004 [Hebrew];
    'Mind of the Suicide Bomber', *CBS News.com*. 25 May 2003.
    http://www.cbsnews.com/stories/2003/05/23/60minutes/ma
    in555344.shtml
2   Ibid.
3   Ibid.
4   Ibid.
5   Michael Radu 'Radical Islam and Suicide Bombers', *Foreign
    Policy Research Institute*, 21 October 2003. http://www.fpri.
    org/enotes/20031021.americawar.radu.islamsuicidebombers.
    html; Raphael Israeli 'A Manual of Islamic Fundamentalist
    Terrorism', *Terrorism and Political Violence* (2002), 14(4): 23–40.
6   Mia M. Bloom *Dying to Kill: The Global Phenomenon of Suicide
    Terror*, 2004, ch. 4 (website), New York: Columbia University
    Press, 2005.
7   Christoph Reuter *My Life is a Weapon: A Modern History of
    Suicide Bombing*, Princeton, N. J.: Princeton University Press,
    2004.
8   Shimon Shapira *Hezbollah: Between Iran and Lebanon*, Tel Aviv:
    Hakibbutz Hameuchad Publishing, 2000, p. 169 [Hebrew].
9   Martin Kramer 'Sacrifice and "Self-Martyrdom" in Shiite
    Lebanon', *Terrorism and Political Violence* (1991), 3(3): 30–47.
10 'Shiites Posthumously Honour Teenager as Suicide Bomber',
    Associated Press, 19 December 1985.
11 'Hezbollah Commemorates Suicide Bombers', *Associated
    Press*, 12 November 1989.
12 Guy Bechor 'Back on the Road to Sacrifice', *Haaretz*,
    6 December 1995 [Hebrew].
13 Shaul Shay *The Shahids: Islam and Suicide Attacks*, Herzliya:
    ICT, 2003, pp. 60–1 [Hebrew].
14 Ibid.
15 Ariel Merari 'Social, Organisational and Psychological Factors
    in Suicide Terrorism' in Tore Bjorgo (ed.) *The Root Causes of*

Terrorism, Proceedings of an Expert Meeting on the Root Causes of Terrorism (9–11 June 2003), Oslo, Norway: The Norwegian Institute of International Affairs, 2003.

16 Ghassan Hage 'Comes a Time We Are All Enthusiasm: Understanding Palestinian Suicide Bombers in Times of Exighophobia', *Public Culture* (2003), 15(1): 79–80.

17 Ehud Sprinzak 'Rational Fanatics: Analysis of the Effects of Suicide Bombers', *Foreign Policy* (2000), 120: 66–73.

18 Rohan Gunaratna 'Childhood: A Continuous Casualty of the Conflict in Sri Lanka', *Weekend Express*, 18–19 July 1998.

19 James F. Dunnigan 'Suicide Terrorist Incorporated', *Strategy Page*, 31 May 2004; Lawrence Uzzell 'Profile of Female Suicide Bomber', *Chechnya Weekly* (11 Feb. 2004), 5(6): 3–6. http://www.jamestown.org/images/pdf/chw_005_006.pdf

20 Rohan Gunaratna *Inside Al-Qaeda: Global Network of Terror*, New York: Columbia University Press, 2002, p. 75.

21 'Recruitment for the Jihad in the Netherlands, from Incident to Trend', *AIVD.NL*: 11–14. http://www.aivd.nl/contents/pages/2285/recruitmentbw.pdf

22 'The Global Salafi Jihad', statement by Marc Sageman to the National Commission on Terrorist Attacks upon the United States, 9 July 2003. http://www.globalsecurity.org/security/library/congress/9–11_commission/030709-sageman.htm

23 Bruce Hoffman 'Al-Qaeda, Trends in Terrorism and Future Potentialities: An Assessment', *Studies in Conflict and Terrorism* (2003), 26(6): 429–42.

24 Rohan Gunaratna (ed.) *Terrorism in the Asia-Pacific*, Singapore: International Specialised Book Services, 2003.

25 Massimo Calabresi 'A Hellenic Haven: The Flight of Kurdish Refugees to Greece Adds to a Cycle of Violence and Vengeance', *TIME* (30 Mar. 1998), 151(13). http://www.time.com/time/magazine/1998/int/980330/europe.a_hellenic_haven.19.html

26 For further discussion, refer to these websites: http://www.child-soldiers.org/cs/childsoldiers.nsf; and http://www.mfa.gov.tr./grupa/ac/acf/FA.htm

27 Michael Radu 'The Rise and the Fall of the PKK', *Orbis: A Journal of World Affairs* (2001), 45(1): 51.

28 Sprinzak 'Rational Fanatics'.

29 Audrey Kurth Cronin 'Terrorism and Suicide Attack', *CRS*

Report for Congress, 28 August 2003. http://www.fas.org/irp/crs/RL32058.pdf.

30 'Root Causes of Terrorism in the Caucasus', *Peace Mission in the North of Caucasus*, Forum on Early Warning and Early Response, February 2003.

31 There are reports that this woman does not exist. According to the Russian authorities, the terrorist Zarema Muzhakhoeva whom they had caught invented the whole story about this mystery woman.

32 Uzzell 'Profile of Female Suicide Bomber'; Kim Murphy '"Black Widows" Caught Up in Web of Chechen War', *Los Angeles Times*, 7 February 2004. http://www.rickross.com/reference/rs/rs43.html

33 Assaf Moghadam 'Palestinian Suicide Terrorism in the Second Intifada: Motivation and Organisation Aspects', *Studies in Conflict and Terrorism* (2003), 26: 83.

34 Jack Kelly 'The Secret World of Suicide Bombers: Devotion, Desire Drive Youths to "Martyrdom". Palestinians in Pursuit of Paradise Turn Their Own Bodies into Weapons', *USA TODAY*, 26 June 2001. http://www.keepmedia.com/pubs/USATODAY/2001/06/26/404192?page=2

35 Amit Navon 'How the Islamic Jihad Terror Machine Operates', *Maariv Internet*, 14 June 2002 [Hebrew].

36 Ilana Dayan and Gal Gabai, research reporters, *Fact* TV programme, 2 June 2004 [Hebrew].

37 Moghadam 'Palestinian Suicide Terrorism in the Second Intifada' 68.

38 Ami Pedahzur, Arie Perliger and Leonard Weinberg 'Altruism and Fatalism in the Characteristics of Palestinian Suicide Terrorists', *Deviant Behaviour* (2003), 24: 405–23.

39 'Iran's Agents of Terror', *US News and World Report*, 6 March 1989.

40 'Raided Base is Breeding Place for Fanatics', *Associated Press*, 3 June 1994.

41 Bechor 'Back on the Road to Sacrifice'.

42 Rohan Gunaratna (ed.) *Terrorism in the Asia-Pacific*.

43 Sanjay Sonawani *On the Brink of Death*, New York: Pushpa Parakashan, 2001, p. 281.

44 Ibid.

45 It should be mentioned that the connection between the idea of suicide for the organization and the leader and high social

status in the organization was not new to the LTTE. It started in the early 1980s when members of the organization were given cyanide capsules to hang around their necks for quick usage in case they were captured. The cyanide capsule wrapped in a leather thong was considered a badge of honour among the organization's members. Bruce Hoffman and Gordon D. McCormick 'Terrorism, Signaling, and Suicide Attack', *Studies in Conflict and Terrorism* (2004), 27(4): 259.

46 Shay *The Shahids*, p. 137.
47 For more information, see www.mfa.gov.tr/grupe/eh/terror/greecebk/annex8.htm.
48 Cronin 'Terrorism and Suicide Attack'.
49 James F. Dunnigan 'Suicide Terrorist, Incorporated'. http://www.strategypage.com/dls/articles2001/20010625.asp
50 Uzzell 'Profile of Female Suicide Bomber'. http://www.jamestown.org/images/pdf/chw_005_006.pdf
51 Kim Murphy 'A Cult of Reluctant Killers: The "black widows" of Chechnya suicide bombers who stalk Russia are driven by hatred, ideology, coercion and fear', *Los Angeles Times*, 4 February 2004.
52 'The Karbala Connection: Where Bombs, Heroin and Islam Meet', *AFP*, 23 March 2004. http://www.keepmedia.com/ShowItemDetails.do?item_id=399522
53 Eitan Rabin 'DNA Tests of Family Members Confirmed Identities of Suicide Attackers', *Haaretz*, 24 September 1997 [Hebrew]; Sami Sockol, Eitan Rabin and Amira Hass 'The Four Terrorists Were Wanted by Israel Already in September 1996 after Escaping from Palestinian Jail', *Haaretz*, 5 September 1997 [Hebrew].
54 Shay *The Shahids*, p. 43; Moghadam 'Palestinian Suicide Terrorism in the Second Intifada' 84.
55 Shay *The Shahids*, p. 44.
56 Ibid.
57 Michael Taarnby 'Profiling the Islamic Suicide Terrorist', a research report for the Danish Ministry of Justice, 27 November 2003: 36, 29. http://www.jm.dk/image.asp?page=image&objno=71157
58 Gunaratna *Inside Al-Qaeda*, p. 73.
59 Yoram Schweitzer 'Suicide Terrorism and the September 11th Attacks', *ICT*, 20 October 2002; 'Translation of the Letter Left

by Hijackers', *ICT*, 29 September 2001. www.ict.org.il. See also the Al-Qaeda manual, lesson 2, on: www.usdoj.gov

60 Zachary Abuza 'Tentacles of Terror: Al-Qaeda's Southeast Asian Network', *Contemporary Southeast Asia* (2002), 24(3): 427–66.

61 Gabriel Weimann 'www.terror.net: How Modern Terrorism Uses the Internet'. www.usip.org/pubs/specialreports/sr116. html

62 Merari 'Social, Organisational and Psychological Factors in Suicide Terrorism' in Bjorgo (ed.) *Root Causes of Terrorism*.

63 Uzzell 'Profile of Female Suicide Bomber'. http://www. jamestown.org/images/pdf/chw_005_006.pdf

64 Kennedy and Power 'The Buddha's Teardrop', *The Old Town Review*, March 2004. http://www.fluxfactory.org/otr/ kennedypowersrilanka.htm; Suba Chandran 'Born to Die: The Black Tigers of the LTTE', Institute of Peace and Conflict Studies, 7 October 2001. http://www.ipcs.org/Terrorism_ kashmirLevel2.jsp?action=showView&kValue=198&subCat ID=1022&mod=g

65 'Mind of the Suicide Bomber'. http://www.cbsnews.com/ stories/2003/05/23/60minutes/main555344.shtml

CHAPTER 8   THE CONSEQUENCES OF SUICIDE
TERRORISM

1 Chris Ryan 'Tourism, Terrorism and Violence: The Risks of Wider World Travel' *Conflict Studies* (Sept. 1991), 244: 1–30; Yoel Mansfeld 'The Middle-East Conflict and Tourism to Israel, 1967–1990', *Middle Eastern Studies* (1994), 30(3): 646–67; Grant Wardlaw *Political Terrorism: Theory, Tactics, and Counter-Measures*, Cambridge: Cambridge University Press, 1989, p. 58; Brien Jenkins 'Numbered Lives: Some statistical observations from 77 international hostage episodes', *Conflict, An International Journal for Conflict and Policy Studies* (1978), 1(1/2): 71–111; Mark Zagari 'Combating Terrorism: Report to the Committee of Legal Affairs and Citizens' Rights of the European Parliament', *Terrorism and Political Violence* (1992), 4(4): 288; Peter Chalk 'The Response to Terrorism as a Threat to Liberal Democracy' *Australian Journal of Politics and History* (1998), 44(3): 377; Leslie Macfarlane 'Human Rights and the

Fight against Terrorism in Northern Ireland', *Terrorism and Political Violence* (1992), 4(1): 93.

2   While the average number of those killed and injured world-wide from ordinary terrorism is 9.3, from suicide attacks, it is 70.3. Figures from the National Security Studies Centre data-bases at Haifa University: http://nssc.haifa.ac.il/

3   Galea Sandro, Jennifer Ahern, Heidi Resnick, David Kilpatrick, Michael Bucuvalas, Joel Gold and David Vlahov 'Psychological Sequelae of the September 11 Terrorist Attacks in New York City', *New England Journal of Medicine* (2002), 346(13): 982–7; William E. Schlenger, Juesta M. Cadell, Lori Ebert, Kathleen B. Jordan, Kathryn M. Rourke, David Wilson et al. 'Psychological Reactions to Terrorist Attacks: Findings from the National Study of Americans' Reactions to September 11', *Journal of the American Medical Association* (2002), 288(5): 581–8; Mark A. Schuster, Bradley D. Stein, Lisa H. Jaycox, Rebecca L. Collins, Grant N. Marshall and Marc N. Elliot 'A National Study of Stress Reactions after the September 11, 2001 Terrorist Attacks', *New England Journal of Medicine* (2001), 345(20): 1507–12.

4   Gary Langer 'Prayers for Victims, Support for Reprisals', *ABCNEWS.com*, 11 September 2001. http://abcnews.go.com/sections/us/DailyNews/wtc_abcpoll010911.html; Mark A. Schuster et al. *After 9/11: Stress and Coping Across America*, paper presented before the United States Senate Committee on Health, Education, Labour and Pensions field hearing on '9/11 and NYC Children', 10 June 2002. http://www.rand.org/publications/CT/CT198/CT198.pdf

5   Langer 'Prayers for Victims, Support for Reprisals'.

6   Mark Gongloff 'When Will We Spend Again?', *CNNmoney*, 26 October 2001. http://money.cnn.com/2001/10/26/economy/economy_consumer/; Michael L. Dolfman and Solidelle F. Wasser '9/11 and the New York City Economy: A Borough-by-Borough Analysis', *Monthly Labour Review* (June 2004): 3–33. http://www.bls.gov/opub/mlr/2004/06/art1full.pdf; David W. Moore 'Corporate Abuses, 9/11 Attacks Seen as Most Important Causes of Economic Downturn', *Gallup Poll*, 5 August 2002. http://www.gallup.com/poll/content/login.aspx?ci=6523; Frank Newport and Dennis Jacobe 'Despite September 11 Attacks, Americans Optimistic about Economic Future', *Gallup Poll*, 25 September 2001. http://www.gallup. com/poll/content/login.aspx?ci=4930

7   Tamar Trabelsi-Hadad 'A Trip? Not in Our School', *Ynet*, 17 March 2002 [Hebrew]. http://www.ynet.co.il/Ext/Comp/ ArticleLayout/CdaArticlePrintPreview/1,2506,L1770370,00. html; *Yedioth Aharonoth* reporters 'Two Years to the Intifada: A War Report', *Ynet*, 6 September 2002 [Hebrew]. http://www. ynet.co.il/articles/1,7340, L-2102594,00. html# top

8   Stevan E. Hobfoll, Daphna Canetti-Nisim and Robert Johnson 'Exposure to Terrorism, Stress-Related Mental Health Symptoms, and Defensive Coping among Jews and Arabs in Israel' (forthcoming).

9   Schlenger, Cadell et al. 'Psychological Reactions to Terrorist Attacks'; Sandro, Ahern et al. 'Psychological Sequelae of the September 11 Terrorist Attacks in New York City'.

10 Schlenger, Cadell et al. 'Psychological Reactions to Terrorist Attacks'; Sandro, Ahern et al. 'Psychological Sequelae of the September 11 Terrorist Attacks in New York City'; Avraham Bleich, Marc Gelkopf and Zahava Solomon 'Exposure to Terrorism, Stress-Related Mental Health Symptoms, and Coping Behaviours among a Nationally Representative Sample in Israel', *Journal of the American Medical Association* (2003), 290(5): 612–20.

11 Sanobar Shermatova 'Caucasians Targeted in Wake of Moscow Blast', Institute for War and Peace Reporting, 13 February 2004. http://www.iwpr.net/index.pl?archive/cau/cau_200402_218_ 2_eng.txt Shermatova 2004; http://www.izvestia.ru/politic/ article25945; Sabrina Tavernise and Steven Lee Myers 'Toll in Russia Climbs to 41 in Bombing at a Hospital', *Sullivan-county.com*, 3 August 2003. http://www.sullivan-county. com/ bush/41_russia.htm;http://bd.fom.ru/report/cat/societas/ Chechnya/act_terrorism/d040732; http://bd.fom.ru/report/ cat/societas/Chechnya/act_terrorism/Nord-Ost/d024506; 'Terrorist Attacks in Russia', Nationwide VCIOM survey, 25–28 October 2002. http://www.russiavotes.org/hostage. htm; http://www.bd.fom.ru/report/cat/societas/Chechnya/ch echenian/of030402

12 Kaz de Jong, Maureen Mulhern, Alison Swan and Saskia van der Kam 'Assessing Trauma in Sri Lanka: Psycho-social Questionnaire, Vavuniya Survey Outcomes', *Médecins Sans Frontières*, The Netherlands, 31 May 2001: 18–20. http://www. msf.org/source/countries/asia/srilanka/2001/psyc-soc.doc

13   Robert D. Putnam 'Bowling Together', *The American Prospect* (11 Feb. 2002), 13(3). http://www.prospect.org/print/V13/3/putnam-r.html

14   Mark A. Schuster et al. *After 9/11: Stress and Coping Across America.*

15   Example for prayer services, see 'Responses to 9/11', *The Text This Week.* http://www.textweek.com/response.htm

16   Ann B. Bettencourt, Kelly Charlton, Nancy Dorr and Deborah L. Hume 'Status Differences and In-group Bias: A Meta-analytic Examination of the Effects of Status Stability, Status Legitimacy, and Group Permeability', *Psychological Bulletin* (2001), 127(4): 520–42; Jennifer S. Lerner and Dacher Keltner 'Fear, Anger, and Risk', *Journal of Personality and Social Psychology* (2001), 8: 146–59; Daniel Bar-Tal and Avner Ben-Amos 'Patriotism as a Social Psychological Phenomenon: Introduction to the Analysis of the Israeli Case' in Avner Ben-Amos and Daniel Bar-Tal (eds) *Patriotism in Israel*, Tel Aviv: Papirus, 2004, pp. 3–18 [Hebrew]; Karen Jones 'Trust and Terror', paper presented at the Conference on Trust, University of California–Riverside, 14th Annual Philosophy Conference, 27–28 February 2004.

17   Darren W. Davis and Brian D. Silver 'Civil Liberties vs. Security: Public Opinion in the Context of the Terrorist Attacks on America', *American Journal of Political Science* (2004), 48: 28–46; Leonie Huddy 'Group Identity and Political Cohesion' in David O. Sears, Leonie Huddy and Robert Jervis (eds) *Oxford Handbook of Political Psychology*, Oxford: Oxford University Press, 2003; Leonie Huddy, Stanley Feldman, Charles Taber and Gallya Lahav 'The Politics of Threat: Cognitive and Affective Reactions to 9/11', paper presented at the Annual Meeting of the American Political Science Association, Boston, August–September 2002.

18   Davis and Silver 'Civil Liberties vs. Security'.

19   The surveys can be located at http://bd.fom.ru/report/cat/societas/Chechnya/act_terrorism/of040602 and http://bd.fom.ru/report/cat/societas/Chechnya/act_terrorism/t906612

20   National Security Studies Centre surveys. http://nssc.haifa.ac.il/

21   Such as the law dealing with internal security: S. J. Res. 23, Public Law No. 107–40; Immigration Laws-Public Law No. 104–208, Section 641; S. 1424, Public Law 107–45; H.R.

3525, Public Law No. 107–73; and more then 134 acts of legislation regarding 9/11. 'Legislation Related to the Attack of
September 11, 2001', The Library of the Congress, 30 October
2002. http://thomas.loc.gov/home/terrorleg.htm

22 Vinay Lal 'Anti-Terrorist Legislation: A Comparative Study of
India', *The United Kingdom and Sri Lanka Lokayan Bulletin*
(July–Aug. 1994), 11(1): 5–24.

23 It should be noted that the arrest should be approved by a
judge. For the full description of the law, refer to
http://civics.haifa.ac.il/civics_files/warriors.htm [Hebrew].

24 For full description of the law, refer to http://www.panorama.
ru/works/patr/govpol/project1–3.html or http://www.duma.
gov.ru/

25 The data were taken from the National Security Studies
Centre databases at Haifa University: http://nssc.haifa.ac.il/

26 Ibid.

27 Ronald D. Crelinsten 'The Discourse and Practice of Counter-
Terrorism in Liberal Democracies', *Australian Journal of
Politics and History* (1998), 44(3): 389–413; Peter Chalk 'The
Response to Terrorism as a Threat to Liberal Democracy';
Fernando Reinares 'Democratic Regimes, Internal Security
Policy and the Threat of Terrorism', *Australian Journal of
Politics and History* (1998), 44(3): 351–71.

28 For more information on this cycle of violence, see Ronald
D. Crelinsten and Alex P. Schmid 'Western Response to
Terrorism: A Twenty-Five Year Balance Sheet', *Terrorism and
Political Violence* (1992), 4(4): 307–40; Chalk 'The Response to
Terrorism as a Threat to Liberal Democracy'; Christopher
Hewitt *The Effectiveness of Anti-Terrorist Policies*, Lanham, New
York: University Press of America, 1984.

29 Mia M. Bloom *Dying to Kill: The Global Phenomenon of Suicide
Terror*, 2004, ch. 4 (website), New York: Columbia University
Press, 2005; Scott Atran 'Mishandling Suicide Terrorism',
Washington Quarterly (2004), 27(3): 67–90.

30 Robert A. Pape 'The Strategic Logic of Suicide Terrorism',
American Political Science Review (2003), 97(3): 356–7.

31 Arie Perliger and Ami Pedahzur 'The Merit of Defensive Coping
with Suicide Terrorism: Lessons Based on the Israeli Case
Study', the American Political Science Association Meeting,
Chicago, Ill., August 2004; William L. Waugh 'Regionalising
Emergency Management: Countries as State and Local

Government', *Public Administration Review* (1994), 54(3): 253–9; Ashton B. Carter 'The Architecture of Government in the Face of Terrorism', *International Security* (2001), 26(3): 5–23.

32 Allan J. Behm and Michael J. Palmer, 'Coordinating Counterterrorism: A Strategic Approach to a Changing Threat', *Terrorism* (1991), 14(3): 171–93.

33 Leonie Huddy, Stanley Feldman, Theresa Capelos and Colin Provost 'The Consequences of Terrorism: Disentangling the Effects of Personal and National Threat', *Political Psychology* (2002), 23(3): 485–509; Brian J. Gaines 'Where's the Rally? Approval and Trust of the President, Cabinet, Congress, and Government since September 11', *Political Science and Politics* (2002), 35(3): 531–6.

34 Pape 'The Strategic Logic of Suicide Terrorism' 346–7; Bloom *Dying to Kill*, ch. 4; Scott Atran 'Genesis of Suicide Terrorism', *Science* (2003), 299(5619): 1535; Assaf Moghadam 'Palestinian Suicide Terrorism in the Second Intifada: Motivations and Organisational Aspects', *Studies in Conflict and Terrorism* (2003), 26(2): 72; Bruce Hoffman 'The Logic of Suicide Terrorism', *The Atlantic Monthly* (2003), 291(5): 40–7.

35 Marc Sageman *Understanding Terror Networks*, Philadelphia: University of Pennsylvania Press, 2004.

36 Bloom *Dying to Kill*, ch. 4.

37 Pape 'The Strategic Logic of Suicide Terrorism' 348–50.

38 For further analysis, see Anonymous *Through our Enemies' Eyes*, Washington, DC: Brassey's, 2003.

AFTERWORD

1 For the structure of Al-Qaeda and its affiliates, refer to Bruce Hoffman, 'Al Qaeda, Trends in Terrorism, and Future Potentialities: An Assessment', *Studies in Conflict and Terrorism* (2003), 26(6): 429–43.

2 For a full description of this approach, refer to Marc Sageman. *Understanding Terror Networks*, Philadelphia: University of Pennsylvania Press, 2004.

Appendix: Suicide Bombings (December 1981–June 2005)

Date	Organization	Location	Target	Dead/ injured
151281	al-Dawa	Beirut	Embassy	61/100
111182	Hezbollah	Tyre	Military	62/28
180483	Hezbollah	Beirut	Embassy	60/100
231083	Hezbollah	Beirut	Military	241/81
231083	Hezbollah	Beirut	Military	59/15
041183	Hezbollah	Tyre	Military	39
121283	al-Dawa (Hezbollah)	Kuwait City	Embassy	6/52
211283	Hezbollah	Beirut	Military	23/144
160684	Amal	South Lebanon	Military	5/9
200984	Hezbollah	Beirut	Embassy	23/70
050285	Hezbollah	Burj al Shimali	Military	0/10
080385	Hezbollah	South Lebanon	Military	12/7
100385	Hezbollah	South Lebanon	Military	12/20
120385	Hezbollah	Ras al-Ain	Military	0/0
090485	Hezbollah	Jezzin	Military	2/2
20485	Hezbollah	South Lebanon	Military	
090585	Hezbollah	South Lebanon	Military	2/4
250585	al-Dawa	Kuwait City	Govt/Police	5/0 (12)
150685	Hezbollah	Beirut	Military	23/17
090785	Hezbollah	South Lebanon	Military	23/28
090785	Hezbollah	South Lebanon	Military	22/6
150785	Hezbollah	Kfar Tibnit	Military	10/11
310785	Hezbollah	Arnoun	Military	2/1
290885	Hezbollah	South Lebanon	Military	15/24
030985	Hezbollah	South Lebanon	Military	7/28
110985	Hezbollah	Hasbaya	Military	0/2
120985	Hezbollah	South Lebanon	Military	21/17
170985	Hezbollah	South Lebanon	Military	30/4
180985	Hezbollah	South Lebanon	Military	0/8

Date	Organization	Location	Target	Dead/ injured
171085	Hezbollah	South Lebanon	Military	6/9
041185	Hezbollah	Arnoun	Military	0/1
121185	Hezbollah	Beirut	Govt/Police	5/13
261185	Hezbollah	Jezzine	Military	20/14
070486	Hezbollah	South Lebanon	Military	1/3
170786	Hezbollah	Jezzine	Military	0/7
201186	Hezbollah	South Lebanon	Military	5/8
050787	LTTE	Jaffna	Military	40
111187	LLO	Beirut	Airport	6/73
141187	Hezbollah	Beirut	Hospital	7/20
191088	Hezbollah	Near Metulla	Military	8/7
120790	LTTE	Trincomalee	Naval vessel	6/0
231190	LTTE	Mankulam	Military	0/0
241190	SBO	South Lebanon	Military	0/2
020391	LTTE	Colombo	Govt/Police	18
190391	LTTE	Silavathurai	Military	5/3
050591	LTTE	Trincomalee	Naval vessel	5/4
210591	LTTE	Sriperumbudur	Govt/Police	19/21
220691	LTTE	Colombo	Military	27/114
151091	LTTE	Palliyagodella	Religious site	166
170392	Hezbollah	Buenos Aires	Embassy	29/142
161192	LTTE	Colombo	Military	6
160493	Hamas	Mehola junction	Restaurant	2/5
010593	LTTE	Colombo	Govt/Police	23
150893		Cairo	Govt/Police	3
120993	PIJ	Gaza	Bus	0/0
041093	PIJ	Beit El	Bus	0/30
021193	Hamas	Singil	Bus	0/0
111193	LTTE	Jaffna	Naval vessel	0
060494	Hamas	Afula	Bus	8/51
130494	Hamas	Hadera	Bus	5/30
180794	Ansar Allah	Buenos Aires	Civilian	96/236
020894	LTTE	Palaly	Airplane	0/0
190994	LTTE	Near Mannar Island	Naval vessel	25/17
191094	Hamas	Tel Aviv	Bus	22/46
241094	LTTE	Colombo	Govt/Police	53
081194	LTTE	Vettilaikerni	Naval vessel	0/5
111194	PIJ	Netzarim junction	Military	3/6
251294	Hamas	Jerusalem	Bus	0/13
201095	al-G al-I	Rijeka	Govt/Police	1/29
220195	PIJ	Beit Lid junction	Bus	18/69
300195	GIA	Algiers	Civilian	42
090495	PIJ	Kfar Darom	Bus	
090495	Hamas	Netzarim	Bus	
180495	LTTE	Trincomalee	Naval vessel	18
160795	LTTE	Jaffna	Naval vessel	0/4
190795	Unknown	Panama City	Airplane	21
240795	Hamas	Ramat Gan	Bus	6/31
070895	GIA	Boufarik	Civilian	8/25
070895	LTTE	Colombo	Govt/Police	22/40
210895	Hamas	Jerusalem	Bus	4/100

Date	Organization	Location	Target	Dead/ injured
030995	LTTE	Trincomalee	Naval vessel	0
100995	LTTE	Kankesanthurai	Naval vessel	0
200995	LTTE	Kankesanthurai	Naval vessel	0
021095	LTTE	Kankesanthurai	Naval vessel	0
171095	LTTE	Trincomalee	Naval vessel	7
201095	LTTE	Colombo	Civilian	23
021195	PIJ	Gush Katif	Military	0/8
111195	LTTE	Colombo	Military	2/3
131195	al-Qaeda	Riyadh	Military	5/11
191195	al-G al-I	Islamabad	Embassy	16/60
051295	LTTE	Batticaloa	Govt/Police	23/41
111295	LTTE	Colombo	Military	17/59
211295	Al-Jihad	Peshawar	Civilian	45/100
301295	LTTE	Batticaloa	Military	0/1
080196	LTTE	Batticaloa	Civilian	0/3
310196	LTTE	Colombo	Bank	91/1400
250296	Hamas	Jerusalem	Bus	26/80
250296	Hamas	Beit Lid junction	Bus	1/0
030396	Hamas	Jerusalem	Bus	19/6
040396	PIJ	Tel Aviv	Mall/shop	20/75
200396	Hezbollah	South Lebanon	Military	1/0
010496	LTTE	Vettilaikerni	Naval vessel	10/12
120496	LTTE	Colombo	Naval vessel	0/0
290496	Kashmir separatists	Lahor	Bus	52
300696	PKK	Tunceli	Military	9/30
030796	LTTE	Jaffna	Govt/Police	37/50
180796	LTTE	Mullaitivu	Naval vessel	35
240796	LTTE	Dehiwala	Train	63/366
060896	LTTE	North of Sri Lanka	Naval vessel	0/4
140896	LTTE	Colombo	Civilian	0/0
251096	PKK	Adana	Govt/Police	5/12
251096	LTTE	Trincomalee	Naval vessel	12/11
291096	PKK	Sivas	Govt/Police	4/1
191196	EIJ	Islamabad	Embassy	16/60
251196	LTTE	Trincomalee	Govt/Police	1/0
171296	LTTE	Ampara	Govt/Police	1/2
060397	LTTE	China Bay Air base	Airplane	0/1
210397	Hamas	Tel Aviv	Restaurant	3
010497	PIJ	Netzarim junction	Military	0/7
010497	PIJ	Kfar Darom	Bus	0/0
190597	Amal	Sea, near Tyre	Naval vessel	0/0
300797	Hamas	Jerusalem	Mall/shop	16/178
040997	Hamas	Jerusalem	Mall/shop	8/200
151097	LTTE	Colombo	Bank	18/110
191097	LTTE	Northern coast	Naval vessel	7/21
281297	LTTE	Maagalle	Govt/Police	0/0
250198	LTTE	Kandy	Religious site	19/34
060298	LTTE	Colombo	Military	9/7
230298	LTTE	Point Pedru	Naval vessel	51
050398	LTTE	Colombo	Civilian	40/270
120398	LTTE	Colombo	Civilian	50/200

Date	Organization	Location	Target	Dead/injured
150598	LTTE	Jaffna	Military	2/0
190798	Hamas	Jerusalem	Mall/shop	0/1
070898	al-Qaeda	Dar es-Salaam	Embassy	11/85
070898	al-Qaeda	Nairobi	Embassy	213/4000
170898	LTTE	Batticaloa	Bank	0/11
310898	GIA	Algiers	Mall/shop	25/61
110998	LTTE	Jaffna	Govt/Police	21/12
291098	Hamas	Gush Katif	Military	1/8
061198	PIJ	Jerusalem	Mall/shop	0/20
171198	PKK	Yuksekova	Govt/Police	0/6
011298	PKK	Lice	Mall/shop	0/14
241298	PKK	Van	Military	1/22
040399	PKK	Batman	Govt/Police	0/4
150399	LTTE	Colombo	Govt/Police	5/8
200399	PKK	Van Province	Civilian	1/3
270399	PKK	Istanbul	Civilian	0/10
050499	PKK	Bingol	Civilian	0/0
110499	LTTE	Colombo	Bus	1/20
290599	LTTE	Batticaloa	Govt/Police	2/0
050799	PKK	Adana	Civilian	0/17
070799	PKK	Iluh	Civilian	0/0
250799	LTTE	Trincomalee	Civilian	1/0
290799	LTTE	Colombo	Govt/Police	2/5
040899	LTTE	Vavuniya	Military	10/18
090899	LTTE	Vakarai	Military	1/2
280899	PKK	Tunceli	Civilian	0/0
020999	LTTE	Vavuniya	Civilian	3/0
040999	Unknown	Jammu	Civilian	
181299	LTTE	Colombo	Govt/Police	26/90
291299	Hezbollah	Qlaia	Military	1/13
010100	Lashkar-e-Taiba	Surankote		11/23
050100	LTTE	Colombo	Govt/Police	11/23
050100	Kashmir separatists	Haiderabad	Civilian	0/18
120100	Lashkar-e-Taiba	Anantang		
210100	Lashkar-e-Taiba	Srinagar		
040200	LTTE	Trincomalee	Naval vessel	0/0
160200	Unknown	Beijing	Civilian	0/1
020300	LTTE	Trincomalee	Military	1/0
100300	LTTE	Colombo	Govt/Police	20/46
230400	Jaish-e-Muhammad	Srinagar	Military	
170500	LTTE	Batticaloa	Religious site	29/78
230500	LTTE		Govt/Police	0/1
020600	Chechen separatists	Alkhan-Yurt	Civilian	2/5
050600	LTTE	Northeast coast	Naval vessel	21/0
070600	LTTE	Colombo	Govt/Police	20/50
070600	Chechen separatists	Alkhan-Yurt	Govt/Police	2/5
110600	Chechen separatists	Alkhan-Kala	Military	2
140600	LTTE	Wattala	Airplane	3/6
250600	LTTE	Northern coast	Naval vessel	10/7
030700	Chechen separatists	Urus-Martan	Military	2
030700	Chechen separatists	Novogrozny	Military	5/20

Date	Organization	Location	Target	Dead/injured
030700	Chechen separatists	Gudermes	Military	10
030700	Chechen separatists	Argun	Military	30/81
090700	Chechen separatists	Alkhan-Kala	Military	27
100700	LTTE	Trincomalee	Religious site	4/1
040800	LTTE	Jaffna	Military	
160800	LTTE	Colombo	Military	6
150900	LTTE	Colombo	Hospital	7/28
021000	LTTE	Trincomalee	Govt/Police	24/50
051000	LTTE	Medawachchiya	Govt/Police	12
121000	Al-Qaeda	Aden	Naval vessel	27/33
191000	LTTE	Colombo	Govt/Police	23/23
191000	LTTE	Colombo	Govt/Police	3/21
231000	LTTE	Trincomalee	Naval vessel	2
261000	PIJ	Gaza	Military	0/1
061100	Hamas	Rafah	Naval vessel	0/0
151100	Hamas	Erez crossing	Military	0/0
221200	Hamas	Mehola	Restaurant	0/3
251200	Jaish-e-Muhammad	Srinagar	Military	9/14
010101	Hamas	Netanya	Bus	35
010301	Hamas	Mei Ami junction	Military	1/10
040301	Hamas	Netanya	Civilian	3/53
240301	Chechen separatists	Mineralnye Vody	Military	20/140
270301	Hamas	Jerusalem	Bus	0/21
280301	Hamas	Neve Yamin	Military	2/4
220401	Hamas	Kfar Saba	Bus	1/50
290401	Hamas	Shavei Shomron	Bus	0/0
180501	Hamas	Netanya	Mall/shop	5/86
250501	Hamas	Gaza	Civilian	0/0
250501	PIJ	Hadera	Bus	0/66
290501	Hamas	Tofah checkpoint	Military	0/2
010601	Hamas	Tel Aviv	Nightclub	22/83
170601	PIJ	Gaza	Military	
220601	Hamas	Gush Katif	Military	2/1
090701	Hamas	Gush Katif	Military	0/1
160701	PIJ	Binyamina	Bus	2/8
220701	PIJ	Haifa	Military	0/0
240701	LTTE	Colombo	Airport	12/17
020801	PIJ	Beit Shean	Bus	0/0
080801	Hamas	Bekaot checkpoint	Military	0/1
090801	Hamas	Jerusalem	Restaurant	15/110
120801	PIJ	Kiryat Mozkin	Restaurant	0/16
040901	Hamas	Jerusalem	Govt/Police	0/13
060901	Jaish-e-Muhammad	Budgam district	Military	2/6
090901	PIJ	Beit Lid junction	Military	0/0
090901	Hamas	Nahariya	Train	3/46
090901	Al-Qaeda	North Pakistan	Govt/Police	2/0
100901	PKK	Istanbul	Govt/Police	3/20
110901	al-Qaeda	Washington	Govt/Police	190
110901	al-Qaeda	Pennsylvania	Civilian	45
110901	al-Qaeda	New York	Civilian	2750
011001	Jaish-e-Muhammad	Srinagar	Govt/Police	38/70

Appendix

Date	Organization	Location	Target	Dead/injured
061001	Unknown	al-Hobar	Civilian	1/5
071001	PIJ	Kibbutz Shluhot	Civilian	1/0
171001	Hamas	Karni crossing	Military	0/2
231001	Lashkar-e-Taiba	Awantipora base	Military	2/2
291001	LTTE	Colombo	Govt/Police	5
301001	LTTE	Jaffna	Military	7/0
081101	Hamas	Baka al-Sharkiya	Military	0/2
091101	LTTE	Batticaloa	Govt/Police	0/1
151101	LTTE	Batticaloa	Civilian	3/0
251101	Taliban	Mazar a-Sharif	Military	3
261101	Hamas	Erez crossing	Military	0/2
291101	PIJ	Hadera	Bus	3/8
291101	Chechen separatists	Urus-Martan	Military	2/2
011201	Hamas	Jerusalem	Civilian	11/170
021201	Hamas	Haifa	Bus	15/35
041201	PIJ	Jerusalem	Civilian	0/5
081201	Lashkar-e-Taiba	Baramulla	Military	2/1
091201	PIJ	Haifa	Bus	0/30
121201	Hamas	Ganei Tal-Gush Katif	Civilian	0/3
131201	Jaish-e-Muhammad	New Delhi	Govt/Police	4/18
151201	PIJ	Tulkarm	Military	0/0
250102	PIJ	Tel Aviv	Civilian	0/23
270102	Fatah	Jerusalem	Mall/shop	1/127
300102	Fatah	Taibe	Military	0/2
060202	Hamas	Maale Adumim	Bus	0/0
160202	PFLP	Karnei Shomron	Mall/shop	3/22
170202	Fatah	Hadera	Military	0/2
180202	Fatah	Jerusalem	Military	1/2
190202	Fatah	Mehola jucntion	Bus	0/0
220202	Fatah	Gaza	Military	0/3
270202	Fatah	Maccabim checkpoint	Military	0/3
020302	Fatah	Jerusalem	Religious site	10/46
050302	PIJ	Afula	Bus	1/20
070302	PFLP	Ariel	Hotel	0/9
070302	Hamas	Jerusalem	Restaurant	0/0
070302	PIJ	Karkur	Military	0/0
090302	Hamas	Jerusalem	Restaurant	11/58
170302	PIJ	Jerusalem	Bus	0/25
200302	PIJ	Vadi Ara	Bus	7/28
210302	Fatah	Jerusalem	Restaurant	3/80
220302	Fatah	Salem checkpoint	Military	0/1
260302	Fatah	Jerusalem	Govt/Police	0/0
270302	Hamas	Netanya	Hotel	29/144
290302	Fatah	Jerusalem	Market	2/22
300302	Fatah	Tel Aviv	Restaurant	1/29
310302	Hamas	Haifa	Restaurant	15/ 31
310302	Fatah	Efrat	Civilian	0/6
010402	Fatah	Jerusalem	Govt/Police	1/ 0
100402	PIJ	Yagur Junction	Bus	8/ 17
110402	al-Qaeda	Djerba	Religious site	19/ 26
120402	Fatah	Jerusalem	Market	6/ 64

Date	Organization	Location	Target	Dead/ injured
190402	PIJ	Gush Katif	Military	0/ 2
200402	Hamas	Kalkilya	Military	0/ 0
070502	Hamas	Rishon Lezion	Nightclub	16/51
080502	PIJ	Megiddo junction	Bus	0/3
080502	al-Qaeda	Karachi	Bus	13/12
190502	PFLP	Netanya	Market	3/60
220502	Fatah	Rishon Lezion	Civilian	2/41
240502	Fatah	Tel Aviv	Military	0/7
270502	Fatah	Petah Tikva	Restaurant	2/30
050602	PIJ	Megiddo junction	Bus	17/42
110602	Fatah	Herzliya	Restaurant	1/12
140602	al-Qaeda	Karachi	Embassy	12/40
170602	Fatah	Tulkarm	Military	0/0
180602	Hamas	Jerusalem	Bus	19/50
190602	Fatah	Jerusalem	Bus	7/39
170702	Fatah	Tel Aviv	Mall/shop	5/33
300702	Fatah	Jerusalem	Mall/shop	0/5
040802	Hamas	Miron junction	Bus	9/48
060802	Fatah	Umm el Fahm	Civilian	0/1
180902	PIJ	Umm el Fahm	Govt/Police	1/2
190902	Hamas	Tel Aviv	Bus	6/66
021002	Unknown	Guilin	Civilian	1/18
061002	al-Qaeda	Sea	Naval vessel	0/12
101002	Hamas	Ramat Gan	Bus	1/20
101002	Chechen separatists	Grozny	Govt/Police	25
111002	Hamas	Tel Aviv	Restaurant	0/0
121002	al-Qaeda	Bali	Nightclub	300/187
211002	PIJ	Karkur	Bus	14/48
271002	Hamas	Ariel	Civilian	3/17
041102	Fatah	Kfar Saba	Mall/shop	2/37
111102	PIJ	Erez crossing	Military	0/0
211102	Hamas	Jerusalem	Bus	11/50
221102	PIJ	Gaza	Naval vessel	0/4
281102	PFLP	Erez crossing	Military	0/0
281102	al-Qaeda	Mombasa	Hotel	16/40
271202	Riyadh-as-Saliheen	Grozny	Govt/Police	83/210
281202	Hamas	Jerusalem	Civilian	
050103	Fatah	Tel Aviv	Market	23/106
170103	Hamas	Gaza	Naval vessel	0/0
080203	LTTE	Sea	Naval vessel	0/0
090203	PIJ	Gush Katif	Military	3/4
050302	Hamas	Haifa	Bus	15/42
220303	Ansar Allah	Halabja	Military	6/9
290303	Unknown	Najaf	Military	4
300303	PIJ	Netanya	Restaurant	0/54
110403	Unknown	Baghdad	Military	2/4
240403	Fatah	Kfar Saba	Bus	1/15
300403	Hamas	Tel Aviv	Restaurant	3/62
080503	Fatah	Gaza	Military	0/0
120503	al-Qaeda	Riyadh	Hotel	34/160
120503	Riyadh-as-Saliheen	Znamenskaya	Military	59/300

Date	Organization	Location	Target	Dead/injured
140503	Riyadh-as-Saliheen	Iliskhan-Yurt	Religious site	16/0
160503	al-Assirat al-M	Casablanca	Hotel	43/0
160503	al-Assirat al-M	Casablanca	Religious site	0/0
160503	al-Assirat al-M	Casablanca	Restaurant	0/0
160503	al-Assirat al-M	Casablanca	Nightclub	0/0
170503	Hamas	Hebron	Religious site	2/0
180503	Hamas	Jerusalem	Bus	7/20
180503	Hamas	al-Aram checkpoint	Military	0/0
190503	Fatah	Afula	Mall/shop	3/50
190503	Hamas	Kfar Darom	Military	0/3
270503	Ansar Allah	Baquba	Military	
050603	Riyadh-as-Saliheen	Mozdok	Bus	18/15
110603	Hamas	Jerusalem	Bus	17/104
190603	PIJ	Sdei Trumot	Market	1/0
040703	Lashkar-e-Jhangvi	Quetta	Religious site	41/100
050703	Riyadh-as-Saliheen	Moscow	Civilian	53/57
070703	PIJ	Yaavez	Civilian	1/6
010803	Chechen separatists	Mozdok	Hospital	50
050803	al-G al-I	Jakarta	Hotel	16/150
120803	Fatah	Rosh HaAyin	Market	1/9
120803	Hamas	Ariel	Civilian	2/4
190803	Hamas	Jerusalem	Bus	24/104
190803	al-Tawhid wa al-J	Baghdad	Hotel	23
030903	Saddam loyalists	Ramadi	Military	1/2
030903	Chechen separatists	Stavropol	Train	5
080903	Hamas	Zrifin	Bus	8/20
080903	Hamas	Jerusalem	Bus	8/30
090903	Ansar Allah	Irbil	Military	3/4
160903	Chechen separatists	Mozdok	Govt/Police	3/25
220903	al-Qaeda	Baghdad	Govt/Police	1/19
041003	PIJ	Haifa	Restaurant	19/60
091003	PIJ	Tulkarm	Military	0/3
091003	al-Tawhid wa al-J	Baghdad	Govt/Police	10
121003	al-Tawhid wa al-J	Baghdad	Hotel	8/40
141003	Ansar al-Sunna	Baghdad	Embassy	1/13
270103	Ansar Allah	Baghdad	Govt/Police	34/224
281003	Saddam loyalists	Falluja	Govt/Police	6
311003	Unknown	Baghdad	Civilian	1
031103	Fatah	Kalkilya	Military	0/0
081103	al-Qaeda	Riyadh	Civilian	17/122
091103	Fatah	Tulkarm	Military	0/3
121103	Saddam loyalists	Baghdad	Military	2/4
121103	al-Tawhid wa al-J	Nasiriya	Govt/Police	31
201103	al-Qaeda	Istanbul	Embassy	27/450
201103	Ansar al-Sunna	Northern Iraq	Military	5
221103	al Tawhid wa al-J	Khan Bani Saad	Govt/Police	12
231103	Saddam loyalists	Baghdad	Military	2
051203	Riyadh-as-Saliheen	Stavropol	Train	42/160
091203	Saddam loyalists	Talafar	Military	0/61
091203	Riyadh-as-Saliheen	Moscow	Military	5/14
111203	Saddam loyalists	Baghdad	Military	1/14

Date	Organization	Location	Target	Dead/injured
121203	Saddam loyalists	Baghdad	Govt/Police	7/40
141203	al-Tawhid wa al-J	Khalidiya	Govt/Police	17/33
141203	Jaish-e-Muhammad	Rawalpindi	Govt/Police	0/0
151203	Saddam loyalists	Baghdad	Civilian	8
251203	PFLP	Petah Tikva	Civilian	4/20
251203	Jaish-e-Muhammad	Karachi	Govt/Police	14/17
271203	Saddam loyalists	Karbala	Civilian	13/100
010104	Saddam loyalists	Baghdad	Market	8/30
090104	Saddam loyalists	Baquba	Religious site	5/37
140104	al-Tawhid wa al-J	Baquba	Govt/Police	2
170104	Saddam loyalists	Baghdad	Military	18.
180104	Hamas	Erez crossing	Military	4/10
180104	al-Tawhid wa al-J	Baghdad	Military	20/100
240104	Saddam loyalists	Khalidiya	Military	3/6
270104	Taliban	Kabul	Military	2
280104	al-Tawhid wa al-J	Baghdad	Hotel	3/15
290104	Fatah	Jerusalem	Bus	11/50
310104	Ansar al-Sunna	Mosul	Govt/Police	9/45
310104	Ansar al-Sunna	Mosul	Military	3
010204	Ansar al-Sunna	Irbil	Religious site	56/200
060204	Riyadh-as-Saliheen	Moscow	Train	39/130
100204	Ansar Allah	Iskandariyah	Govt/Police	55/67
110204	al-Tawhid wa al-J	Baghdad	Military	47/55
180204	al-Tawhid wa al-J	Hillah	Military	11/106
220204	Fatah	Jerusalem	Bus	8/68
230204	Ansar al-Sunna	Kirkuk	Govt/Police	10/45
280204	Unknown	Rawalpindi	Religious site	0/4
020304	al-Qaeda	Karbala	Religious site	101/230
020304	Ansal Allah	Baghdad	Religious site	70/200
020304	Lashkar-e-Jhangvi	Quetta	Civilian	44/154
060304	Fatah	Erez crossing	Military	2/15
090304	Islam fundamentalists	Istanbul	Civilian	2/6
140304	Fatah	Ashdod	Civilian	8/16
170304	al-Tawhid wa al-J	Baghdad	Hotel	7/24
180304	al-Tawhid wa al-J	Basra	Hotel	3/2
200305	Unknown	Falluja	Military	2
290304	Hizb-ut-Tahrir	Tashkent	Market	4/21
300304	Saddam loyalists	Hillah	Govt/police	1/7
060404	Riyadh-as-Saliheen	Nazran	Govt/Police	2/7
170404	Fatah	Erez crossing	Military	1/3
210404	al-Tawhid wa al-J	Riyadh	Govt/Police	10/125
210404	al-Tawhid wa al-J	Basra	Govt/Police	73/200
240404	al-Tawhid wa al-J	Basra	Naval vessel	6/0
280404	Hamas	Kfar Darom	Military	0/4
060504	al-Tawhid wa al-J	Baghdad	Military	6/25
070504	Lashkar-e-Jhangvi	Karachi	Religious site	15/200
170504	Arab Resistance	Baghdad	Govt/Police	7/7
220504	al-Qaeda	Baghdad	Govt/Police	5/1
010604	Saddam loyalists	Bayji	Govt/Police	11/18
060604	al-Tawhid wa al-J	Taji	Military	9/30
080604	Saddam loyalists	Mosul	Govt/Police	9/25

Date	Organization	Location	Target	Dead/injured
130604	Saddam loyalists	Baghdad	Govt/Police	12/13
140604	al-Tawhid wa al-J	Baghdad	Military	5/1
170604	al-Tawhid wa al-J	Baghdad	Govt/Police	35/138
240604	al-Tawhid wa al-J	Baghdad	Military	5/5
240604	al-Tawhid wa al-J	Mosul	Govt/Police	62/220
240604	DHKP-C	Istanbul	Civilian	4/15
040704	Saddam loyalists	Baquba	Govt/Police	2/1
060704	Ansar al-Sunna	Khalis	Civilian	14/70
070704	LTTE	Colombo	Govt/Police	4/7
140704	al-Tawhid wa al-J	Baghdad	Govt/Police	11/40
170704	al-Tawhid wa al-J	Baghdad	Govt/Police	5/8
170704	al-Tawhid wa al-J	Mahmudiyah	Govt/Police	2/47
190704	Saddam loyalists	Baghdad	Govt/Police	9/62
260704	Saddam loyalists	Mosul	Military	3/6
270704	Saddam loyalists	Baquba	Military	0/0
280704	Islam fundamentalists	Baquba	Govt/Police	68/56
280704	al-Qaeda	Kohat	Military	2/3
290704	IMU	Tashkent	Embassy	3/1
290704	IMU	Tashkent	Embassy	2/4
290704	IMU	Tashkent	Embassy	2/1
300704	Hizb-ut-Tahrir	Tashkent	Embassy	4/7
310704	al-Qaeda	Fateh Jang	Govt/Police	9/25
010804	Saddam loyalists	Mosul	Govt/Police	5/53
050804	Unknown	Baghdad	Govt/Police	5/21
050804	Unknown	Baghdad	Govt/Police	5/21
240804	Riyadh-as-Saliheen	Rostov-on-Don	Airplane	46/0
280804	Unknown	Mosul	Military	0/0
310804	Hamas	Beer Sheba	Bus	16/100
310804	Riyadh-as-Saliheen	Moscow	Train	11/50
040904	Unknown	Kirkuk	Govt/Police	21/30
060904	Unknown	Siirt	Unknown	0/0
090904	al-G al-I	Jakarta	Embassy	10/180
180904	Unknown	Kirkuk	Military	21/67
200904	Unknown	Mosul	Unknown	4
220904	Unknown	Baghdad	Military	5/10
220904	Fatah	Jerusalem	Civilian	2/15
300904	Unknown	Baghdad	Govt/Police	10/60
041004	Unknown	Baghdad	Embassy	10/76
101004	al-Tawhid wa al-J	Baghdad	Govt/Police	17
101004	Unknown	Baghdad	Civilian	5/10
151004	al-Tawhid wa al-J	Baghdad	Civilian	10/20
151004	Taliban	Kabul	Mall/shop	2/8
201004	Unknown	Baghdad	Govt/Police	16/40
231004	Unknwon	Khan al-Baghdadi	Govt/Police	16/30
251004	Unknown	Mosul	Govt/Police	3/9
251004	Unknown	Mosul	Govt/Police	1/0
011104	PFLP	Tel Aviv	Market	3/32
031104	Unknown	Baghdad	Govt/Police	0/9
041104	Unknown	Tikrit	Govt/Police	1/10
061104	Tanzim Qa'idat	Samarra	Govt/Police	42/62
081104	Unknown	Baghdad	Religious site	3/45

Date	Organization	Location	Target	Dead/injured
111104	Unknown	Baghdad	Market	19/15
131104	Unknown	Hillah	Govt/Police	1/4
191104	Unknown	Baghdad	Govt/Police	2/10
261104	Unknown	Baghdad	Govt/Police	2
291104	Unknown	Ramadi	Govt/Police	12/10
031204	Unknown	Baghdad	Religious site	14/19
041204	Unknown	Baghdad	Govt/Police	8/38
131204	Tanzim Qa'idat	Baghdad	Military	13/15
141204	Unknown	Baghdad	Military	7/13
231204	Unknown	al-Latify	Govt/Police	9/13
241204	Unknown	Baghdad	Embassy	9/19
271204	Unknown	Baghdad	Govt/Police	13/50
291204	al-Qaeda	Riyadh	Govt/Police	1/6
291204	al-Qaeda	Riyadh	Govt/Police	1/6
291204	al-Qaeda	Riyadh	Govt/Police	0/4
291204	Unknown	Samarra	Unknown	1/10
010105	Ansar al-Sunna	Baghdad	Govt/Police	3/25
040105	Tanzim Qa'idat	Baghdad	Govt/Police	10/60
050105	Unknown	Hillah	Govt/Police	20/25
050105	Tanzim Qa'idat	Baquba	Govt/Police	6/13
060105	Hamas	Ganei Tal-Gush Katif	Civilian	1/0
080105	Unknown	Baghdad	Civilian	4/19
100105	Unknown	Rubai'a	Military	4
100105	Unknown	Baghdad	Govt/Police	7
110105	Unknown	Basra	Govt/Police	2/7
110105	Tanzim Qa'idat	Tikrit	Govt/Police	7/12
110105	Unknown	Basra	Govt/Police	1/0
130105	Fatah	Karni crossing	Military	9/15
160105	Unknown	Kut	Civilian	8
170105	Unknown	Bayji	Govt/Police	10/20
180105	Unknown	Baghdad	Govt/Police	4/8
180105	Hamas	Gush Katif	Military	2/6
190105	Tanzim Qa'idat	Baghdad	Govt/Police	2/8
190105	Tanzim Qa'idat	Baghdad	Govt/Police	18/21
190105	Tanzim Qa'idat	Baghdad	Govt/Police	2/3
190105	Tanzim Qa'idat	Baghdad	Govt/Police	0/7
200105	Unknown	Sheberghan	Civilian	1/21
210105	Unknown	Baghdad	Religious site	15/42
210105	Unknown	Youssifiyah	Civilian	12/16
230105	Ansar al-Sunna	Hillah	Civilian	0/9
240105	Tanzim Qa'idat	Baghdad	Govt/Police	1/10
260105	Tanzim Qa'idat	Sinjar	Govt/Police	15/30
270105	Tanzim Qa'idat	Baquba	Govt/Police	5/9
280105	Unknown	Baghdad	Govt/Police	6/4
290105	Tanzim Qa'idat	Khanaqin		3/5
300105	Unknown	Baghdad	Govt/Police	1/4
300105	Tanzim Qa'idat	Baghdad	Civilian	1/10
300105	Tanzim Qa'idat	Baghdad	Civilian	1/5
300105	Tanzim Qa'idat	Baghdad	Civilian	3/9
300105	Tanzim Qa'idat	Baghdad	Civilian	1
300105	Tanzim Qa'idat	Baghdad	Civilian	1/16

Date	Organization	Location	Target	Dead/injured
300105	Tanzim Qa'idat	Baghdad	Civilian	1/5
300105	Tanzim Qa'idat	Baghdad	Civilian	2/2
020205	Unknown	Musayyib	Hospital	19/26
030205	Unknown	Baghdad	Military	
070205	Tanzim Qa'idat	Mosul	Govt/Police	12/6
070205	Tanzim Qa'idat	Baquba	Govt/Police	15/17
080205	Tanzim Qa'idat	Baghdad	Military	21/27
110205	Unknown	Balad Ruz	Religious site	12/23
140205	Support and Jihad	Beirut	Car	20/120
180205	Unknown	Baghdad	Religious site	8/10
180205	Unknown	Baghdad	Govt/Police	3/0
180205	Unknown	Baghdad	Religious site	17/23
180205	Unknown	Baghdad	Religious site	10/10
190205	Unknown	Baghdad	Civilian	6/55
190205	Unknown	Baghdad	Civilian	5/40
190205	Unknown	Baghdad	Bus	17/41
190205	Unknown	Baghdad	Religious site	7/55
190205	Unknown	Baghdad	School	1/0
220205	Unknown	Baghdad	Govt/Police	4/30
240205	Unknown	Iskandariyah	Govt/Police	2/8
240205	Unknown	Tikrit	Govt/Police	15/22
250205	PIJ	Tel Aviv	Nightclub	5/50
280205	Tanzim Qa'idat	Hillah	Civilian	125/140
280205	Unknown	Musayyib	Govt/Police	1/3
020305	Tanzim Qa'idat	Baghdad	Military	8/28
030305	Tanzim Qa'idat	Baquba	Govt/Police	1/18
030305	Tanzim Qa'idat	Baghdad	Govt/Police	7/15
070305	Tanzim Qa'idat	Baquba	Govt/Police	11/20
090305	Tanzim Qa'idat	Baghdad	Govt/Police	4/40
100305	Prophet's Companions	Mosul	Civilian	53/100
140305	Unknown	Baghdad	Military	4/0
150305	Unknown	Baghdad	Govt/Police	1/4
190305	Army of the Levant	Doha	Theater	1/16
200305	Tanzim Qa'idat	Mosul	Govt/Police	3/2
210305	Unknown	Samarra	Hospital	1/12
240305	Islamic Army in Iraq	Ramadi	Govt/Police	11/14
280305	Unknown	Musayyib	Military	5/10
280305	Unknown	Karbala	Civilian	7/9
300305	Taliban	Jalalabad	Govt/Police	1/1
310305	Unknown	Tuz Khormato	Military	5/16
140405	Unknown	Mahaweel	Market	4/6
150405	Unknown	Baghdad	Military	0/5
190405	Unknown	Baghdad	Military	4/38
220405	Unknown	Baghdad	Religious site	9/24
240405	Unknown	Tikrit	Govt/Police	7/27
250405	Unknown	Ramadi		1/0
290405	Unknown	Baghdad	Civilian	40/100
300405	Unknown	Cairo	Civilian	1/7
300405	Unknown	Cairo	Bus	2/0
010505	Unknown	Tal Afar	Civilian	25/50
010505	Unknown	Baghdad	Military	5/12

Date	Organization	Location	Target	Dead/injured
020505	Unknown	Baghdad	Military	1/0
040505	Ansar al-Sunna	Irbil	Govt/Police	60/150
050505	Unknown	Baghdad	Civilian	13/20
050505	Unknown	Baghdad	Govt/Police	1/6
060505	Unknown	Suwayra	Market	16/40
060505	Unknown	Tikrit	Govt/Police	7/3
080505	Unknown	Baghdad	Military	22/33
110505	Unknown	Hawija	Civilian	20/30
110505	Unknown	Tikrit	Civilian	30/40
110505	Unknown	Baghdad	Govt/Police	4/22
120505	Unknown	Baghdad	Market	12/56
120505	Unknown	Baghdad	Military	0/5
230505	Unknown	Tuz Khormato	Govt/Police	5/13
270505	Unknown	Islamabad	Civilian	19/65
280505	Unknown	Baghdad	Civilian	14/44
300505	al-Qaeda	Hillah	Govt/Police	31/108
310505	al-Qaeda	Karachi	Religious site	5/20
010605	al-Qaeda	Kandahar	Civilian	20/42
020605	Ansar al-Sunna	Tuz Khormato	Restaurant	12/37
020605	Unknown	Kirkuk	Military	2/12
020605	al-Qaeda	Baquba	Military	5/4
020605	Unknown	Baghdad	Govt/Police	0/15
020605	Unknown	Balad	Religious site	10/12

Sources: ABC net <http://www.abc.net.au/>; Associated Press; BBC <http://www.bbc.co.uk/>; CBS <http://www.cbs.com/>; CDISS Terrorism Program <http://talkjustice.com/links.asp?453053937>; cnn.com <http://www.cnn.com/>; Haaret'z Daily newspaper; ICT database <http://www.ict.org.il/>; Maariv Daily newspaper; MITP Knowledge Base <http://www.tkb.org/Home.jsp>; Reuters <http://today.reuters.com/news/default.aspx>; *New York Times* <http://nytimes.com/>; US Department of State <http://www.state.gov/>; United Press International <http://about.upi.com/>; *Washington Times* <http://washingtontimes.com/>; Ynet <Ynet.co.il>

Index